EUROPE SIMPLE

EUROPE STRONG

EUROPE SIMPLE
EUROPE STRONG

The Future of European Governance

Frank Vibert

Polity

First published in 2001 by Polity Press in association with Blackwell Publishers Ltd

Editorial office:
Polity Press
65 Bridge Street
Cambridge CB2 1UR, UK

Marketing and production:
Blackwell Publishers Ltd
108 Cowley Road
Oxford OX4 1JF, UK

Published in the USA by
Blackwell Publishers Inc.
350 Main Street
Malden, MA 02148, USA

ISBN 0–7456–2852–4
ISBN 0–7456–2853–2 (pbk)

A catalogue record for this book is available from the British Library and has been applied for from the Library of Congress.

Typeset in 10.5/12 pt Sabon by Kolam Information Services Ltd, Pondicherry, India.

Printed in Great Britain by MPG Books Ltd, Bodmin, Cornwall

This book is printed on acid-free paper.

Contents

Preface

For more than a decade, the existing European union has been en-
gaged in a process of institutional navel-gazing while dragging its feet
on the great task of unifying Europe after the end of the Cold War.
This book puts itself at a deliberate distance from the detail of institutional questions facing Europe and focuses instead on the basic
structure of a political framework for the continent. It assumes that
the reader will have some general familiarity with the existing union,
the treaties on which it rests and the institutions to which it has given
rise. In certain cases there are doctrines of the European Court of
Justice, such as the direct effect of Community law, that are important
for understanding how the current union works but that are not to be
found in the treaties. Where appropriate, these are referred to in the
text. Discussion in the union is now turning towards constitutional
questions, and a new Inter-Governmental Conference is scheduled for
2004. This is to be welcomed. However, the merits of a constitution
depend on its content. This book takes a look at some basic theory
that might help us establish the substance of a viable political framework for Europe.

Frank Vibert, London, April 2001

Acknowledgements

Quotations in this book from Alexis de Tocqueville, *Democracy in America* (1835–40), have been taken from the 1946 version published by Oxford University Press in 'The World's Classics' series (trans. H. Reeve; ed. H.S. Commager). The epigraph from Adam Smith, *Essays on Philosophical Subjects* (1795), is taken from the 1980 Clarendon Press edition (ed. W.P.D. Wightman). I would like to thank Dr Walter Eltis (Emeritus fellow, Exeter College, Oxford) for encouraging me to write this book, and Professor Richard Rose, Professor Ed Page, Dr David Henderson, Dr Mark Thatcher and Anthony Barnett, as well as an anonymous reviewer for Polity, for reading and commenting on a first draft. I would also like to thank Sarah Summers for preparing the manuscript for the publisher, and Justin Dyer for his most helpful editing. Finally, for her support throughout, I would like to thank my wife, to whom the book is dedicated.

Introduction

It is both necessary and desirable that the government of a democratic people should be active and powerful: and our object should not be to render it weak or indolent, but solely to prevent it from abusing its aptitude and its strength.

Alexis de Tocqueville, *Democracy in America*

The Need for a Radical Rethink in Europe

This book is about Europe's developing continent-wide system of government. The European Union of the future will include not just the present fifteen member states of Western Europe but more than thirty states, including Turkey, whose membership has been accepted in principle. It will contain a population of more than 500 million people and will extend up to the borders of Russia, with which some form of special association will be needed.

The goal of a continent-wide political union is extraordinarily ambitious. The underlying assumption of this book is that it is also extraordinarily desirable. But its attainment is not assured; the form of the governance of such a union has not been thought through. There has been a blithe assumption that the institutional framework originally suited for just six member states in the original European Economic Community, and which has already been expanded to include fifteen members, can now once again be more than doubled in size. There has been an equally unthinking assumption that a union that started with limited economic goals can be transformed to meet the completely different standards of political union without at the same time transforming the way in which it works. Even if the outside world had stayed still since the original model started operations in the late 1950s, these assumptions would be highly questionable. In reality, the environment facing all the world's governments has changed out of all recognition. When we think about the form of union suited for Europe, we simply cannot project what seemed good fifty years ago.

There is a growing realization that just extending the order of the existing European union will not suffice for a continent-wide system of government. Because the member states of the existing union are finding it increasingly difficult to agree on the reforms needed, a more far-reaching debate about the constitutional principles for political union in Europe seems to have started. Even at the outset, the debate is thoroughly confused. The approach taken in this book is to identify the fundamental issues underlying a system of government for Europe and to advocate a radical rethink.

Rethinking European Union: The Need for a New Starting Point

A radical rethink of the shape of political union in Europe must start with first principles. Part of the reason why thinking about Europe's future remains so limited is that the starting points for the debate are so often rooted in fear. First, there is fear of the past and the destructive nationalism that tore Europe apart twice in the last hundred years. This past should never be forgotten – but it no longer provides a starting point for thinking about the shape of a continent-wide political union. Germany, France and Great Britain may have rivalries and tensions still remaining in their relationships, but it is unthinkable and implausible to think that they will ever again go to war to settle their differences. The same is true for all European countries, with the exception of the Balkans, and even they show signs of recognizing that fighting is not the answer to ethnic tensions. Secondly, there is fear of the future – a fear that is particularly reflected in fear of globalization and market processes. Rooting the debate about Europe's system of government in such fears about the past, or about the future, results in basic errors. It leads to a misdiagnosis of the setting in which contemporary systems of government have to operate and to a misreading of the challenges facing them. A continent-wide system of government based on fear is not the way ahead.

Connecting Two Systems of Choice

The approach taken in this book thus adopts a different starting point: the recognition that individual and social choices can be made either through the system of political choice or through the system of market choice. It is the way in which the two systems of choice connect that is critical. If the connections are right, then both systems of choice can work together in ways that enable people and communities to make the best of their choices and opportunities. If the connection goes wrong, both systems are damaged and work in ways that make it more difficult for people to make important choices in their lives.

The key issue for a continent-wide system of government for Europe is therefore to get these connections right. If the connections fail, Europe will end up with a system of political choice and a system of market choice that do not work. The result will be enormous frustration in people's lives and a reaction against Europe's system of government that will stimulate exactly the kind of local nationalisms and other forms of extremism that Europe needs to avoid. If, on the other hand, it can get these connections right, then people will find that Europe makes it easier for them to make critical choices in their lives. Europe's system of government will become something to celebrate.

In order for Europe to get the connection right between the system of political choice and the system of market choice, two conventional attitudes need to be rejected. First, there is the legacy of the post-war belief in the 'social market'. The tradition has been perverted and debased from the intentions of its founders so as to encourage a completely misplaced confidence that when anything goes wrong in the market then the system of political choice can easily correct for it. Unfortunately the relationship between the two systems of choice is not that simple. Systems of political choice and market choice can, and often do, interact in ways that make it more difficult rather than easier for people to make the critical choices they face in their lives. If a European system of government is to make it easier for people to make the pivotal choices in their lives and to make the most of their opportunities and aspirations, then a much more fundamental rethink of the relationship between state and market is required.

The second conventional attitude that needs to be rejected is that a large European union will be better equipped to help people in their lives simply by virtue of superior size alone. Conventional wisdom views size as the answer to the insecurities of globalization and the bewildering speed of change in what is called the information revolution. This attitude is also mistaken. The significance of these and other changes in the setting for governance lies not in their impact on the optimum scale of governments, but in their effect on the two systems of choice. In order to get Europe's system of government right, the need is to rethink what is happening to the two systems of choice and their relationship.

An Unequal Shock

The diagnosis given in this book is that the new setting for systems of government is one where the two systems of choice – the political system and the market – have been impacted in a highly unequal manner. The new setting has encumbered systems of political choice while giving new vitality to systems of market choice. The competitive advantage has been given to the marketplace as a system for making individual and collective choices. Politicians, meanwhile, seem increasingly irrelevant to people's lives.

This contrast between the two systems of choice can be seen in the way in which the market has demonstrated a much greater adaptability to the new setting. Businesses connect with extraordinary efficiency from the global market to the very local, the private sector has become more and more responsive to signals in the commercial marketplace, and private providers are increasingly outperforming governments even in the provision of social benefits or so-called 'public goods'.

What this means is that when individuals and societies look to make their choices in the marketplace, or through politics, they find an increasingly sharp contrast between responsive private markets and unresponsive political systems. Governments, in comparison with markets, look more and more disconnected, unresponsive and leaden-footed. The economic market is exploiting new ways of doing business and finding superior ways of responding quickly to what people want. By contrast, the system for making individual and social choices through politics suffers under an increasing handicap. This unequal effect of external circumstances is what economists refer to as an 'asymmetric shock'.

Thus, in shaping Europe's system of political choice to the new setting, governments face a crucial decision: they can put in place for Europe a system of political choice that matches the responsiveness of the market; or rules can be made that handicap market choice so as to match the inefficiency of the current systems of political choice. This is the basic decision confronting Europe. If Europe's leaders have the courage to think radically about ways of putting in place a more responsive system of government, then people in the continent will be able to make the most of their lifetime opportunities. What people need genuinely to be afraid of is that Europe's political leaders will think of ways to handicap market choice rather than ways to improve the system of political choice. If they turn in this direction, Europe will indeed end up with the worst of all worlds – where neither system of choice works properly.

What Needs to be Rethought

When we turn to think about the ways in which Europe's system of political choice can be reformed in order to match the responsiveness of systems of market choice, this book identifies three fundamental challenges.

The first of these challenges is that the boundaries of public policy no longer correspond to the territorial boundaries of states. This is true regardless of whether the state is small, such as New Zealand, or large, such as the United States. It is true for a small member state in the European Union, such as Finland, and it is true for a large one, such as Germany.

This disconnection undermines two traditional ways of thinking about how to organize the future of political union in Europe. On the one hand, it undermines traditional federal theories that have relied heavily on fixing territorial distributions to divide up public policy responsibilities so as to distribute powers in a large political system. Thus we can consign to the past the idea that public policy responsibilities in Europe can be divided along the lines of Germany's traditional federal system in any long-lasting way, by assigning particular fields of policy responsibilities to particular territories. On the other hand, this disconnection also undermines the claim that it is possible to think about a continent-wide union in terms of a straightforward scaling up so that Europe becomes analogous to a large nation state. Many of Europe's leaders like to claim that, because it will be large, a continent-wide European union is better placed to take on many of the functions of the traditional state. This claim is at best a half-truth and, at worst, simple deception. The fact of the matter is that the disconnection between the boundaries of public policy and the boundaries of territory has just as much impact on how to organize systems of governments in the largest political associations as it does in the smallest.

The second challenge is to think about how the functions of modern governments are changing and what this means for Europe. Since the end of the nineteenth century, and particularly with the European post-war models of the welfare state, it has become customary to think of the state in terms of its role as provider. The provider role means visualizing the state as the reallocator of resources, as the redistributor of income, and as a principal source of financial security when people come up against risks they face in their lifetimes, such as unemployment and sickness. However, the provider role of the state has reached its peak; increasingly, the primary function of the state is to make rules and regulations. One key reason for this shift is that the rule-making function of governments seeks to address at source the risks facing people during their lifetimes. For societies that are increasingly preoccupied with the treatment of risk, this direct treatment of risk at source is enormously attractive. Thus, in trying to assess what it is that a continent-wide system of government can do best, there is a need to focus especially on this changing role of the state. It would be a huge mistake to think that a continent-wide system of government will do on a large scale what a traditional European nation state does on a smaller scale.

The third challenge is that the nature of democratic expression is changing. Citizens today in every democracy want to see much more direct control over what governments do. They are simply no longer prepared to input their votes into political systems and let their elected representative act for them in the way that traditional forms of representative democracy provide. Citizens want their systems of government to be responsive to their wishes in much more direct ways.

The most visible symptom of popular discontent with traditional ways of political expression is the way in which people assert claims about 'rights'. Such claims have become the principal means by which people express their political beliefs and principles. Elections retain one vital purpose: to provide people with a means to throw politicians out of office. But when it comes to signalling what people want out of politics, rights have largely replaced in importance the significance of the vote and the elected representative. The framework for any system of government for Europe, or anywhere else in the world, thus has to come to grips with such political signals.

This new setting for systems of government has not arrived overnight. In the United States, for example, the advent of the rule-making or regulatory state can be dated from the 1930s and the shift to rights-based politics to the 1960s and 1970s. But the new landscape presents an enormous challenge to traditional ways of thinking about systems of government. In thinking about the ways in which Europe's system of political choice can best connect with the system of market choice, it is these challenges that render imperative a radical rethink of the shape of continent-wide union.

Rethinking the Activities of the Union

Europe can respond to these challenges and to the shock to the two systems of choice in part by focusing clearly on where the continent's comparative advantage as a system of government really lies. The shift in the functions of government towards the rule-making role is not only important for the way in which the functions of European government are viewed but also hugely to its advantage. This is because it is in the rule-making role rather than in the provisioning role that the comparative advantage of Europe as a system of government resides. In the language of economists, there are increasing returns to scale from rule-making on a Europe-wide basis. By contrast, the amount that people can be taxed in order to finance public expenditures has natural limits – limits that have already been reached or exceeded in all countries in Europe – and with finite financial resources, the larger the political association, the less money there is to spread around.

Recognizing that the functions of government are changing also makes it possible to think more clearly about how best to make use of Europe's comparative advantage in the rule-making and regulatory role. The approach taken in this book is to distinguish between rules with 'reach' and rules with 'richness'. It is suggested that

Europe's system of government should focus on the provision of rules with reach while allowing other jurisdictions to provide supplementary rules with richness. Essentially what this division of activities does is to provide Europe's citizens with choice. They can rely on a Europe-wide rule for a standard and predictable product in all parts of the union and for rules of conduct that enable businesses and people to operate freely across the union. But, at the same time, they can look to different regulatory regimes to provide different products that can offer a richer content. An analogy can be made with 'fast' food. The union will provide a McDonald's product – predictable and convenient wherever you are. At the same time people will also want 'slow' food. Different regulatory regimes can provide this alongside the standard product.

Thinking about the comparative advantage that a continent-wide system of government has in rule-making applies equally to the international functions of a union. One of the outstanding features of international life has been the post-war growth in international rules of behaviour. How the union relates its own regulatory and rule-making activities to the international rule-making arena is a critical issue and one that the existing union already shows signs of misunderstanding.

Rethinking Europe's 'Democratic Deficit'

Recognizing that people want to communicate more directly in systems of political choice also suggests that Europe's democratic practices have to be radically rethought. It has become a commonplace in thinking and talking about European political union to diagnose that the current union suffers from what is called a 'democratic deficit'. This is conventionally attributed to the lack of a genuine European public opinion, the absence of European political parties and a perception that the European Parliament is in various ways 'unrepresentative'. The approach taken in this book is different. If systems of political choice are to match the responsiveness of systems of market choice, what we need to focus on is the contrast between the direct methods of communication in the system of market choice and the indirect methods of communication in systems of political choice.

In contemporary systems of political choice it is the vote that reflects the indirect method of communication in politics and claims based on rights that reflect the direct method. Thus, allowing greater space in systems of political choice for the direct method means allowing greater space for claims based on rights. The difficulty for systems of political choice arises because there is a potential tension between the two forms of expression. Claims about rights attract impassioned minorities. Voting, on the other hand, gives no special weight to how strongly we feel about issues. Each person's vote counts the same. The democratic challenge for Europe centres on how to resolve the potential tension between political opinions expressed in the form of claims about rights and opinion expressed through the ballot box.

To resolve the potential tension between the strongly held views of minorities, expressed through claims about rights, and the views of majorities, expressed through the ballot box, the key decision for Europe is where claims based on rights should be recognized. This hinges on distinguishing between the use of rights to argue about the 'right allocation' of resources in a society and their use as a guide to 'right reason' in society. This means rejecting dated thinking about rights and looking much more closely at how the language of rights is used in contemporary social and political debate so that the design of Europe's system of political choice can best profit from the way this language can help in social reasoning.

Rethinking Organization

The shock given to systems of market choice and political choice invalidates any idea that Europe's system of government can just be seen as a scaled-up version of the kind of nation state familiar in Europe. Irrelevant too are traditional forms of federalism with their territorial divisions of function. Answering the challenge for a new form of organization have come models from business and sociology.

There are indeed insights to be gained for Europe's system of government from the way in which businesses organize their activities. In systems of market choice, businesses have learnt how to connect from the global to the local level. A supermarket, for example, may have gathered the products on its shelves from sources all over the world and yet, at the same time, the selection it offers the consumer in a particular location will reflect what shoppers in that particular locality have signalled they want. Businesses thus have learnt how to be both global and local. Governments, on the other hand, have not. They treat globalization as a threat and local differences as a nuisance.

One particular form of organizational model offered by business is the network model. This draws attention to the way in which many businesses have changed from hierarchical command and control organizations to flatter organizations where authority is more dispersed. At the same time there are also important limitations to the network model, and in particular there is a difficulty in linking the network model with democratic principles. In thinking more radically about Europe's future, the approach taken in this book is to look at a further model of business organization: the nexus model. The light the nexus model sheds on the organization of authority links it more closely both with the rule-making functions of a European system of government and with democratic norms. It helps define where Europe's government needs authority and where a more open architecture would be desirable.

Tolerance

The challenges facing a continent-wide system of government for Europe come together around the issue of pluralism. The task of building a continent-wide system of government leads many of Europe's leaders to place the emphasis on the need for Europe's political system to provide 'coherence' in the form of a consistent and uniform approach to important policies and values so that the union does not consist of a patchwork quilt of different obligations and responsibilities. At the least it seems to suggest that Europe should look to enforce a common set of rules and values where these overlap in areas of core concern.

The approach taken in this book is different. It suggests that in a highly diversified continent such as Europe, it would be a great mistake to equate the coherence of the system of government with virtues such as uniformity and consistency across the union. Instead, the key issue is the way Europe's political system is arranged around the requirements for toleration – or the agreement to disagree.

Knowledge-Based Systems of Government

A political framework for tolerance appears to run counter to the most common normative justification for a European system of government. The conventional approach to justifying such a system of government is to appeal to ethical qualities, and in particular the extent to which it incorporates and implements 'European' values such as social cohesion and solidarity and other fundamental human rights. The desire to reflect common European values leads in turn to setting limits on tolerance.

The approach taken in this book appeals to a different European tradition. This is because the relationship between moral systems and political systems is not a straightforward one. In the final analysis, our most important moral values stand as an independent yardstick as to whether we should respect and obey the system of government. The responsibility for those standards rests with the people themselves. It was not the lack of fine words in the Polish constitution that brought down the communist regime; it was the moral courage of the workers of Solidarity. The approach taken in this book is that instead of looking to Europe's political system to incorporate important moral values, we should look on our systems of political and market choice as learning systems. The justification for Europe's system of government is thus to be found in the way in which it provides for knowledge-based government.

Simplicity

The theme of this book is that in a radical rethinking of the future shape of a continent-wide political union a simple form of democratic government will enable Europe to reap the best of what can be achieved both through the system of political choice and the system of market choice. Thinking in terms of a simple structure makes it easier to identify what is important in a continent-wide system of democratic government and what is not. It will also make the system understandable to people.

In scientific reasoning, simplicity has long been seen as a virtue. The untidiness of everyday democratic politics lies far from the neatness of scientific theorizing, but what, in practical terms, 'simplicity' means for Europe's system of government is, first, that it should keep simple what it does and concentrate on what it and only it can do. This is to provide rules and regulations that reach across the continent-wide union as a whole. The union should not be trying to perform the functions of the traditional state in Europe. It should not be taxing and spending, or trying to reallocate resources and redistribute income, or attempting to provide people with financial security against all the risks they face in their lives. This approach to defining the core function of a continent-wide union focuses on the kind of activities that will add value rather than on trying to pre-allocate subject areas for Europe-wide public policy.

Secondly, in order to resolve the potential tensions between rights-based politics in Europe and vote-based politics, a simple structure means that the political framework for Europe's system of government should do only two things. It should establish rights that are about the preconditions for political and market choice (such as the right of freedom of expression) as the preconditions for membership of the union. But once these have been met, the framework should set out the decentralized procedures under which rights claims within the system of political choice can be contested and explored. It should not attempt to provide centralized interpretations.

Thirdly, a simple structure means that Europe's system of government should define its span of authority in terms of its rule-making function. Within the union, the rule-making function helps determine where it needs authority. In other areas an open architecture is desirable. Many European activities will flow through Brussels as the nexus for their connections and make use of the institutions there. But many will have their own, different forms of organization.

The rule-making role also provides guidance on how best to align the union's connections with international rule-making regimes. In this context, Europe needs first and foremost a system that will recognize and respect the different types of relationship involved. The right form of connection is the one that will provide the union with the incentives to support the right rules of international behaviour.

The best way for members to provide such incentives is to maintain their own relationships with outside international regimes and alliances and partners. While members will very often choose to authorize the union to act on their behalf, the possibility that they will not, and the possibility that members may choose other partners, will together act as a necessary restraint on the union's own behaviour and encourage it to support international rules of conduct. The paradoxical effect of allowing the different states of the union to maintain their own independent relationships with the different international regimes is that it will make them more, rather than less, likely to use the union as their main intermediary. Here too, therefore, an open architecture is required.

Finally, Europe's system of government has to simplify the tasks of its central institutions. They suffer from over-ambition. The Commission wants to become the 'government' for the continent of Europe, the European Parliament wants to become a representative assembly in the same way that national parliaments claim to represent public opinion within each member state, and the European Court of Justice wants to become a constitutional court for the union in the same way that many member states have constitutional courts to try to protect the fundamental rules of their political system. These ambitions are excessive and inappropriate because they fail to recognize the key ways in which a continent-wide system of government will be different from the kinds of government we are accustomed to within the traditional member states. The institutions need to focus on a simpler and more restricted range of functions reflecting the rule-making role of the system of government and the span of authority related to that role.

Stronger

That a simple form of government for Europe will be a stronger form is, at first sight, a surprising claim. It would seem, for example, as though Europe's system of government would be stronger if it were to be organized with superpower status as the aim. However, this perception is false. If Europe is to become strong in the world it will not be because it sets that as its aim. It will arise as the indirect result of a system of government that makes the best of the mechanisms of both political choice and market choice. The great danger facing Europe is not that it will repudiate democracy or repudiate the market, but that it will clog up both systems of choice so that neither works effectively. If this happens, Europe will not be a force in the world. It will have neither strength nor influence.

It would also seem as though a continent-wide union would be stronger if it were to set out deliberately to construct a sense of European identity around the uniform interpretation of our most important shared values. This perception is also false. The key to building a sense of identity is not by Europe's system of government promoting allegedly 'special' European values but through people feeling that they are part of a responsive political process. The 500 million people who could be in Europe's system of government must feel that the system is 'theirs'. This means that Europe's system of government has to take into account the growing dichotomy between the speed and responsiveness of the private market, where the consumer increasingly calls the shots, and the mechanisms of public choice, where Europe's political leaders still behave as though people must be told what is good for them. Business leaders recognize that customers increasingly control processes in the economic marketplace; political leaders do not wish to recognize that people look increasingly for similar control and responsiveness in politics.

It also might seem as though Europe's system of government would be stronger the more extensive the authority exercised by the union over its members. This too is a mistaken view. What will make Europe's system of government strong is to ensure that it is knowledge-based. In this way it will provide the framework for better individual and social choices. In order to be knowledge-based, the system of government should exercise authority only where it has a comparative advantage in so doing, it must contain internal mechanisms for change and adaptation, and it must be open to the outside world. Each of these requirements will restrict its range of authority.

If Europe fails to recognize that a strong system of government for the continent will also be a limited one, the outlook will be sombre. The continent will combine continued economic prosperity together with continued failure to find for itself the right system of government. Any such failure will carry a very high cost. Public opinion will be permanently suspicious of a mythical beast called 'Brussels' – a malignant belief that the institutions of European government can be lumped together as one in a system that answers to a different tune than that of public opinion. Majorities outside Brussels will be suspicious of hidden elites that are alleged, correctly or incorrectly, to pull the strings in Brussels. Extremist minorities will also be stimulated – not only those with a nationalist tinge but others with whatever the paranoia of the time may bring. It could take the form of religious fundamentalist groupings or of groups who see their life as shaped by a 'Brussels conspiracy'. In the United States there are groups that see the FBI as the arm of a federal government 'conspiracy'. Europe could similarly see groups arise for whom Europol is seen as part of a European 'conspiracy'. Nor will what is going on be recognized for what it is: a symptom of the shortcomings in Europe's system of government. On the contrary, these reactions will be depicted as justifying the need for more 'Brussels', for more public relations, for more spin doctors, for more state-directed education as 'good Europeans'. The end result will be a system of government where public choices become extremely difficult to make and essential qualities such as consent and participation are replaced by the cancerous qualities of suspicion and disaffection.

Europe's system of government can avoid this fate. But to do so, it must not set out to attempt more than it can achieve or claim what it cannot do. It needs to build and maintain a system of political choice that matches the strength of choice in the market. This means putting in place strong rules in limited areas. By confining its tasks to the maintenance of the few essential rules necessary for the union to keep together, Europe's system of government will, over time, move beyond today's sometimes grudging acquiescence and come eventually to inspire and even be seen as a model for others to emulate.

Europe's Classical Liberal Tradition

The approach taken in this book towards these fundamental issues in rethinking the shape of a continent-wide European union fits within Europe's classical liberal tradition.[1] At the same time the presentation of the message differs in a number of crucial respects from the way in which that tradition has been presented in recent times. For example, it is not suggested that society can do without a system of political choice and rely simply on the market – both are needed. Similarly the rule-making and regulatory functions of government are not seen as leading inexorably towards total state control. On the contrary, while there is a vital need to guard against an abuse of the regulatory role, rules and regulations can also play an enormously helpful role in widening the scope for individual and social freedom, particularly in large-scale political associations. Neither is it suggested that political association is about the individual and not about communities. The antithesis is a false one. Liberalism is about the individual within a social setting.

Where this book fits within the classical liberal tradition is in its acceptance of the virtues of market choice and in placing a central emphasis on the importance of the institutional and procedural arrangements for tolerance in the union. It sets out the framework for limited government in the continent. It is liberal also in looking to justify the framework for political association in terms of the knowledge base for making individual and social choices.

Organization of the Discussion

The subject of the fundamentals of European political union necessarily cuts across the boundaries of traditional academic disciplines. For this reason the argumentation in this book draws heavily on the interdisciplinary tradition of constitutional economics. This approach uses the perspective of economics to explore the mix of economic, political, legal and philosophical issues involved in a continent-wide system of government.

The book starts by highlighting the crucial importance of systems of government in determining the success or failure of societies (chapter 1: 'How to Look at European Governance'). The analysis examines the different ways in which the debates about European political union typically start and argues in favour of a less commonly used starting point: namely, the position of the outside observer. The outside observer looks at what makes people in a society decide to make their crucial lifetime choices either through the market or through politics. The system of government is key in this because it connects the two systems of choice. The way in which Europe's future system of government connects choices made in the market with choices made through political processes will determine the long-run success or failure of Europe as a political association.

In order to have a system of government for Europe that gets the relationship right between market choice and political choice, there is a need to be clear about the setting in which contemporary systems of government have to operate. This discussion is introduced in the following chapter ('Adapting to Shock: The New Setting for Governance'). The analysis places both systems of choice in the well-known context of 'globalization', the 'communications revolution' and the ageing of society. These developments are discussed in terms of 'opportunity costs': their effect on the ease or difficulty people have in using the two systems of choice. This leads to the diagnosis of 'asymmetric shock': a situation, as noted above, where private markets have been stimulated to become more responsive mechanisms for people to make their choices, while, by contrast, political markets have become less responsive. The chapter continues by discussing the various adaptations that can be made to systems of government in the light of this diagnosis.

The discussion continues in chapter 3 with a look at some of the leading political ideas prevalent about how Europe's system of government should evolve ('Projecting the Past: Conventional Scenarios for Europe's Future'). It suggests that politicians have fallen into the same trap as have economic forecasters, who, in looking to the future, often end up by projecting the past. The chapter identifies how much conventional political thinking about the future of Europe's system of government is backward-looking.

The following three chapters look in greater detail at the key aspects of the contemporary setting for governments identified earlier. First there is an analysis of the rule-making functions of government. Chapter 4 ('The Reach of Rules') describes why the main functions of government are turning away from the role of government as provider towards the role of government as regulator and rule-maker. It discusses how the union will need to specialize in putting in place rules with reach across the continent. It looks at the implications for the union of allowing for different rules alongside the rules with reach.

Secondly there is an analysis of the way in which the language of rights has come to dominate contemporary political communication. Chapter 5 ('Signals and Noise: The Role of Rights') looks at the reasons why this has happened and the importance of rights in correcting for the indirectness of representative democracy. The chapter continues by looking at the different uses to which the language of rights is put in order to see how contemporary systems of government can best exploit these uses. It makes a major distinction between those rights that are about the preconditions of systems of political choice – such as the right of free expression without which a system of democratic choice cannot work at all – and those that are about the priorities within a system of political choice.

Thirdly, in chapter 6 ('Networks and Nexus') there is a discussion of the architecture of 'connections'. The discussion dismisses the traditional response of political scientists that government can just be scaled up in size. It then turns to consider models borrowed from business. One currently fashionable borrowing looks at government as a network analogous to business networks; the other looks at the idea that firms can usefully be viewed as providing a nexus of contracts. The chapter evaluates where such borrowings appear applicable and where they do not. It suggests that the union's span of authority can be defined by its specialized rule-making function and by the way in which its rule-making authority is organized in relation to various international regimes.

Chapter 7 brings together the discussion on what the union should be doing, the way people make their preferences known and the way in which the authority of the union should be organized, in terms of an argument in favour of 'simplicity'. It describes the form a simplified system of government for Europe would take and compares this simple democratic structure for a continent-wide union with the conventional views outlined earlier.

The two following chapters respectively discuss the two main criticisms that can be levelled against simple governance: that such a system will not provide the coherence that a political system requires, and that it will not answer the moral dimension of European political union.

The concluding chapter brings together the wider implications of designing for a simple system of government for Europe, including the constitutional consequences.

Getting It Right

Europe's system of government is still at a formative stage. But already there are danger signals. It already runs the risk of trying to monopolize connections, over-prescribe rules and abrogate the interpretation of rights. Its institutions are already tainted with corruption and venality. It is already beginning to be seen as a cumbersome and distant system where decisions are taken by a symbolic 'Brussels' disconnected from the cares and desires of ordinary people. It is tempted by models of government that are rigid and unsuited to modern conditions.

Citizens are looking for new ways to exercise control and ensure immediacy of response in their system of government, analogous to the new powers they have acquired in the economic marketplace. Thus, an essential quality for Europe's system of government is that it should provide a sense of 'affinity' so that the people within its borders feel that it is 'their own' and not 'over there'. In a large political association this is difficult to do. In the United States there is the well-known phrase of 'beyond the beltway,' implying a divorce between the federal government politics of Washington, DC (inside the ring-road called the beltway), and the vast majority of the American public (living outside it). References to an emerging system of European government as 'Brussels' is a symptom of exactly the same phenomenon: a political centre that is 'over there' and seen to be divorced from the people it is meant to serve.

The answer offered by this book to the problem of distant government in large political systems is to 'make it simple'. Paradoxical it may be, but a simple form of democratic government for Europe will also be the strongest. By focusing on what it and only it can do, the union will not constantly be accused of unnecessary interference; by limiting its span of authority, it will not be seen as a constant threat to other jurisdictions; by offering tolerance of differences, it will respond to Europe's pluralism; by providing for variety and innovation, it will be better able to meet the challenges that lie ahead.

Europe's system of government has a mountain to climb in order to win allegiance, let alone affection. By trying to do too much, it will only disappoint and disaffect. By confining itself to the essentials, however, a base of respect will be established that will provide a platform for an enduring popular support.

1 How to Look at European Governance

It is not, then, merely to satisfy a legitimate curiosity that I have examined America; my wish has been to find instruction by which we may ourselves profit.
Alexis de Tocqueville, *Democracy in America*

Systems of Government: The Source of Success

The system of government determines the success or failure of a society. As Europe moves toward building a continent-wide political union, it starts from a base of great economic prosperity in much of the continent, the resource of a highly educated population and individual states that have embraced democratic ways of life. But this enormously promising base will not provide the platform for the success of a continental union unless a system of government can be devised that is suited to the continent as a whole.

Such a system is not yet in sight. The governments of the individual nation states realize hesitatingly and with reluctance that the present union will not do. They do not see clearly what can replace it. The existing member states cling to what is in place, apply patch-jobs where necessary and increasingly act together in ways that may well be beneficial and productive, but depart more and more from what was envisaged in the current union's formal treaty base. There is a movement to 'constitutionalize' what is important in the present treaty base and to bring in what is missing. This is a welcome sign of the start of a more fundamental debate. However, the virtues of constitutionalization depend entirely on the content of what is to be put in constitutional form. The danger is of badly thought-out transpositions from national experience.

Unless a new system can be devised, this great European venture will fail. The history of the last century is full of examples of countries with great initial promise, with abundant natural resources and enterprising populations that failed to deliver on that promise. At the start of the century Latin America had countries such as Argentina and Brazil with every prospect for success yet which failed to find it. At mid-century several of the newly independent countries of Africa had rich resource bases on which to build – but again the promise has not materialized. Towards the end of the century, countries in East and Southeast Asia appeared to have found a formula for success in the footsteps of a resurgent Japan. But for Japan, the last decade has been wasted and the prospects for many other Asian countries seem much more fragile and elusive than before.

The American Example

When the position of Europe's leaders, as they try to build a continent-wide system of government, is compared with the position of the founding fathers of the United States as they sat down to debate the provisions of the American Constitution, there is a striking contrast in the framework for the debate. The founding fathers of the American system started with one enormous advantage: they conducted their debates within common terms of reference about the principles of good government. The transition from a confederal to a federal form of government, and the translation of abstract principles into actual practice, provoked fierce dispute and sometimes acrimony. The outcome reflected not the triumph of pure theory but partisan political objectives, hard political bargaining and ruthless ratification tactics. Nevertheless, when it came to the underlying principles of good government the founding fathers turned, by and large, to a shared heritage of English legal theory and practice and drew in common from the political theories of Hume, Locke and Montesquieu. Crucially, they also accepted without question that most commercial activity would be undertaken by private enterprise.[1]

As Europe's political leaders seek now to build a political union in Europe, they lack such common terms of reference. All are committed to the ideal of democracy. But beyond this starting point, important as it is, there is no agreement on the principles of good government. One strand of tradition in Europe emphasizes the importance of 'rule-based' democratic government: the idea that powers in a democracy must be placed within a system of rules. A different strand emphasizes the importance of 'rights-based' systems of government: the idea that a system of government does not gain legitimacy just by the fact of its existence but only if it respects certain fundamental rights, including social rights, which define the just society within which the system of government must work. In addition, most countries in Europe subscribe to the idea of 'representative' democracy: the idea that those who exercise political power do so on behalf of those who have voted them into office. Finally, most governments in Europe accept the philosophy of the 'social market': that is, the market moderated by government interventions in the face of any social distress.

At the same time, there is no consensus on these components, or how to express them or how to draw them together. Not all member states subscribe to the idea of rule-based government or agree where the rules should constrain democratic impulses. Equally, member states do not agree on the role of rights in a constitutional setting. While all countries subscribe to the practices of representative democracy, many also allow, particularly in the context of Europe, for a different tradition, that of direct or 'participative' democracy where people have the chance to express themselves directly on the great issues of the moment. While the attachment to the social market is pervasive, there is, at the same time, a growing realization that different versions of the model need to be rethought.

As a result of these different strands, when, at the end of the day, the existing treaties of the European Union are examined in order to see what has been agreed to date about the shape of political union in Europe, there is to be found a *mélange* of provisions that reflect not a common understanding of the principles of good government, but opportunistic, self-seeking and unprincipled bargaining by politicians and European institutions, with outcomes so complex that the text is unintelligible except to the experts. When governments try to justify to public opinion what they have agreed in the treaties, the stress is always on the good policy outcomes they hope and promise to achieve – never on the underlying principles of political association.

The confusion in the treaty base of the existing European union stems not just from the lack of common terms of reference about the principles of good government, but also from the difficulties of the modern setting facing systems of government. Many of the old anchor points about how democratic government should be organized have been lost. The functions of government are changing, people's expectations of what politics can deliver are changing and geography no longer provides a secure basis on which to allocate functions between different layers of government. This loss of the compass for governance spills over into further evasion and muddle in the treaty base itself.

If the process of building a system of government in Europe continues down this path of confusion and ever-increasing complexity, the continent will end up in the worst of all worlds. Democratic forms of government in Europe will have been eroded, market economies will have been damaged. Instead of Europe being able to take advantage of dynamic global opportunities, it will find itself a backwater of thwarted aspirations, political discontent and the breeding ground for extremism. What lies behind the success of the United States has been the adoption of a hugely robust system of government. What lay behind so many of the stories of failed endeavour or semi-success in the twentieth century was an inability in other parts of the world to do the same.

Alternative Starting Points

In order to sort out the principles of a system of government for a continent-wide political union the choice of the starting point for the debate is itself highly important. Debates about the shape of political union in Europe typically start from assumptions that are highly questionable and that will lead the continent in the wrong direction. They appeal to fears and unfounded beliefs that stand in the way of a clear perception of the foundations for a European system of government.

The Counterfactual: Nation against Nation

The most common starting point of all for discussions about the shape of Europe is fear of the past. The finger is pointed at the aggressive nationalism that ravaged Europe in the first half of the twentieth century and it is suggested that political union in Europe is designed above all to avoid a return to that earlier condition of nation against nation. For a whole generation of European politicians, now gone from the scene, any major speech on European union would incorporate a reference to the Second World War.

This kind of starting point about what would happen in the absence of a union has ancient roots in political theorizing. Its ancestry derives from theories that start from a postulated 'state of nature'. In most cases the 'state of nature' is not an Arcadia but a condition of brutality and lawlessness. The logic of the argument relies on a counterfactual, argument,[2] which runs that: 'If we did not have our system X, we would have the desperate condition of Y.' Perhaps the best-known example in political theory of this starting point is the state of nature described by Thomas Hobbes.

The counterfactual is seductive as a starting point because it provides a means of justifying an existing political system. Essentially, the warning is that if a brick is removed from the political edifice, a wall will crumble, the building will fall down and there will be a return to the disastrous former state that everybody wishes to avoid.

Just such a line of argument is employed to justify the existing European union. It has become an article of faith among European politicians and an actual article in the current treaty base that the so-called '*acquis communautaire*' should be maintained in full and built on. What this is intended to mean is that there can be no going back from whatever institutions, policies and procedures are in place now in the union. Taken at face value this provision would simply build redundancy and sterility into the treaties because any system of government must have the ability to change, repeal and revise. But more importantly the implied message is that if the existing union gives an inch in modifying what it has got, everything may start to unwind and Europe will be back, not to nature, but to competitive and destructive nationalism. A variant of this message is sometimes given in the metaphor of a bicycle climbing a hill: if the existing union does not go forward, momentum will be lost and everything will slip back.

One basic weakness in this whole approach is that the counterfactual can be challenged. In today's Europe it is implausible that, in the absence of the existing union, European states would indeed revert to their behaviour of the first half of the twentieth century. The overwhelming majority of people in Europe and their governments have learnt their lesson that aggression does not pay. The only exception to this lies in the Balkans. To justify an extension of the arrangements for the existing union to the whole of Europe on the grounds that otherwise all nations in Europe will once again be at each other's throats defies belief. And the more that the counterfactual is disbelieved, the weaker it becomes as a foundation on which to build the edifice of a continent-wide system of government. The real-world challenge to the counterfactual can be sidestepped. It is possible to say that the counterfactual is simply a theoretical construction. Even a theoretical 'state of nature' may still be a useful device for illuminating some essential feature of a system of government. Yet those who argue that, in the absence of the European Union, the continent would revert to the behaviour of the first half of the twentieth century are using the example as a literal rather than a hypothetical state of affairs. They are asking Europe's citizens to believe that, in the absence of a political union, Europe would indeed sooner or later find itself in a situation where nation would once again be pitted against nation.

The counterfactual approach to the construction of European political union not only defies belief but it does not get off first base for a different reason. The disasters that Europe invited on itself and succumbed to in the first half of the twentieth century provided enormously important motivation for the generation of leaders that started the move towards European political integration. But good motives are not enough. A better starting point is needed in order to provide theoretical or practical insights into the principles of a continent-wide system of governance. People need to know what kind of system of democratic government Europe can put in place, how it will operate and why they should respect it. It is not good enough to say that the existing union is better than no union at all. Such an argument could be used to justify any kind of political union in Europe. The present union has succeeded far beyond the hopes of the founding fathers of the original coal and steel community and the original economic community and this achievement should indeed be respected. But Europe cannot start by assuming that the present union provides the right structures for the continent-wide union that is now possible following the collapse of communism.

Dealing with Uncertainty

As memories of twentieth-century disasters fade away and as generations of politicians in Europe change, discussion about a European system of government increasingly starts from a different point. Attention is drawn not to dangers past but to new and future dangers. From fear of the past, Europe's politicians go straight to fear of the future. The most frequently cited spectre on Europe's doorstep is that of 'globalization'. No matter that globalization is as much a cause for celebration as it is for trepidation and as much an opportunity as it is a threat, it is always the downside, the negative and the unknown that are pointed out. The union, it is suggested, has to be constructed so as to provide a protection and security against these new dangers.

Sometimes the same line of thinking is presented in terms of 'the end of the nation state'. The proposition is once again that the traditional so-called 'nation state' can no longer perform its accustomed functions and Europe needs to face up to a new and uncertain world where a continent-wide union offers better protection against the unknown.[3] It is also suggested that the legitimacy of modern political structures has been built around the state as an instrument for helping people to cope with the insecurities in their lives, and that now that the nation state can no longer offer any such sense of security, that legitimacy is vanishing.[4] In the context of Europe it is the wider political union that is said to provide the new and improved basis for helping people cope and around which a new political legitimacy is to be built.

Arguments such as these, based on uncertainty about the future, have also traditionally provided a starting point for the discussion of the principles of political organization. The theoretical device employed in this discussion is provided by the so-called 'veil of ignorance' or, more accurately, the 'veil of uncertainty'. According to this approach, it is argued that the rules of political association must be valid and applicable to meet circumstances that cannot be foreseen. Consequently the basic principles of political association must be those that will be universally acceptable in general circumstances. This approach had a great vogue among political theorists in the second half of the twentieth century,[5] although its roots go back much further.

One of the difficulties with approaching political construction on the basis of uncertainty about the future is that it draws too sharp a distinction between the past and the future. In the real world, the veil of uncertainty is approached not just through a fog of ignorance but also through experience both of what has been tried and found lacking and what has been tested and found to work. The past cannot be used indiscriminately to justify anything currently in place, but neither can it be ignored. Systems of government do not deal just with future abstractions, and there is a need to be clear and explicit about what it is exactly that is being carried forward into the debate from the past, and why.

There is, however, a more basic deficiency in any approach built on uncertainties about the future and that is that it opens the door to far too wide a speculation about what might be generally acceptable in unknown and unknowable circumstances. It will be argued in the next chapter that the world indeed provides a new setting for systems of government. But a precise diagnosis of this new setting is needed in order to adapt the framework. The particular response given to the new setting has also to be justified against other possible responses. Thus, in thinking about a continent-wide system of governance for Europe, it is not sufficient to say that something is needed at the European level in order to safeguard people against an uncertain future. Instead, there is a need to be much more precise about the setting to be faced, the nature of the different responses that can be given, and the justification of those that are finally chosen. Indiscriminate fear of the future is no better a guide to building a European system of government than is indiscriminate fear of the past.

The Moral Standpoint

A third traditional starting point for exploring the principles of government for Europe is to emphasize the moral dimension of governance. The moral standpoint goes beyond the claim that any system of government for Europe will be a morally superior alternative to a state of conflict between nations. It also goes beyond the claim that a European system of governance can reduce the uncertainties people face in their lives from globalization. The essence of the moral standpoint is that any system of government for Europe must be built around the concept of 'justice'.[6]

Since, in the abstract, everybody is in favour of 'justice', it seems like a firm basis on which to start thinking about a system of government for the continent. The difficulty lies in how to translate an abstract goal into the provisions of a system of government.

In the context of debate in Europe, 'justice' is usually defined to include both procedural justice and substantive justice. Procedural justice means that the system of government must respect basic standards such as free expression.[7] Substantive justice means 'social justice': in other words, the system of government must be equipped to offer social protection to those who need it and express the social virtues of solidarity between rich and poor, between generations and between the 'social partners' in Europe. The basic idea is that of the 'social state'. The individual nation state in Europe may no longer be able to perform the role of a social state, but Europe's system of governance can still be designed to embody the philosophy and design of such a state.

The ideal of the social state represents a rich and widely shared tradition in Europe. The breadth of this tradition can be illustrated by the many different ways in which the concern for justice can be formulated. The formulations, drawing on very different sources of inspiration, include the following:

- Solidarity with the community is an integral way in which people conceive their identity, and this sense of solidarity has to be built into the rules of political organization.[8]
- Some measure of agreement on the principles of social justice is necessary for a human community to be viable and durable.[9]
- A notion of what is just will help a society to select and sustain the norms, rules and institutions that are needed in any system of government.[10]
- Welfare provision by the state is necessary in order to underpin the legitimacy of government structures.[11]
- Legal systems also need to be based on 'just laws' in order to gain legitimacy since it is not any system of law and law enforcement that is legitimate.[12]

These different ways of appealing to a concept of justice in thinking about Europe's system of government are undeniably attractive, particularly for Europe's politicians. Witness the recent proclamation of the existing union's Charter of Fundamental Rights with its *mélange* of procedural and substantive rights. Yet, at the end of the day, this tradition of the social state does not provide a good starting point from which to think about the structures of a continent-wide system of government.

There are two important difficulties to starting to discuss the shape of governance in Europe from the point of moral concern about social justice. The first concerns how to express the values of procedural justice in relation to those of social justice. Placing the two definitions of justice side by side can encourage the idea that there is a 'trade-off' between the two. This is pernicious. A state that provides a high level of social protection does not as a result have to offer less respect for procedural norms.

A number of different and conflicting solutions have been suggested in order to avoid the trap of 'trade-offs'. From one side it can be argued that notions of procedural justice have priority. From the other side it can be argued that what matters is rules that embody substantive justice and that procedural standards are subsidiary. Between these two contradictory positions there have been a number of attempts to express standards of procedural justice in ways that incorporate the social dimension. These attempts make use of concepts such as 'fairness' and 'equality', which seem to bridge the divide.[13] As mentioned above, the concept of 'basic rights' has also been employed to argue in favour of equal status for procedural and social justice on the grounds that the right to a social state is a basic right numbering alongside other basic rights such as procedural rights of participation. This is a complex debate that has not resolved the inherent tension between the two notions of justice.

The second difficulty concerns how to express the relationship between the norms of the political world and the norms of the moral world. The underlying issue is about what gives legitimacy to a political system. This will be discussed further in chapter 9. At this stage it suffices to say that, if the organization of political life involves issues that are different from those that people confront in making moral judgements, then it is not possible to move easily from propositions about the moral order of society to propositions about the political order. In other words, moral propositions (such as the virtue of social solidarity) cannot be used in any straightforward way as a basis on which to rest a political order because they will not address the particular type of issues that have to be confronted when the special properties of systems of government are taken into account. For example, systems of government have the power to coerce: to make people do what they do not want to do. Power as such is morally neutral: it can be used for purposes that are good or for purposes that are bad. But in the design of a system of political choice there is a need to address the issue of the power to coerce as a central issue, perhaps indeed as *the* central issue. Thus, how to frame the checks and balances that must accompany this power – even if it is to be used for good ends and to achieve substantive justice in society – has to be treated as a critical feature of any political system.

At first sight the moral standpoint is an attractive position to adopt in starting to think about Europe's system of government. But it overlooks the ways in which a political system differs from a system of morality and blurs the problem of how to express a concern about substantive justice alongside procedural justice. It opens wide the door to a system of government that can act without constraints as long as it proclaims fine intent.

The Outside Observer

There is finally a different starting point that avoids the debate about the counterfactual, that does not play on fears and uncertainties about what the future might bring, and that keeps views about the moral standards in society separate from the different concerns to be given a central focus in looking at systems of government. This different starting point is that of the outside observer.

Historically, the most famous example of the outside observer is that provided by Alexis de Tocqueville, who visited America over nine months in 1831 and 1832 in order to examine the American system and to find out, if he could, why a democratic form of government had taken hold in the United States but not in Europe. What is striking about Tocqueville's analysis, published in two parts, in 1835 and 1840, is that he saw the key to the way in which America's then system of government worked as lying in the way in which it connected two systems of choice: that of politics and that of the market.[14]

Updated to contemporary debate, Tocqueville's model draws attention to three features of governance. First, the outside observer will see that it is possible for people to make choices through two systems: through the mechanisms of political choice and through the mechanisms of the marketplace. Secondly, people can be viewed as starting from a position of neutrality as to which system of choice is best. There is no initial predisposition in favour either of the market or of politics. If the political system looks to be the best system for making choices, the outside onlooker will assume that participants will be attracted to that route; conversely, if the market offers greater advantage, it seems safe to assume that participants will look instead to that route. Thirdly, the outside observer does not need to prejudge what types of choice are best made through each system, nor, furthermore, is the onlooker prejudging where the borderline between the two systems of choice should be drawn. Participants will likely favour one channel for some choices and the other for other choices.[15]

What Tocqueville saw as key to a system of government is to get the connection between the two systems right. He saw the possibility that the two systems could transform each other in mutually beneficial ways.

The insight that the two systems of choice are connected seems to imply that, up to a point, they can be viewed as alternatives. If one channel is clogged, participants will simply turn, or be forced to turn, to the other as a means for making choices. At first sight this would seem to suggest in practical terms that if, for some reason, the system of market choice is not working properly, it may be possible to compensate by doing more through the system of political choice. Conversely, if the political system does not work effectively, then it may be possible to compensate by making more choices in the market. However, Tocqueville's diagnosis does not invite any such easy deductions. Instead, he seems to suggest that if the connections between the two systems of choice are faulty, then both mechanisms for choice may become clogged and the outside observer will see that people have nowhere to turn to express either individual or social choice. In other words, the system of government will fail to provide society with any effective means for making individual or social choices and social and political breakdown will result.

Contemporary social theorists may wish to bring in additional analytically distinct social sub-systems: for example, adding to Tocqueville's two categories the additional categories of social institutions such as the family and culture. Each has had its advocates in recent times. Cultural values such as civility or trust have been pointed to as essential ingredients of a successful society,[16] as have social values such as the importance placed on the family.

Some of this advocacy of the importance of additional sub-systems has been rapidly dated by the success of the United States in recent decades. Even if the United States were now to slip into recession, this success has undermined theories about social or cultural values that foresaw the inevitable decline of the country. But Tocqueville himself would not have denied the importance of cultural or social values. His own discussion of America devoted considerable space to each. These possible refinements do not weaken his basic insight that politics and economics interact in ways that make it impossible for either to be independent of the other.

When Tocqueville looked at the two systems of choice he saw the legal system as providing the link between political choice and the market. History since Tocqueville's time has eroded the independence of legal systems. He himself foresaw correctly that government in a democratic society would be active government. In practice, the result of active government has been that government has become the overwhelming source of law. It is government that acts as the connector of both systems.

If Tocqueville's position as the outside observer is adopted as the starting point for thinking about Europe's system of government, it implies thinking about Europe's system of government in terms of two connected systems of choice: that of politics and that of the market. It is not possible to deal with each as though it were separate. Thus in thinking in terms of systems of government the focus should not just be on the system of political choice by itself. Instead, it has to be on the system of political choice together with the system of market choice.

Moreover, Tocqueville avoids easy assumptions about the nature of the connection. He does not suggest that the relationship should be seen as a mere question of how output is divided – where either the political system is regarded as a predator on the market system or, conversely, where the market is regarded as an encroacher on choices better decided within politics. Tocqueville's diagnosis is that if the connection is established correctly, then the strengths of one system of choice reinforce the strengths of the other. If, on the contrary, the connection is set wrongly, then he warns that both systems of choice can be impaired and the weaknesses of the one can accentuate the weaknesses of the other. In other words, if the two systems of choice are working well together, then the sum of the system is worth more than the sum of its parts. The converse also applies. If the connection is faulty, the system will deliver less than its parts.

There are three compelling reasons why the standpoint of the outside observer should be preferred as the starting point for looking at a system of government for Europe. First, there is the negative reason that it avoids the weaknesses of the alternative approaches discussed earlier. It does not rest on disputed historical counterfactuals, nor on alarmism about future hypotheticals; neither does it rest among the philosophical quicksand surrounding concepts of justice and fairness.

Secondly, it offers a measure of the success of a system of government. It is a measure that does not depend on scaremongering about the dangers of globalization. Nor does it depend on unreal promises about the particular benefits – social or otherwise – that a system of governance can deliver. Tocqueville was impressed by the commercial vigour of the early United States but he was not equating success with prosperity. Instead the message can be interpreted as the need for a system of government that enables people to make the best of their choices – whatever they are, whatever existing resource endowments are, whatever future opportunities might bring and whatever their preferences might be. In other words, if the connection between political choice and market choice is right, people will have the widest possible choices in whatever circumstances and be able to make the best use of both channels of choice. In Europe, people might choose to maximize the possibilities of economic growth, but, on the contrary, they might choose to give priority to a green and safe environment. There is no prejudice against the market. Equally there is no prejudice against political choice.

Thirdly, the standpoint of the outside observer challenges some key orthodox beliefs in Europe. In particular, orthodox formulations of the social market model in individual nation states in Europe encourage people to think of the relationship between political choice and market choice as one of benign opposites where the precise correspondence between them does not matter too much. Tocqueville warns against that kind of assumption. It is an orthodoxy that is already extremely costly in individual countries in Europe and one that will be much more damaging if adopted as a guide to what a continent-wide system of government should be doing and how it should be constructed. A fresh look is required.

Connecting Two Systems of Choice

There are two basic reasons why Europe has shied away from taking a fresh look at the relationships between the system of market choice and the system of political choice. The first stems from the view that it is unnecessary to look too closely at the relationship because there is something inevitable about the way in which democracy and 'the mixed' or the 'social market' economy go together. The second stems from the view that, when anything goes wrong in the market, the system of political choice can easily make amends. Both views are mistaken. If they are followed, Europe will fail to appreciate what is happening to the two systems of choice and what this means for systems of government. As a result, its own system of government will fail.

Democracies and the Mixed Economy

In the real world all democratic societies seem to end up with mixed economies. The combination arises because market outcomes may not be seen as desirable by democratic opinion and those who do badly in a market economy may have the power through democracy to demand intervention.[17] The seeming inevitability of this combination lulls opinion into complacency. The temptation is to stop thinking about the way in which the state and the market interrelate.

The basic reason why the relationship needs continuous attention is that the two systems of choice interact in ways that matter enormously for the way in which people live their lives. Moreover, they may interact in ways that can be hugely damaging to the choices open to people. The most telling illustrations can be seen by looking at the points where market choice and political choice intersect. The importance of this point of intersection in the daily lives of citizens can be appreciated because what people typically confront in making some of the most critical decisions in their lives is precisely the product of both systems of choice. In other words, some of the most important decisions in people's lives have to be taken exactly where systems of market choice and systems of political choice interconnect. If individuals decide to make payments into a private pension or insurance scheme in order to be able to enjoy later life more than they could by relying on a state pension, or if they decide to pay for extra tuition out of their own purse to go to a particular university because they think the subsequent job rewards will be higher than if they opted for a cheaper state-supported university place, they are making hugely important life-cycle choices that take into account an environment that is neither pure market nor pure politics.[18]

The key question at these points of intersection when individuals and families make hugely important and far-ranging decisions is whether people's choices are being widened, narrowed or just being muddled and made more complicated. The answer across much of Europe is that at these critical moments of choice, governments muddle people's options rather than assist them to get the best out of the market and the best out of politics. If the current practices of the member states are transferred to Europe as a whole, similar muddle in people's most important choices will be inevitable. As a result, Europe's system of government will become associated with all the frustrations in people's lives.

The Fiction of Benign Opposites

The idea that Europe does not have to think too closely about democracy and the mixed economy is further buttressed by the complacent way in which a 'mixed economy' or the 'social market' is accepted as the norm in Europe. The model of the social market, which started from a much more rigorous approach to the way in which the mechanisms of political choice were linked to market choice, has evolved to become a quite unreflective presumption that if there are deficiencies in one system of choice – the market – then they can be easily offset by the other – politics.

In fact, the conventional assumption made in Europe that the system of politics compensates easily for the defects of the market is faulty and would seem, in large part, to be the product of wishful thinking. The reality is that there is no easy demarcation line between the two and there can be no counting on the system of political choice to automatically correct for deficiencies in the system of market choice because:

- both systems of choice reflect both individual and aggregate choice – the market is not just about individual choice, neither is politics just about aggregate choice;
- both reflect the selfish as well as the social – the market can meet social concerns, and equally politics can reflect selfish concerns;[19]
- both the market and politics produce impure goods that are neither wholly public nor wholly private – the market is not just about private goods, and politics is not just about public goods;
- both contain inherent inequalities – the market is unequal because money counts and politics is unequal because information and access count;
- both are a source of injustice as well as justice – people can be victimized by politics through no fault of their own and they can do badly in the market through no fault of their own;
- both present risks – there are market risks when markets change and there are political risks when public policies change; and
- both suffer from systemic sources of failure – political systems because they suppress information, and market systems because they become unstable in the search for information.

For fifty years, countries in Europe have proceeded on the assumption that the strengths of each of the two main systems of choice could be effortlessly combined because the strengths of one system – politics – could be relied upon to offset the weaknesses of the other – the market. This assumption is now being carried over into the continent-wide union as a whole. There is a casual assumption that the right connections exist in individual member states, or near enough so that it makes no difference, and an equally casual assumption that these same relationships can now be extended to the whole of Europe's system of government. This is wrong.

Re-examining the Setting for Governments

If Europe's system of government is to connect together the two systems of political choice and market choice so as to enhance their mutual strengths rather than aggravate their mutual weaknesses, there is a need to look afresh at the modern setting facing systems of government:

- There is a need to assess precisely where it is in this new setting that systems of political choice add value to systems of market choice.
- There is a need also to look precisely at the way in which preferences and priorities are being signalled in this new setting so that both systems are responsive to the choices people want to make.
- Finally, there is a need to look at how systems of political and market choice are best organized in this new setting so as to deliver what they are good at delivering and can best respond to signals about what people want.

Europe has an opportunity now to re-examine the connection between the two systems of choice and to try to arrange the rules for a continent-wide union so that individuals and communities can get the best out of each system. It will not achieve success unless it does so. When the relationship between the two systems of choice is examined more carefully rather than relying on conventional wisdom about how the two relate, it can be seen that one system – the system of market choice – has been rapidly adapting to offer what it is that people want, while the other system – the system of political choice – is floundering. It is this disjunction between the two systems of choice that challenges systems of government. The next chapter therefore looks at the reasons underlying this disjunction and what this setting means for building a successful system of government for Europe.

2 Adapting to Shock

The New Setting for Governance

Europe faces the realities of the information society and global-
isation. There is a need to provide for an ageing population and
respond to the expectations of young people.
European Council Millennium Declaration, Helsinki,
December 1999

An Asymmetric Shock

The New Setting for Governance

The portentous-sounding 'Millennium Declaration', issued by the highest body of the European Union – the European Council – at the end of 1999, referred to the forces of the information revolution, globalization and to the changing age structures of society as the fundamental challenges facing Europe.

There are plenty of commentators who are quick to claim that there is nothing new about any of these developments. The nineteenth century saw major advances in the speed and technology of infor-mation transfer, for example with the invention of the telegraph. The same century also saw the beginnings of major advances in public health and the start of sustained increases in life expectancy. It also witnessed a huge increase in international trade and capital flows.[1] Yet, despite all the many qualifications that can be made about what is really new and what is old, and what is hype and what is reality, few would disagree that the global interlinking of economies and societies, the information revolution, and the pace of medical progress feeding dramatic demographic shifts are bringing about real changes in the day-to-day world in which people live and make their choices. These are the factors that define the setting for modern systems of government.

What is of paramount importance for the future of European union is to go beyond just identifying and describing globalization, the information revolution and the ageing of populations and to analyse their implications for a system of government that is intended to embrace all of Europe. This the Millennium Declaration did not do.

It is the theme of this chapter that the changes in the external setting in which people live their lives are delivering to systems of government what economists refer to as an 'asymmetric shock'. What this means is that when the two systems of choice – politics and the market – are looked at, the effect of the changes in the external setting can be seen to be highly unequal. The market system is benefiting enormously from the changes and exploiting them so that it has become much more responsive in providing what people want. By contrast, making choices through the traditional vote-based mechanisms of politics has become more difficult. These mechanisms are looking much weaker and much less able to respond in similar fashion to what people want. In other words, the changes in the external setting have benefited one system through which people make their individual and social choices – the market – but have worked against the other system – politics. In plain terms, people are finding politicians less relevant to their lives and politics a turn-off. This asymmetric shock has critical implications for systems of government, and, specifically, for how to think about a continent-wide system of government for Europe.

New Economies – Old Politics

When comparing the different ways in which market systems and political systems have responded to the changes cited by the European Council, three immediate and striking contrasts present themselves. The first concerns core activities. On the side of the market, convergent technology has provided new consumer products such as the mobile phone, demolished old industry boundaries and forced businesses to reassess their core activities. By contrast, there has been no comparable reassessment of the core functions of government on the side of political choice. Governments continue to offer their traditional products and to try to perform their traditional activities.

The second contrast concerns the customization of products. The market has been able to exploit the ease and directness of contact made possible by the information revolution to customize products and services to the particular client. The most striking illustration of the way people can access comparative information on what they want, when they want it, is through the internet and e-commerce. By comparison, the way in which people can communicate what they want to governments remains slow and indirect.

The third contrast concerns the reorganization of the way business is done. Businesses have restructured their organization so that the market connects increasingly efficiently from the global to the local. By contrast, systems of government hesitate to restructure the way they do their business. The result is extremely poorly functioning connections between different political domains. In absolutely no way can systems of political choice be said to offer seamless connections from the global to the local.

Such contrasts between the way in which the two systems of choice have responded to change are of critical importance for Europe's system of government. This is because they directly concern the most fundamental questions that have to be looked at in a continent-wide political union: the functions that European government should be trying to perform; the way in which people signal what they want out of politics; and the way in which units of government connect across boundaries and large political spaces.

Before examining these fundamental questions about Europe's system of political choice, it is necessary to look more closely at the precise nature of the shock to systems of market and political choice. This will help identify the necessary focus of attention when considering how systems of government can best adapt.

The Ease of Using Systems of Choice

The language of economics helps diagnose the ways in which it is becoming easier for people to make their individual and collective choices through the market and more difficult to make their choices through politics, and what this means for Europe's own system of governance. The metaphor borrowed from economics is 'cost'. The outside observer will see participants in society using whichever system of choice – politics or the market – has the least 'costs' attached.

In a broad sense the costs are 'opportunity costs'. The image is one where people will have certain choices to make in life, have certain initial preferences about them, and use whichever system of choice seems easiest in order to get what they want. What 'asymmetric shock' implies in this context is that external forces such as the information revolution have made it easier for people to take advantage of the opportunities offered by the market to get what they want relative to the opportunities offered through the system of political choice.

To talk about choice in this way is an abstraction. In the real world, in different European countries, people may not have the choice whether to invest in private supplementary pensions for their old age or in private health care or to go to private universities, or the choice may be heavily weighted by existing patterns of provision. Changes in the reliance on political choice or market choice as a result of dissatisfaction with one or the other can take place only at the margin. But what is important in the real world is dissatisfaction and frustration with existing options. It is the ease or frustration in the making of important choices in people's lives that provides the true pointer to what should be looked for in constructing Europe's system of government.

At first sight, the economist's notions of opportunity costs may seem rather remote from the language of politics. But the economist's metaphor of 'cost' should be taken not in a literal sense, but rather as a way of symbolizing the ease or difficulty that people experience when trying to get what they want from the market and from politics. The identification of different types of opportunity cost provides a way of seeing why systems of market choice have become more responsive to what people want while political systems have not, and what this means for a continent-wide system of government.

Three Different Types of Opportunity Cost

Three different types of cost can be distinguished that together make up the opportunity costs of using one system of choice or the other.[2] First, there are entry costs. Traditionally in economics these represent the costs for existing or new producers of breaking into a market as a new provider of goods or services. Entry costs might not, at first sight, seem relevant to the choice between politics and the market. Most people do not become entrepreneurs offering new products either in the market or in politics. However, the opportunity costs of entering a market serve another purpose. When entry into a market is easy it forces existing producers to keep their service or product constantly under review and to make sure that they respond to what people want. The costs of entry are thus intimately connected with the contestability of markets. When the costs of entry come down, contestability rises. What convergent technology and the information revolution have done to the market has been to bring down entry costs by demolishing old industry product and service boundaries. As a consequence, existing products and services face pressure for renewal. Thus, in the market, the lowering of entry costs is forcing businesses to revamp their core activities and to refashion what they offer. By contrast, the maintenance of high entry barriers in systems of political choice reduces contestability in what is offered by systems of political choice and means that political markets are not renewing or rethinking what they offer. Hence, in complete contrast to what has been happening in the market, nothing forcing a comparable renewal has been operating in politics. In other words, in politics there has been little or no incentive for the providers of political choice – the politicians or political parties – to reassess the core of what they are offering.

Secondly, there are information costs. These are the costs of acquiring the information needed to make informed choices, as well as the costs of processing and transmitting information about what people want.[3] The market is exploiting information sources to offer more customized goods and services. By contrast, the system of political choice remains caught in the procedures of representative democracy, where the methods of communication are indirect and imprecise and where the underlying assumption is that politicians can tell voters what is best for them. In other words, signalling systems in the market have become more direct and more immediate and exert a constant pressure on business to respond more precisely and more quickly to what the consumer wants. Traditional signalling systems in politics offer no such immediacy.

Thirdly, there are transactions costs. In economics these represent the costs of production and market organization, including those of the internal organization of the firm. Forced by the market to cut their costs, businesses have been compelled to reorganize the way they conduct their business and the way they connect markets from the global to the local. In business-school jargon, they have been forced to become 'lean' and 'agile'. Systems of government, by contrast, are struggling. It is the traditional nation state that connects the global with the local and that, in the system of political choice, performs the tasks analogous to the firm in the market. At the global level, nation states manage a badly coordinated patchwork of different international regimes and, at the local level, there is huge diversity in the way in which governments treat local preferences. The ways in which nation states make connections between the global and the local remain cumbersome and inflexible. None could be described as either lean or agile.

The overall opportunity costs of the two systems of choice and the way in which the different cost factors affect their behaviour have a direct relevance to the kinds of decisions that Europe faces in designing its system of government. If they are ignored, an unresponsive system of political choice for Europe will be designed right from the start. Moreover, the disparity between the two systems of choice would also mean that its politicians would constantly be on the defensive because Europe's system of political choice would not be producing what people want. In order to avoid in-built frustration with Europe's system of government, the lessons have to be absorbed about how markets have adapted to shock while political systems have failed to adapt. The key lessons are discussed further below.

Entry Costs and the Refashioning of Core Business

Entry Costs in the Market

The so-called 'information revolution' stems from 'convergence'. One dimension of convergence has been the link between computer technology and communications technology. The other is between different sectors of the media and communications companies. The impact of convergence has been to obliterate the traditional boundaries between industries. Companies in the computing, communications and media sectors themselves have been in the front of the firing line and have been first to feel the impact. They have had to decide whether their futures lie as providers of carriage or as providers of content, or some combination of both. But the impact is far broader.

A traditional gas distribution company, for example, might realize that it has information on households that provides a platform from which it can offer many other consumer services, whether in selling other forms of energy, or other products entirely, such as insurance or banking services. Similarly, a supermarket can use its information systems to offer financial services, or, conversely, a financial service company can use its client base to offer non-financial products.

One of the most important effects of the collapse of old industry boundaries has been to lower the costs of entering new areas of activity. When industry boundaries are static and products well-defined and traditional, it is difficult for newcomers to dislodge incumbents. Incumbents may have well-established brand leadership, they may have installed themselves in the best locations, they may exploit economies of scale, and, furthermore, buyers may have little incentive to switch their source of supply. For new entrants the perceived risk of failure may be seen as high. There is equally a lack of incentive on established incumbents to branch out into new areas.[4]

The technological advances of the information revolution have changed all this. New entrants can come in with new technology and new products and the collapse of old industry and sector boundaries means that few companies can hide behind static markets, static suppliers and static buyers. Instead of the costs and risks being biased against new entrants, convergent technologies and products mean that well-established incumbents are just as much at risk as new start-ups. The assertion that a market advantage is conferred on the business that is the 'first mover' in introducing a new product or service indicates not only how important it is for even established businesses to be on their toes, but also how market advantage has shifted from incumbent firms.

The main impact of technological advance and reduced costs of entry has been that, over a wide swathe of the market, businesses have been forced to reassess their core product or core service. From the utilities that come to homes, to the manufacture of the consumer durables used in households, to the way in which shopping is done or financial services accessed, goods and services are being reformulated, repackaged, freshly presented and delivered in different ways.

By contrast, the system of political choice has faced no such external pressure to review its core business or key functions and to consider what it is that political systems need to deliver in today's world. It has simply tried to defend old products. One of the main reasons for this is that the costs of entry in politics remain very high.

Entry Costs in Politics

Entry costs in politics consist of organizing political parties to bring public policy offerings in front of the public rather than organizing new companies to bring products; they consist of mobilizing the headquarters and branch infrastructure and workers for a party-political cause rather than setting up a plant and recruiting workers for a company; and they consist of getting new political messages across to a target audience rather than getting a new product across to a target sales market.[5]

These costs in politics have not come down. It is difficult to get voters to switch to new parties in the way that they may change their brand loyalties in the market; the advantages of incumbency remain huge, not least because of the way in which political parties are able to exercise patronage not only within politics, but also in the wider setting of, for example, appointments to administrative jobs or to executive agencies. In addition, politicians can use the mechanisms of politics to defend their own positions. For example, they can change electoral systems to make challenges from minorities less likely, or they can control the rules for party funding to suit incumbents. Moreover, party leaders can tighten their own control by increasing their powers in the political selection processes, or by dispensing patronage, or by devising rules to fend off challenges to their own position.

In the case of Europe the incentives for the market to renew its products compared with the lack of incentives for renewal on the side of political choice are magnified for other reasons in addition to the changes associated with the information revolution. Entry costs for business have been reduced and market contestability increased, not just because of the technological impact of the information revolution but, more generally, because of the lowering of tariff and non-tariff barriers between national markets in Europe. At the same time, the lowering of international trade barriers has further compounded this effect.

Yet, by contrast, when entry costs in Europe for the political system are looked at, they appear to have risen. Contestability in political systems is closely associated with the ability of different political parties to offer competing platforms with different policy options on offer to the electorate. However, it is inherently more costly for political parties to organize over a large political space and, within the existing union, truly union-wide parties have not been able to get off the ground. Instead, national parties have used the territorial and financial advantages of incumbents to occupy the political arena and to claim their seats in the European Parliament. At elections they fight on local platforms and not on European ones. Proposals to finance Europe-wide political parties publicly through the European Parliament and in proportion to existing party strengths would only reinforce the advantages of incumbents and the difficulties for new entrants.

In short, the lack of incentives for systems of political choice to update their products, which applies to all systems everywhere, applies with particular force when Europe is looked at as a political space. The entry barriers against new contestants who could offer fresh alternatives are huge, and the existing parties are already protecting their turf. Instead of new actors offering new products for a new market, what can be seen is a new political market occupied by old parties, organized in the old way and peddling old products.

Information Costs and Customization

Customization

When commentators first looked at the growth of modern communications techniques, their gloomy prediction was that the power of communications systems would be placed in the hands of politicians and those with political power. In other words, signals and commands would run from politicians to the citizen. Governments would be telling everybody what to do. The reality, however, is far from the Orwellian nightmare.[6]

In the marketplace the information revolution has made the market increasingly client-driven. On the one hand, customers have much greater comparative information quickly at their disposal. At the same time, the market has been able to use convergent technologies to shorten communications within supply chains and to be more discerning in treating the customer. The information revolution is being used to collect and sort client information in ways that make it increasingly possible to customize the product or service and to deliver quickly. Increasingly the market is offering bespoke products for particular clients. Thus, from the point of view of the supplier, the scope for analysing and evaluating the market has opened up, while, for the customer, the scope for comparing products and shopping around has also increased enormously.

By contrast, there has been no such communications breakthrough in systems of political choice. On the contrary, the political system has barely begun to consider the implications of customization. Politics repeats old mantras about the need for 'universal provision' or 'uniform standards' as a way of justifying common products where 'one size fits all'. Far from the communications revolution having placed additional power in the hands of politicians, governments have lost important points of leverage. Governments no longer own communications utilities such as phone companies, government-owned media companies are increasingly beleaguered and government control over content is also being lost. Systems of politics have lost power rather than gained it. For the citizen, there is indeed a justified fear of loss of privacy and invasion of personal space. But it comes from the market as much as or more than it does from politics: for example, from the ease with which personal information can now be collected from different market sources. Governments also find it more rather than less difficult to keep secrets. They may still abuse their increased ability to collect personal information on individuals and groups but, in general, they cannot be accused of controlling the information revolution to increase their power over the citizen. What they can be accused of is failing to acknowledge that people want customized products. In the market, a CEO knows that the customer is king; in politics, political leaders still behave as though they themselves are the kings.

Direct Versus Indirect Communication

At root, the explanation for why the market has responded to the information revolution by customizing its products while systems of political choice have not is due to the way in which people signal their preferences in the two markets. Traditionally this has been represented as a problem of individual choice in the market against the problems of aggregating choice in politics. Information costs suggest different sources of difficulty, however.

The essential reason why markets have been able to customize their products and services is because they have used the information revolution to improve direct communication. This involves not only more direct communication with final consumers and end users of goods and services but also direct communication with suppliers and other companies involved in creating the product or service. By contrast, the system of political choice is founded on the practices and conventions of representative democracy, which stand above all for indirect choice and communication. Elected representatives have a rather loose connection with those who elect them and traditionally feel that they can act with considerable discretion and not just attempt to reflect the views of those who actually voted for them.[7]

The indirectness of representative democracy can be seen in two ways. First, in the electoral process. This has one absolutely essential attribute, namely that it provides people with a chance to remove politicians from office or to vote new ones in. This is a crucial function in a democracy. But at the same time it is a blunt instrument for conveying messages on the products that politicians offer – the public policy mix. In part this is because when governments or politicians are voted out it is usually on the basis of their past performance or lack of it. Signals about the future are more difficult to give and discretion is needed to deal with what cannot be foreseen. In addition, in offering products for the future, major parties with the greatest possibility of ending up as a governing party offer general policy products in order to appeal to the 'average' voter. Minority parties can offer more precise policies geared to a more particular group. But this has different drawbacks. It is unpredictable whether minority parties will form part of a governing coalition and it is also unpredictable what kind of policy influence they will have even if they do. Minority parties in a coalition often become prisoners to other parties within the coalition and unable to deliver what they have promised to their own supporters. In short, elections can convey brutal messages about the past but rather crude messages about future preferences.

Secondly, elections are by their nature episodic. In other words they provide not a continuous way of conveying information about the policy products that people want but an opportunity once in four or five years. Influencing policy products between elections is a much more oblique process where politicians monitor focus groups and opinion polls but where voters tend to fade in importance at the expense of pressure groups or interest groups.

For these reasons, in representative democracies, the election market and the legislative market can be seen as two different information markets.[8] What they have in common is that neither offers an easy way for direct expressions of opinion on particular items in the public policy mix. Consequently, while the market is increasingly customizing its products, by contrast the techniques of representative democracy are not able to respond in the same way by customizing political products. The vote-based signalling systems of representative democracy continue to give mainly indirect messages.

Customization and Ageing

When the European Council referred to the ageing of Europe's population as one of the main millennium challenges, they had in mind the impact on government budgets of the cost of present methods of financing public pensions. They also had in mind the cost of health care for the elderly. These are enormously important problems for government finances, but the more fundamental impact of more individualized health treatments from advances in molecular biology and understanding of the human genome could well be in increasing demands of people for customized products from systems of choice.

The fact of the matter is that no one knows how people will react to the probability of living much longer and much healthier lives. What does seem clear is that the way the life-cycle is looked at in traditional terms as being divided between a period of maturation, a working life and a period of retirement is likely to change profoundly. People are likely to change their attitudes towards education, careers, leisure, health and their family formation in ways that cannot be foreseen. Moreover, and more importantly, people will make different choices. In other words they will want to make individualized choices. What this in turn means is that they will want customized instruments to help them navigate in new ways over a longer life-cycle.

The contrast between direct communication producing customized products in market systems of choice compared with indirect communication being unable to shape customized products in politics thus poses an enormous challenge for a continent-wide system of government. Over the extensive political space of Europe as a whole, messages conveyed through the political system will be general at best. Therefore, in thinking about the system of political choice, there is a need to think both about the product to be delivered and about how the indirectness of signalling through the vote can be supplemented by other means of more direct expression.

Transactions Costs and Connecting Markets

What is broadly referred to as the information revolution has caused the market to refocus what it offers people and the way it offers products, and at the same time it has enabled businesses to offer an increasingly customized product or service. In addition, globalization has cut transactions costs for businesses in dealing with different markets and business has responded by developing extraordinarily efficient ways of linking local markets with global markets. The market has become adept at sourcing supplies or service functions from distant points, at the same time as adapting a product or service to the tastes and product preferences at a local point of sale.

By contrast, the transactions costs for systems of government in dealing with globalization have not come down to anything like the same extent. It is the so-called 'nation state' that provides the predominant link between the local and the global. But how best to put together the links in the chain from the global to the local defies the structure of most systems of government. Some types of cost have come down. For example, it is easier to coordinate between national capitals because of improved communications between governments and government departments. Nevertheless governments have much greater difficulty in connecting across international boundaries than do businesses. At the global level there is a patchwork of international regimes with equally patchwork mechanisms for trying to achieve an overall coherence. At the local level there is a huge variety in governmental forms.

An important part of the success of the market in linking the local and the global can be attributed to a willingness to change methods of organization. This has meant a willingness to change the internal organization of the firm: for example, to flatten management structures and to reduce the number of layers of management. It also has involved a willingness to reorganize relationships outside the firm. For example, connections with suppliers or end purchasers may be organized differently so that communications do not have to take place from head office to head office but can do so from subsidiary to subsidiary. The lesson for systems of political choice is that government too has to rethink its organization.

One implication of this analysis is that the transposition of any of the existing structures from any of the countries of Europe is most unlikely to provide an answer for the way in which Europe's system of government is best organized. No national system of political choice has been able to revise its organization and reduce transactions costs to an extent that begins to approach the kind of transformations to be seen in the business world.

The formation of a continent-wide political union is itself in part a response to a desire to play a more effective international role and thus to link European citizens with what is happening globally. However, while the aspiration is there, the basic questions about how precisely to formulate the links remain unresolved. The European response has been limited to thinking in terms of scaling up the size of the basic political unit – from the nation state to a continent-wide system. In many cases, businesses have also responded to the new setting by scaling up the size of their activities, through internal growth, mergers and acquisitions. But in addition, they have done much more, and size, in and of itself, is not seen as the guarantor of success. Businesses, even – indeed particularly – the largest, have also reshaped both the way they are organized internally and the way in which they deal with the outside world. Yet in the context of organizing Europe's system of political choice, the most important questions of organization remain in dispute. There is no consensus either as to how units of government can best be linked internally within the union, or as to how the connections are best made to the external world beyond. Europe's political system is far from providing the kind of flexible connections that systems of market choice can offer.

The Cumulative Nature of Cost Differences

The discussion so far of the different ways in which the two systems of choice – politics and the market – can be viewed through the metaphor of 'costs' has simplified the analysis by linking particular costs to particular ways in which the behaviour of the two systems can be compared. Thus 'entry' costs have been linked to the refashioning of core business, 'information' costs to the ways in which markets respond to signals, and 'transactions' costs to the way in which people are connected by firms and governments across territorial boundaries. However, this is an oversimplification and understates what has happened.

In practice these different types of cost work in tandem and re-inforce each other. Businesses have been forced to reassess their core activities not just because entry costs have been lowered, but also because the customization of products has forced them to re-examine where exactly they have comparative advantage in responding to a more client-driven environment, and, in addition, because more inter-connected markets have exposed them to new competitors.

By contrast, systems of political choice have resisted changing the core of what is offered not only because the costs of entry remain high in politics, but also because more cumbersome signalling systems do not provide sufficiently sharp incentives to rethink what products should be offered, and because poor connections between political domains also impede what can be offered through systems of political choice.

Similarly, the success of the market in connecting the global and the local is also due to the combination of factors discussed: the willing-ness of businesses to redefine their core activities and exploit direct forms of communication as well as their willingness to reorganize the way they conduct their business both within the firm and with exter-nal business clients. As a result of this combination, the market increasingly functions as a single global entity while the system of political choice remains largely segmented and disjointed.

Because these cost factors are working together, they accentuate the asymmetric impact on the two systems of choice. They work together to make market choice more responsive. At the same time they work together to impede the responsiveness of systems of political choice. Thus, when taken together, rather than considered singly, they re-inforce the original diagnosis that one system of choice, the market, has been able to exploit the global market and the communications revolution to respond more quickly to customer signals, to offer more precisely honed goods and services and to link different markets rapidly and effectively. By contrast, the other system of choice – politics – does not connect domains effectively or efficiently, does not offer customized products, and still treats citizens as people who can be told what is good for them.

For each of these reasons, therefore, the outside observer is looking at a setting for modern governance where the system of market choice has improved its ability to deliver individual and social choices while the system of political choice has not been able to lower its cost base. Other things being equal, people will turn to the system of market choice and away from the system of political choice.

The Risks from Asymmetry

Does It Matter?

It is tempting for Europe to ignore this situation and to do nothing about it. This would mean accepting that more and more individual and social choices will be made through the market. The gyrations of politicians as they slip further and further into irrelevance could be viewed with the equanimity of anarchists. In the context of Europe, special attention would be paid to the market framework so that it offers choices at the least cost, but the political construction of Europe could be put to the back of one's mind because it really would not matter too much.

A much more sophisticated justification of a 'do nothing' approach argues that it is possible for societies to draw the boundary between political choice and market choice in many different ways and therefore there should not be too much concern about an upset to the kind of balance people have become used to. Different kinds of balance have different strengths and weaknesses but many combinations are viable and consistent with social success.

Although a 'do nothing' approach may be tempting for both reasons, it would in practice prove to be a huge mistake. The idea that it is possible to be agnostic about the various types of balance to be struck between market choice and political choice came into vogue around the time of the collapse of communism. It then became immediately apparent that, even with the ending of the only rival to market choice, there were still several different ways of expressing the relationship between market choice and political choice. Thus 'Asian capitalism' was seen to provide one type of model that made political choice less a system for social welfare but more a system for steering the market. At the same time, in contrast both to 'Asian capitalism' and to 'Anglo-Saxon capitalism', 'Rhineland capitalism' provided a strong welfare net through the system of political choice. The Swedish 'corporatist' model provided yet another type of combination between the market and the state. These different ways of expressing the relationship between politics and the market were seen as having different strengths and weaknesses but offering, at the same time, valid alternatives. Each faced different challenges but their longer-term viability was not basically questioned.[9]

Practical experience since the fall of communism has, however, eroded the degree to which the particular equilibrium reached can be regarded with indifference. A lot of previously favourable commentary on the so-called 'Asian model' has been discredited by the political and economic crises that struck Asia in the 1990s. In addition, both political and economic difficulties in Europe have made the so-called 'Rhineland model' also look much less robust than it once did. Experience is thus suggesting that while different solutions are possible, it may matter enormously which one is chosen.

A 'do nothing' approach also seems justified to those who regard the system of political choice as a 'predator' on the system of market choice.[10] However, Tocqueville warns against this attitude. According to him, politics and the market do not work to divide up a fixed amount of social and individual choice. If the two work well together, the sum of the possibilities for a society is expanded; if they connect badly, the sum of choices is reduced.

It is this relationship between the two systems of choice that shows why Europe has to take seriously the diagnosis of asymmetric shock. The shock could trigger an interaction between the two systems that works to reduce the future possibilities and choices for Europe. This could happen in three quite distinct ways. First, those in political power might actively try to halt the decline of the system of political choice by engaging in restrictive practices. Secondly, they might try to handicap market choice, so as to even the playing field. Thirdly, they might act more passively just to resist change. Any of these reactions will prevent Europe from making the most of its opportunities.

Adoption of Defensive Strategies in the Political System

In the business world a failing industry will often try to halt its decline by engaging in restrictive business practices. It may collude with other businesses in the same industry in order to try to share out the market. Businesses may also collude to try to stabilize the prices for their product. A first possible reaction of Europe's politicians trying to stem the decline of their system could be to reach for analogous restrictive practices.

Restrictive practices within systems of political choice mirror those of the business world. The first option is collusion between politicians. This may take place within particular political jurisdictions or, in the case of Europe, between different political units. The most common form of collusion between different political jurisdictions is through the sharing of powers and responsibilities. As a consequence, it becomes very difficult to judge the performance of different political units. Different policies are not on offer and responsibility is shared whatever the outcome of policies.

These forces can be seen at work in the case of the political system of the existing European union. The institutions are arranged so that power is shared in several different ways. It is shared between governments within the Council of Ministers, between the institutions in Brussels – Council, Commission and Parliament – and whenever the treaties do not make clear who is responsible for what. When things go wrong, everybody can blame someone else and no one takes responsibility.

The drawback to this strategy over the long term is that in the political world, as in the world of the market, restrictive practices tend to mask decline but cannot in the end prevent it. The reason for this is that a system of political choice cannot be operated as a closed system any more than can a system of market choice. In the case of the market Europe's marketplace is part of a global market. Europe is a very large market and foreign trade is a relatively small part of total activity. Nevertheless, if Europe tried to cease trading with the rest of the world, or if international capital and technology flows were blocked, Europe's marketplace would become increasingly inefficient and people would come to recognize that it was not producing the goods and services or the opportunities provided by markets in other parts of the world.

A political market that suppresses competition and engages in collusion can also only delay its eventual decline. It cannot reverse it. In the long run, people will still be able to make performance comparisons with outside systems, and outside systems will still exert their own performance pressures. More importantly, the system of market choice will continue to exert competitive pressure. Restrictive practices in one system of choice measured against efficiencies in another will lead people to increasingly prefer the less restrictive system.

However, in the interim, during the period when these effects are working themselves out, the cost for Europe would be high. In the marketplace, restrictive practices tend to be identified quite quickly. Both competitor industries and the consumer have an interest in identifying them. In the case of restrictive practices in politics, detection takes longer. Comparisons are more difficult for people to make and rival systems of government have no interest in pointing out deficiencies in another system. Thus people in Europe might not realize for a very long time that their system of government is letting them down.[11] For example, in the United Kingdom, an undetected source of relative decline has been the restrictive practice operating in politics that most ministers and all party leaders must be drawn from the House of Commons. This has restricted entry to a narrow, parochial and often ill-informed pool.

Handicapping the Market

There is in addition a second defensive strategy available for those with political power. That is, for governments to attempt to handicap the market so that the disadvantages of the system of political choice are not shown up by the system of market choice.

Governments are able to handicap market choice because of their power to set the rules of the market, and hence take steps to raise the opportunity costs of making choices in it. Thus they can raise entry costs in the market by regulating businesses in ways that retain old industry demarcations. For example, the United States is alleged to have delayed the information revolution by some twenty to thirty years by preventing the main computer manufacturer of the time – IBM – coming together with the main telecommunications company of the time – Bell.[12] Governments can also raise information costs by trying to control the way information is conveyed or by trying to control its content. For example, the uptake of mobile telephony or the installation of fibre-optic cables has taken place at quite different speeds in different markets because of the attempts by different governments to control methods of carriage. They can raise transactions costs by trying to put in place non-tariff barriers to competition – frequently through imposing regulatory barriers. For example, the French government currently protects the domestic electricity industry from competition by insisting on the right to control the energy mix (the proportions of electricity generated from different fuel sources).

Passive Resistance

Thirdly, Europe's political interests could simply resist change. In all sorts of ways, from the way that institutions of the existing union, such

as the European Parliament and the European Court of Justice, behave
to protect their interests, to the way that member states behave to
protect theirs, there is already turf protection and resistance to change.
This could simply grow and make the shaping of a continent-wide
system of government increasingly difficult. The prospect would be for
a long-lasting disequilibrium between the two systems of choice.

The collapse of communism has shown that it is difficult for a
political system to survive if it tries to suppress both means of choice
– the economic and the political – but there are still examples in the
world, notably China, where the market is allowed expression but the
system of political choice is suppressed. Nobody is suggesting that
Europe might follow in this direction and actively suppress choices
through politics. What does seem very much possible, however, is that
Europe's political leaders will react in ways that clog up both channels
of choice so that neither works well. Indeed, Europe's largest state –
Germany – has been suffering from this problem for a number of years.
Unless the risk is clearly recognized, the problems arising from the
asymmetric shock to the two systems of choice could be very long-
lasting.

The Need to Rethink

What these three different types of interaction would result in is a
narrowing of the benefits that individuals and communities in Europe
can derive from both politics and the market. They can also be seen as
triggering the risk of what is known as 'path dependency', where a
negative dynamic is established that becomes extremely difficult to
reverse.[13]

The diagnosis of 'asymmetric shock' therefore presents great risks
for the future of a continent-wide union unless the response is to
rethink Europe's system of political choice so that it matches the
efficiency of the system of market choice. 'Efficiency' in this context
does not mean a political system deprived of democratic, human and
social qualities. It means looking for a system of political choice
through which individuals and communities can use democratic politics to widen the choices they face over their lifetimes, express their
principles fully, and make the most of their opportunities.

Thus, the right conclusion to draw from the diagnosis of asymmetric shock is that in looking at the design of Europe's political structures the need is to focus on the key areas where systems of market
choice have gained an edge. This means:

- looking again at the core business of government so that the system of political choice in Europe is focused on the areas where it offers a comparative advantage;
- looking at the way in which the directness of communication can be improved in political systems; and
- looking at the way connections are organized between different political jurisdictions so that much less disjointed connections between different political units become possible.

Unfortunately there is no guarantee that Europe's leaders and governments will learn the lessons of what has happened to systems of choice and rethink Europe's system of political choice. The reason for this is that much of the thinking about Europe's future is backward-looking and rooted in the past. This conventional thinking is discussed in the next chapter.

3 Projecting the Past

Conventional Scenarios for Europe's Future

A new science of politics is indispensable to a new world. This, however, is what we think of least; launched in the middle of a rapid stream, we obstinately fix our eyes on the ruins which may still be descried upon the shore we have left.
Alexis de Tocqueville, *Democracy in America*

Four Conventional Scenarios

In the absence of a common vision of what good government is all about and what the new setting for governments really means, when Europe's political leaders negotiate on the shape of the political system for a unified continent, they bring a mix of ideas and vision to the table. Currently, when Europe's politicians lift their heads from more pressing day-to-day concerns and talk about their long-term vision of Europe's future, they typically mingle together four main themes.

First, they talk about Europe being able to play a larger part in world affairs so that it carries a political punch equivalent to its weight in the world economy. When they talk in this way, they invite comparisons with the United States, holding out the prospect of a Europe that, even if not a 'hyperpower' in the same league, will become nevertheless a global political powerhouse.

Secondly, politicians talk at the same time about Europe's social tradition and the need to preserve and protect the social market model amidst the pressures of globalization. The image is of a Europe that will be able to offer, on a large scale, the kind of social protection against the insecurities in life that individual member states offered their populations after the Second World War. The message is that a continent-wide union will be better placed to deal with the impact of large-scale international trade and capital movements that appear to be diluting the degree of social protection that can be offered by individual states.

Thirdly, Europe's political leaders refer to diversity in Europe, the importance of national characteristics and traditional ways of life, and offer the soothing image that the union will still allow people to retain their own national and regional personalities.

Finally, Europe's leaders talk of a union based on the rule of law and put in play a different picture: that of a union where the same law applies equally to everyone, wherever they may be located.

This chapter discusses each of these visions of Europe's future. When politicians talk about these, they often mix the components together in the same speech. From their point of view this is understandable. They may want to send more than one message to more than one audience. Thus when British Prime Minister Tony Blair talks about Europe as a 'superpower but not a superstate', he is sending a message to his fellow prime ministers that he wants to see the union develop its powers and capabilities while, at the same time, he is sending a message to domestic public opinion that the union can continue to be viewed as a 'union of states'.

However, the discussion disaggregates the different elements in these themes because attached to each is a different rationale for European union, with different implications for its form and functions. Each of the four scenarios illuminates different questions about Europe's future. Their weakness does not lie just in the divergent and contradictory answers they offer about important aspects of Europe's future. Their common weakness is that in crucial respects each remains rooted in the past. As a result they give seriously misleading guidance about what needs to be done in order to put in place a new continent-wide system of governance.

Superpower Europe

Starting from the fact that Europe is already a major economic force in the world, the model of 'Superpower Europe' goes on to argue that Europe should develop in a way that will give it commensurate weight as a political player in world affairs. This objective can be defined in the passive terms of the need for Europe to be able to stand on its own feet and look after its own interests anywhere in the world. Alternatively, it can be defined in the more active terms of the need for Europe to be able to have a positive influence on developments outside its borders and be able to have greater influence in shaping world developments in conformity with its own agenda.

Presenting a scenario for the future of Europe where the continent aims to become a superpower conveys a number of additional messages. One concerns Europe's relationship with the United States, namely that a single country – the United States – should not be able to exert the degree of dominance in world affairs that it is currently able to do. The suggestion is that in order to counterbalance this situation, Europe should develop so that it can provide an alternative perspective and a countervailing influence. This can be phrased in a cooperative way – with an emphasis on the help that Europe can provide the United States in sharing more of the burden in upholding the rules of good international behaviour. Or it can be phrased in terms of rivalry – Europe should set out to try to establish a different approach to international questions, formulating an approach that is, above all, not the position of the United States.

A second message is about bargaining power in the world. The assertion is that in today's world only the largest and most powerful states will have political influence. At one time the individual states of Europe, such as France and the United Kingdom, could wield influence by themselves in world affairs. Those days are largely gone. The UK sees its influence in the world through playing some kind of bridging role between the United States and the European Union. France sees its role in the rather less perfidious and more straightforward terms of persuading other countries in Europe to see the world in the same way that France itself views it. Germany, which, within Europe, is the most influential of the traditional nation states, sees Europeanization as a way of legitimizing its power and influence. Each of these large states, for their different reasons, as well as the many smaller states in Europe, see European union as the main instrument for wielding influence in the world outside their borders.

Eco-social Europe

In many ways 'Superpower Europe' is an old-fashioned concept. It looks back with nostalgia to the days when European powers counted for more in the world. It is old-fashioned too in equating security with diplomatic and military power. Many would argue that it is old-fashioned in yet a further respect in that it looks on international relations as a game of power politics between rival centres of influence.

The alternative vision of 'Eco-social Europe' looks at 'security' in quite different terms. Europe has no hostile neighbours surrounding it and also has many allies or potential allies in the world outside the continent. Instead, the threats to security are seen to come from new and different sources: the threat that environmental degradation will change life on earth as we know it, and the threat that external global economic forces bring to personal security and social solidarity inside Europe. International relations are not seen as a matter of power politics but, instead, Europe is seen as part of a global system where all actors are interconnected. The environmentalist slogan of 'think globally, act locally' captures this system-wide perspective.

Seeing 'security' in these terms projects a different image of Europe's future. The continent has to come together not against external threats of a military nature, or in order to protect Europe's vital interests in an unfriendly world, but instead to provide a setting where society is at peace with itself. The vision is one where the continent is bound together by social, environmental and inter-generational concerns and linked to the world outside by being part of the same overall system.

The appeal of this vision rests on two distinct elements. One is holism. It takes a holistic approach to Europe's place in the world and the place of communities large and small within Europe. It is holistic in a different sense in that it also places social and political values within a larger belief system.[1] The second element of appeal is the strong ethical element in the vision. Both environmental and social ethics can run across the usual political divides of left and right. Moreover, this ethical framework can contain a spectrum of opinion, from those who reject the market, on the one hand, to those, on the other, who see market instruments as offering better environmental and social protection than the administrative remedies of government.[2]

An Order of States

The vision of Europe as an 'Order of States' differs fundamentally from the two previous models. This is because it does not see a continent-wide form of governance in unitary terms. Europe does not need to be bound together in a unitary form, either by the need to protect itself against the outside world, or by a unifying belief system. Instead the union is defined more in terms of the pooling of national interests. The union is one that is bound together more by common interests than by any overarching sense of common values.

This model sees the union of the future remaining one where the traditional states would continue to play the leading role in shaping what would be done and the way in which it would be done. Since these interests will differ between the states of the union, it is inherent in this model that the union will have to operate to a large extent by consensus and allow for differences. The implication is that the arrangements of the union will allow for considerable flexibility in policies and in the way in which the states organize their shared interests.[3]

Jurists' Europe

The model offered by 'Jurists' Europe' is of Europe conceived as a legal structure. This means above all that the continent is to be seen as an area of the rule of law. The rule of law in this context has two components. First, there is the concept that laws that apply in one part of the union to one set of its citizens must apply uniformly in other areas to all other citizens so that there is equality of treatment given to all union citizens. Secondly, there is the concept of government under the law. In other words, the institutions of the union must keep within the bounds of the roles set out for them and, in addition, the agreed procedures of the union must be followed. Consequently, if an institution oversteps the limits of its powers, or if a law is passed, or a measure taken, that does not follow set procedures, then the resulting law or measure can be overturned.

At first sight the vision of 'Jurists' Europe' seems rather dry and somewhat disengaged from the reality of a political union for Europe. Nothing could be further from the truth. There are two aspects that give the model of 'Jurists' Europe' great immediacy as a practical approach to European government. One arises through the integrating effect of the law. Uniform law uniformly applied is a powerful integrating instrument.[4] Within the existing union the Court of Justice has developed a jurisprudence involving the ideas of the supremacy of union law, the direct effect of union laws and the pre-emption doctrine, which have, taken together, been widely credited in making the powers of the union concrete and extensive.[5] The judges at the court have, by their own account, pursued a certain 'Idea of Europe'. This has meant in practice that, when faced with a dispute over the powers of the union in relation to the powers of the member states, the court has generally favoured the powers of the union so as to help bring about what the treaty base refers to as an 'ever closer union'.[6]

The second way in which the model of 'Jurists' Europe' gains immediacy comes from the linking of the concept of the rule of law with substantive concepts of justice. In other words, the idea of the union as the rule of law is linked to the idea of the union as an area of social justice.[7] As already mentioned, one way of expressing this idea is to think of the union as 'a union of rights', where included among the rights of all citizens are not only procedural rights, such as the right of free expression, but also social and environmental rights. Here too, within the existing union, the court has developed a basis for an expansive jurisprudence.

The Same Questions – Different Answers

Any vision of Europe's future system of government, including those conventional scenarios outlined above, has to provide answers to four key questions:

- *Identity*: There have to be reasons given why people should feel part of the system of government, identify with it and feel that they owe it a sense of loyalty or allegiance.
- *Structure*: The model of the system of government must offer an account of the political structure. That is to say, it should give an idea of how powers are to be organized in the system.
- *Function*: A sense must be given of the functions people can expect the system to perform or try to perform.
- *Legitimacy*: The model must offer some justification for why people should regard it as a legitimate system or one that they should obey. Legitimacy goes beyond identity. People may feel they should obey a system of government just because they identify with it. But legitimacy is about giving reasons why a system should be regarded as a worthy system of government – reasons that can be understood even in the absence of any sense of identity.

It is a concept closely bound up with procedural standards. For example, a system of government may not be regarded as legitimate if it does not follow democratic procedures.

The conventional visions of Europe's future outlined above offer different and conflicting answers to each of these key questions. The way in which the responses vary can lead Europe towards very different political futures. They embody underlying assumptions that need to be made transparent, with the result that they can be seen to be questionable, contradictory or, in some cases, just thoroughly misleading.

Identity

The key feature of the 'Superpower' approach to identity is that it appeals to a negative sense of identity. That is to say, it expresses what Europe is not. Above all, Europe is not the United States. Having gained superpower status, Europe will not depend on the United States for influence in the world. It will be able to project a different view on international matters and its own views will be taken much more seriously by other countries.

Expressing identity in the negative – conveying what Europe is against – seems in some ways less robust than expressing identity in positive terms – what Europe is for. But historically, negative identity seems to have been just as powerful a rallying cry for societies and ideologies as has identity expressed in positive terms. There is a latent anti-Americanism in many countries in Europe and the appeal of negative identity should not be underestimated.

The idea of an 'Eco-social Europe', by contrast, does try to define Europe's identity in positive terms. It offers the idea of a society that gives a special place to social inclusion, to solidarity between generations, as well as one that undertakes to care for the poorest of its citizens. By implication it depicts a society that is prepared to put family, group and community ties ahead of self-interest and personal gain, and that downplays economic motivation in favour of 'higher' values.[8]

The idea of the union as an 'Order of States' approaches identity in yet a different way because it does not place the stress on any unifying sense of European identity, either positive or negative. Instead it envisages a world of 'overlapping' identities where people can feel that they belong to more than one community and where the sense of identity with the nation is likely to be as strong, or stronger, than any sense of belonging to the union. In addition it allows for people to have a sense of community with groupings outside and beyond the union, whether as part of a Hispanic world, or a Francophone world, or as members in some sense of a global community.

In the case of 'Jurists' Europe' the approach to identity has a strong underlying ethical element. There is appeal to a shared history – in particular the need to turn the page on a history when governments in Europe subverted the law. A stress on social justice as well as procedural justice also represents an ethical appeal. In addition, there is a strong emphasis on equality. The uniform application of law is seen as a way to achieve equal treatment for a common citizenry of Europe.

The different approach to identity between the union conceived as an 'Order of States' and the union conceived as a future European 'Superpower' is particularly important. The 'Superpower' model sees a future superpower status as one important way to help build a sense of identity in Europe. By contrast, the 'Order of States' appeals to the sense of identity with the nation state and its regions that already exists, and suggests that this should mould the way political union in Europe is shaped. This difference has an important effect on the way in which the powers of a continent-wide union and its institutions might be defined and organized. If the construction of a sense of European identity through superpower status is itself one of the tasks of political union, then its powers, as well as the tasks of the institutions, could be seen in a much more expansive light.[9]

A second consequence arising from the different ways in which these models approach identity concerns the unifying role of shared values in a continent-wide union. Implicit in three of the models is the idea that Europe's sense of identity revolves around some overarching belief system, related mainly to a sense of social justice. In the other model – the 'Order of States' – the approach appeals to the more limited idea that in a Europe with diverse national histories and diverse values there nevertheless exist areas where values overlap and provide sufficient glue to help hold a continent-wide union together. This difference may seem rather esoteric and a question of emphasis. But it can lead to very different attitudes towards basic qualities of European union such as pluralism and tolerance. An emphasis on the importance of an overarching belief system may lead in the direction of a union whose task is to promote that belief system in order to bolster a sense of European community.[10] An emphasis on diversity may lead more in the direction of designing for the tolerance of differences.

Structure

Not only do these different political models for Europe's future offer different responses to questions about why people should identify with the union, they also offer different views about how to structure power in the union.

The idea of 'Superpower Europe' essentially suggests that the traditional state can be scaled up in size and thereby gain superpower prestige and status. The model makes an implicit appeal to the example set by the United States. Indeed, sometimes the idea of a European superpower is expressed in terms of a 'United States of Europe'. What references to a United States of Europe exactly mean in terms of structures is less clear. They are usually taken as meaning that Europe's future is as a federal state. But American federalism today is very different from the American federalism of the early days of the republic. In most respects the current American system of government provides a unitary form of government where the sense of one nation is strong. The reference to the American example therefore in many ways suggests that Europe should look to becoming, over time, a unified and unitary state.

For the vision of 'Eco-social Europe', the powers needed in the union are essentially those needed to provide social and ecological security in Europe. This means that the union must be organized so as to be able to reallocate and redistribute resources in the way that nation states can do. The model does not lie across the Atlantic, but is provided by the welfare states of Europe themselves. These, however, provide quite different power arrangements. Some, like Sweden, are quite centralized. Others, like Germany or Spain, are much more decentralized. But what is important is the assumption that, in one form or another, there are transpositions from the nation states in Europe that will work for the union as a whole. This assumption is the touchstone of this model.

The idea of the union organized as an 'Order of States' is, however, much more sceptical about transpositions. On the contrary, the implication is that the union can be organized around functional tasks in which national institutions will play a continuing role and the governments of the member states will continue to provide the overall direction needed. This approach further implies that different tasks may require different institutional and procedural arrangements. At the same time, because the model is sceptical towards transpositions, whether from the United States or from any single country in Europe, it assumes instead that the union will develop, in one way or another, as a unique form of governance. In practice, it is precisely this combination of ongoing national involvements, task-specific arrangements for the union and the resulting uniqueness of the arrangements that lies behind many of the complications of the existing union.

'Jurists' Europe' sees structure more in legal terms. This in turn tends in the direction of thinking hierarchically. Political institutions are to be arranged, as courts may be, in a hierarchy of importance related to the relative importance of the laws and measures to be passed.

There is, in addition, a further question highlighted by these different approaches to structure: that is, the relationship between the structuring of the union to deal with the external world and the structuring of the union to deal with its internal priorities. 'Superpower Europe' approaches structure from the outside in. That is to say, it sees an external objective for the union – the goal of superpower status – as providing the guide to how the union should be generally structured. By contrast, 'Jurists' Europe' has in practice, in the case of the existing union, seen the external powers of the union as flowing from its internal objectives. For example, in the case of the existing union it has been argued successfully that because the union has put in place a single internal market, so too it must have, as a natural consequence, a common external commercial policy. By further contrast, the model of an 'Order of States' sees no necessary connection between the internal order of the union and the external. According to this model, different tasks demand different structures.

These different models for looking at the structuring of powers in a continent-wide union reveal great confusion in the way politicians represent Europe's future. One model – an 'Order of States' – suggests that European union should be viewed as something with new and unique structures, while others suggest that structures can be borrowed from inside the union, or from the United States. One model – 'Superpower Europe' – suggests that in order to deal effectively with the outside world, Europe should be seen as a way to scale up existing forms of government, while another model – an 'Order of States' – suggests that the way the union is organized for dealing with questions of external policy may be different from the way it is organized to deal with internal policy questions.

Function

The different conventional models for Europe's future offer not only different prescriptions about how to structure the union, but also very different approaches about how to define its powers. Two of the models, 'Superpower Europe' and 'Eco-social Europe', offer a way to pre-select the areas where the union needs powers, according to predefined ideas about which policy areas are important. By contrast, the other two models – 'Jurists' Europe' and the vision of the union as an 'Order of States' – are open-ended.

If Europe is viewed as an 'Order of States', there is no pre-ordering of areas of importance as to where powers will be needed or pre-selection of activities but, instead, a sense that powers can be delegated in limited ways, as and when the usefulness of a pooling of powers can be demonstrated. 'Jurists' Europe', equally, does not try to pre-select areas of functional importance. It too is open-ended. What it envisions, however, is not the politically determined dynamic of an 'Order of States', but a legal and legislative dynamic flowing from integration through the law. In other words, from a core area of law, wherever it might start, legislation and law will spread out into related areas so as to achieve consistency. The legal doctrines of pre-emption and the supremacy of union law give expression to this colonizing dynamic.

Within the existing union it is clear that open-ended dynamics can lead to problems. For example, following a legal dynamic, the Court of Justice has taken on occasion a more expansive view of the powers necessary for the union than the member states may have intended from their political perspective. This has led to a tension between the political and the legal approaches.

Open-endedness, regardless of whether it is politically or legally driven, is a disadvantage more generally to those who would like to see the powers of the union defined on a once-and-for-all basis. Thus within the existing union there is a long-standing debate about whether the union should rely on the doctrine of subsidiarity, which allows for the political dynamic, or whether instead there should be an attempt to define a long-term attribution of powers among the different political units of the union.

The underlying issue concerns how to define the powers of a European union. Two of the models suggest that it is possible to predetermine the powers needed. Moreover, from this starting point it would be possible also to redistribute, or reaffirm, the remaining powers among the sub-units of the union: the member states and their regions. The other two models essentially question the feasibility of predetermined arrangements of powers.

In their different ways, both avenues are very dated. In today's world it is arbitrary to try to divide powers according to territory. At the same time it is also asking too much of public trust to suggest that the problem of who does what can be safely left in the hands of politicians or judges to decide what is best for people according to an open-ended dynamic. None of these conventional models appears to offer a convincing way out of this dilemma.

Legitimacy

Each of the four different visions of Europe's future opens up a different path to justifying a system of government for Europe. For 'Superpower Europe' the justification is based on the idea of the primary importance to a society of the defence of its vital interests and its territorial integrity. For the model of an 'Eco-social Europe' the path to legitimation lies in the reference to the social and moral values that the union will be pursuing. In the case of an 'Order of States', the union has a derived legitimacy. The states remain 'Masters of the Treaty' and they confer a legitimacy on the union on behalf of their peoples. The legitimacy of 'Jurists' Europe' derives from the concept of government under the law – the idea that the government and the institutions of government must operate within the confines of rules and that these basic ground rules will be maintained by a judicial body following judicial procedures. The traditional model of judicial review is that provided by the Supreme Court of the United States.

The key division between these different approaches concerns the role to be played by ethical considerations in the justification of a political system. For both 'Jurists' Europe' and, above all, 'Eco-social Europe' there is an assumption that the ethical dimension must be built into the system of government in order for it to claim legitimacy. Neither of the other two models has to incorporate this ethical assumption. 'Superpower Europe' may include the idea that the union should exercise an ethical foreign policy but the model is basically about power politics. The model of a European 'Order of States', meanwhile, is essentially conferring an inherited legitimacy on the union that flows from the perceived legitimacy of each of the member states themselves. According to the logic of this model, the legitimacy of the union itself is not something that needs to be established independently of the legitimacy of the member states.

The Costs of the Past

The four conventional conceptions of Europe's future, described above, offer different answers as to how the union should be structured, how it should provide a sense of identity to its citizens, what core functions it should perform and how it should seek to legitimize itself. When Europe's political leaders mingle these different elements in the same speech, as they often do, they may not be aware of the diverse and sometimes contradictory rationales they are giving about the future shape of Europe. On the other hand, they may also be wanting to cover all the bases and protect their own backs. In the final analysis, however, it is not the contradictions or inconsistencies of politicians that undermine these different visions of Europe's future. The overwhelming weakness in these conventional views is that, in one way or another, each of the models is backward-looking.

The backward-looking logic of these different scenarios can be seen most clearly in the case of the union envisioned as an 'Order of States'. This attempts to base a continent-wide union on the traditional nation state and with minimum impairment to it. But in addition, the vision of 'Superpower Europe' is also backward-looking. It essentially offers to scale up the traditional nation state so that people recognize on a larger scale the kind of government functions and institutions that are familiar in the national setting. Also backward-looking is the vision of 'Eco-social Europe'. Despite its apparently forward-looking concerns with environmental degradation, in the final analysis, what is being offered is an attempted reassurance that the kind of post-war welfare state people are most familiar with can be better protected in the larger union. 'Jurists' Europe' also appeals to the familiar. The comfort offered by this model is the beguiling notion that everybody else will become more like each other in the rules they obey. A sleight of hand is involved in the sense that each community hopes that it is their own rules that others will adopt. The self-deception encourages the expectation that common rules will not diverge too far from what is familiar.

Despite their common fault in looking to the past, these different models do offer something of great value. Each brings into focus particular questions that any approach to a continent-wide union will have to address. Some have already been identified. Among the most important are the following:

- The idea of 'Superpower Europe' raises the question about whether scaling-up provides an answer to how to structure a continent-wide government.
- The vision of 'Eco-social Europe' highlights the question as to how far, in order to justify a system of government for the continent, there is a need to build into it Europe's most important social and moral values.
- The concept of an 'Order of States' draws attention to feelings of identity and diversity in Europe and spotlights the question of how the union is going to manage a pluralist society.
- 'Jurists' Europe' poses the equally fundamental issue of how Europe's system of government is going to achieve coherence.

The cost to Europe of being guided by the conventional models offered by politicians is that precisely because the models are rooted in the past, they prejudge and circumscribe prematurely the possible answers to these key questions. It is this that makes it more likely that, in negotiating a political agreement for a Europe-wide system of government, the negotiating governments will set Europe down the wrong path, or build in a permanent disequilibrium between the system of market choice and the system of political choice.[11] The politicians who advance these conventional scenarios for Europe's future lack the political courage and political vision to break away from the past and to leave behind what is familiar.

It is understandable that Europe's politicians should try to reassure public opinion about what a continent-wide union will mean for them by sounding themes that are familiar. Yet, at the same time, they are trying to disguise the deeply contradictory nature of the different visions on offer. Even more importantly, they are giving seriously misleading visions of the future of a continent-wide system of governance because they encourage people to think that a European system of governance can be built with the minimum of disruption to existing systems, including the existing union, without thinking through the new setting in which governments have to operate.

It is to this new setting that the following chapters return. They take a much closer look at the implications for European governance of the way in which the functions of government are changing, the way in which the communication of what people want out of politics is changing, and the way in which the organization of a continent-wide union will need to change. They suggest that the conventional scenarios put forward by Europe's political leaders offer bogus reassurances. If Europe's system of political choice and system of market choice are to work together in ways that improve the lives of everyone in Europe, a new and different type of union will be required.

4 The Reach of Rules

After having ... successively taken each member of the commu-
nity in its powerful grasp ... the supreme power then extends its
arm over the whole community. It covers the surface of society
with a network of small complicated rules, minute and uni-
form ... such a power does not destroy, but it prevents existence;
it does not tyrannize, but it compresses, enervates, extinguishes,
and stupefies a people.

Alexis de Tocqueville, *Democracy in America*

Redefining Core Functions: From Provisioning to Rule-Making

The Shift to Regulation

The purpose and function of governments are changing. A fundamental shift is taking place from the role of government as 'provider', to the
increasingly crucial role of government as rule-maker or regulator. It is
the regulatory role that is gradually becoming the most important
function of government and the focus of public attention. In looking
at the need for systems of government to adapt to shock by reassessing
their core activities, it is this shift of functions that is central. In trying
to identify where a continent-wide union can best add value, it is to the
regulatory function that the spotlight should turn.

In the first half of the nineteenth century Alexis de Tocqueville had speculated on the consequences of what he saw as the inevitable spending propensities of democratic forms of government. In Europe, by the end of the nineteenth century, Bismarckian Germany had launched the state into the role of provider with state-provided education and pensions. It was an example quickly followed by other countries in Europe. From the 1930s onwards a new surge in the role of the government as provider took place as government spending came to be seen, both in Europe and in the United States, as the answer to the worldwide depression and to the social ills that accompanied it. The symbol and the symptom was in the continual rise of government expenditure as a proportion of the income generated by economic activity.

In recent decades the idea of the state as the efficient manager of levels of demand in the economy has been eroded. Nevertheless, for most of the second half of the twentieth century an orthodoxy was in place, almost worldwide, that held that public spending remained absolutely necessary in order to secure the best allocation of resources, to achieve a reasonable distribution of income and also in order to achieve welfare objectives that left no one excluded from the resources of society.[1]

Yet despite this orthodoxy, by the end of the twentieth century the increase in the share of public expenditures in total income had come to a halt. In some cases there were even signs of reversal. In the United States, years of focusing on excessive budget deficits have begun to shift towards the unfamiliar ground of tax cuts and what to do with budget surpluses. In Europe, the need to prepare for the single currency has also introduced a new curb on expenditure increases and some participating states have begun to reduce the burden of accumulated government debts. Tax-cutting is also beginning to appear in Europe. Some see this peaking in the government share of total expenditure in the economy as a temporary and passing phase. The discussion below sees it as the symptom of a much more fundamental shift in the functions of government.

Government has long had a regulatory function. In its modern form, this has its roots in the nineteenth century as, for example, factory conditions for women and children increasingly became the target of regulation. But its increase in contemporary society can be dated to the 1930s and the response to economic depression. Now it is on the way to becoming the dominant function of government.

The idea that the long-term future of Europe's system of government lies in the rule-making and regulatory role is, at first sight, a frightening prospect. This is because many individual countries in Europe are already over-regulated rather than under-regulated. If the continent-wide union follows a regulatory path, it therefore seems inevitable that yet another layer of regulation will be added and individual countries will be further encouraged to step up their already over-burdensome regulatory propensities. It seems to invite Europe's system of government to handicap market choice instead of thinking about ways of improving the system of political choice.

However, there are relative advantages for governments in seeing their principal role as regulator rather than as provider, and the attractions of the former role seem likely to increase. Moreover, the earlier analysis suggested that a reassessment of core activities of government is essential if systems of government are to try to match the ease of systems of market choice. The shift towards rule-making and regulation by governments is, in principle, a way in which they can make use of their comparative advantage and perform the kind of function that people will find more useful and more attractive than the traditional provisioning functions. At the same time it does mean that Europe will have to face up to the dangers of over-regulation by placing a critical emphasis on how it sets about the regulatory role. It is the abuse of regulatory power, rather than regulatory power itself, that is the legitimate target of concern.[2]

The idea that Europe's system of government can best exploit its comparative advantage as a system of choice by developing the rule-making role can be criticized from two quite different directions. It will dismay those for whom all regulatory activities of government are seen as undesirable. It will equally dismay those who would like to see Europe's system of government carry out, in due course, most of the functions of a traditional state, including the provisioning role of governments. Both views are mistaken. There are fundamental reasons why a reassessment of the core activities of systems of government favours a shift from provisioning towards rule-making.

Rule-Making and the Comparative Advantage of Governments

From Diminishing Returns to Increasing Returns

The general reason why the rule-making role of governments is likely to progressively eclipse their provisioning role is that the former is an activity that offers governments increasing returns to scale. By contrast, public expenditure in the individual countries of Europe produces diminishing returns as it increases and governments cannot get out of this box by turning to union-wide taxing and spending.

The reasons for diminishing returns in the provisioning role of governments occur on both the revenue side and the expenditure side. On the revenue side, rising tax burdens bring perverse incentives once they go much beyond the proportions of income that people would pay voluntarily. In some societies that proportion may be quite high; it is said, for example, that a tradition of social solidarity in Sweden makes high marginal income tax rates of 50 per cent or more acceptable. But in other countries the proportion may be much lower – closer to 20 per cent. When the proportion significantly exceeds voluntary levels, then people behave so as to reduce the taxes they must pay. Devices such as paying for services in cash, under-declaring income or bargaining for 'tax-efficient' or after-tax rewards from employers are the symptoms and they are familiar throughout Europe. Governments can try to conceal the tax bite by deducting tax payments at source, so that people get used to looking at their pay cheques after tax and disregard before-tax income. But there are limits to the persuasiveness of this kind of sleight of hand.

On the expenditure side, there are also diminishing returns from increased public expenditures. The general reason for this is that the social problems that welfare payments try to alleviate, or the resource allocation issues that public investment tries to target, are rarely matters of money alone. Unless these other causes are addressed, then putting more money into the problem yields less and less in the form of results. In some cases perverse incentives also arise. The best known is the so-called 'welfare trap'. This is created when social welfare payments of one type or another deter recipients from seeking jobs that would enable them to stand on their own feet.

Governments cannot avoid these diminishing returns from taxing and spending by turning to Europe's system of government. In current practice, in the case of the existing European union, diminishing returns from public expenditures arise long before the points at which they arise within individual member states. This is because the common budget for the union largely comes from the tax resources of the member states, and thus, for the countries that are putting more money into the budget than they are taking out, the payments compete with domestic uses. This puts a much lower limit on the amounts countries are willing to contribute. The union budget can therefore be seen as a typical 'club good'. That is to say, the benefits are in limited supply for members of the club. The more members there are in the club, the less the benefits to share around for each. Moreover, most of the existing budget of the union represents an unproductive 'churning', whereby member states put money in for some purposes and take money out for others, and the net gain or loss is small for most countries.

Even if the union were to be provided with its own power to tax and spend, it would still quickly be up against diminishing returns. The tax revenues would hit the same tax ceilings as already exist in the member states and the expenditures would continue to substitute, probably unproductively, for domestic expenditures.

The significance of increasing returns was recognized by classical economists, who saw it as a key to economic growth. Adam Smith gave the famous example of a pin factory. According to his observations, each person working by him- or herself at home could produce only one pin per day. In a factory, where the pin-making operation was divided into eighteen different operations, one worker could make the equivalent of 4,800 pins per day.[3] The lesson was clear. The classical economists were emphasizing the importance of achieving a shift from agriculture, which offered constant or diminishing returns, to manufacturing industry, where, with the same effort, it was possible to produce a more highly valued bundle of goods.

In contemporary discussions of increasing returns, a distinction is made between economies of scale based on the pooling of resources and economies based on specialization. Both are needed.[4] The analogy with the current functions of contemporary government is that by specializing in the rule-making function of governments and by pooling the efforts of governments in the rule-making area, Europe's system of government can potentially offer a more highly valued bundle of services to people compared with the orthodox role of government provisioning.

There are four main reasons why this should be so. The rule-making activity for Europe's system of government:

- offers network economies;
- concentrates directly on the risks affecting people's lives instead of offering compensation for the consequences of risk;
- offers an instrument whereby governments can target their interventions rather than offer generalized products that fail to meet demands for customized products; and

- involves a shift in charging that moves the boundaries associated with the diminishing returns from general revenue-raising for general expenditure purposes.

The Network Advantage

The first reason why the function of government is shifting towards a regulatory role and why the rule-making role is particularly appropriate for a continent-wide union is that rules increase in value the greater the number of people who observe them. This is sometimes described as a 'network advantage'. The idea is that the larger the network, the more value there is in it.[5]

The 'network advantage' is a fashionable name for what has long been accepted: that there are benefits for society from widely observed rules. People know what is expected of them and equally know what to expect of others. They do not have to make special efforts to find out what different behaviour patterns or practices there might be, and they do not have to make extra efforts to adapt to different practices in different places. The disruption that can arise from different and possibly conflicting rules can be avoided. The classic example given by David Hume in the eighteenth century was of the rules of the road: everyone gains if these are the same everywhere, generally known and generally observed. In short, expressed in economic terms, widely observed rules bring savings in both information costs and transactions costs for people. In the case of a continent-wide European union, when individuals and groups and businesses know that common rules are in place for the continent as a whole, rather than thirty or more different sets of rules, one set for each member state, there are similar potential advantages. It is a matter of plain convenience.

From Compensation for Risks to Direct Risk Reduction

A second key reason why the regulatory role can potentially offer a more highly valued package of benefits is because rule-making helps to address the risk in people's lives directly. By contrast, social expenditures are mainly compensation devices that deal with the consequences and aftermath of risk.

It is the compensation view of public expenditure that has underpinned much of the philosophy of the social market across Europe.

According to this view, in order for people to accept the risks of the market economy, where they might not do well through no fault of their own, it has been necessary to offer the assurance that the rules needed to support the market will be accompanied by the promise that the state will provide a social safety net to those who need it. In other words, the state will compensate for the insecurities of the market, and those, for example, who find themselves without a job, or without shelter, or without savings for their old age, will be looked after by state provision.

A compensation approach is less attractive than one that tries to prevent the adverse circumstance happening in the first place. Rules and regulations can be targeted to prevent the risks occurring that will otherwise lead people to seek help in the form of compensation for adversity. For example, people will find it easier to provide for their old age if the state regulates private pension providers so as to encourage them to offer some low-cost products with easily understandable terms and conditions. Similarly, if governments introduce measures to deter the consumption of products that damage health, such as health warnings on cigarettes or taxes on alcohol, then, other things being equal, job insecurity associated with chronic ill health will be reduced, as will unemployment benefit payments.[6]

There is no hard evidence to suggest that people are, in general, more exposed to risks during their lives now than they were in previous eras. On the contrary, rising life expectancy and better health are evidence that risk reduction is the norm for most people. However, as people live longer and lead more active lives, they seem to have become more generally conscious and aware of risks and, at the same time have, rather indiscriminately, come to regard most risks as preventable. Thus, risk awareness does seem to have increased and adds a new and defining element to political debate.[7] Divisions within societies and between societies can no longer be characterized in terms of 'left' or 'right' but instead reflect different attitudes towards risk. The rule-making role of government is therefore enormously attractive. It addresses what has come to be one of the main concerns of people and it tackles risk at source.[8]

From Universal Provision to Selectivity

An additional reason why regulation is attractive is that it offers governments an instrument that is better adapted for selective interventions, while provisioning is biased towards the universal. Rules and regulations can be general or they can be specific. A rule that bars the use of recreational drugs, such as ecstasy or cocaine, is of general applicability. A rule that says that directors of public companies must be 'fit and proper' in order to take on the responsibilities of a public company is specific to the profession of company managers. Thus, rules can, and do, run the gamut from the very general to the targeted and the specific.

By contrast, when it comes to government expenditures, it is often difficult for governments to move away from universal provision. For example, child benefits in the form of tax credits or tax reductions are difficult to deny to all taxpayers with children regardless of their economic circumstances, even though their rationale is to redress childhood deprivation in the poorest households. Similarly, state pensions tend to be paid to all and not just to those who have no other means of support. Equally, the mantra of the British National Health Service, 'free at the point of delivery for all', is designed to avoid differences in the provision of health care, even if a large part of society could afford to pay for privately funded health care.

The targeting of rules thus takes governments in the direction of the customization of their product. However, government spending programmes are difficult to shift from general benefits and notoriously difficult to target effectively.[9]

From General Charging to Connected Charging

A final reason why rule-making offers advantages to governments compared with provisioning is related to charging. Welfare payments and government resource allocations usually come out of general revenues. The 'earmarking' of particular revenues for particular spending purposes is relatively rare. When it does occur, it is often abused and the money used for other purposes. For example, in the case of the UK, vehicle licence fees have no relation to road spending, and national insurance payments bear no relation to any particular health benefits (their original respective justifications).

By contrast, the costs of regulation usually fall, in the first instance, on the activity regulated. If higher safety standards are required of European truck operators, the costs will be borne initially by truck-owners and fall next on those who use truck transport, who may face higher haulage charges. Since many governments preside over taxation levels that are at or beyond the level where compliance is willing and where perverse effects are legion, there is a clear benefit for governments to shift the burden of charges away from taxation systems to other types of charging. Citizen acceptance of this shift in charging principles is also likely to be higher than in raising tax burdens. This may partly be because by the time the costs of regulations show up at the consumer level (for example, by the time higher road haulage charges filter through into higher prices for goods transported by road), the effect may well have been dispersed and be difficult to detect. But, in addition, there appears to be a rough justice involved: if people want safer road haulage practices, then they must be prepared to pay for them.

The shift in charging from the general to the particular should not be misinterpreted. In both cases it is ultimately the citizen or consumer who bears the cost. The citizen pays for market interventions, either through the tax system, or through the costs of regulation. However, because of more targeted charging, the threshold at which people become unwilling to pay may be higher in the case of the costs of regulation.

Rule-Making in Europe

The advantages are such that the regulatory and rule-making function of governments is not only here to stay but, for fundamental reasons, is likely increasingly to displace provisioning as the principal activity of government. Thus, a reassessment of where the comparative advantage of systems of political choice lies and where core activity must be refocused will put the spotlight on rule-making and regulation. It is the activity of government that is best adapted to extend over the wide political spaces of a large union.

Because the existing European union's activities have only involved provisioning in a limited way (and even then with enormous waste), the current union has already been described as a 'regulatory state'.[10] And as it is in rule-making that the comparative advantage of systems of government lies – and particularly so for a continent-wide system – the union's long-term future seems likely to remain characterized by this role.[11]

In order to place the rule-making function within a continent-wide framework for political choice there are three key questions that have to be answered. First, the nature and scope of the union's own rule-making role must be defined. The danger is that too much rule-making, in too much detail, will stifle a society. It will lead to a situation where neither the system of political choice nor that of market choice is able to work.

Secondly, the relationship between the union's role and the regulatory activities of the member states of the union has also to be defined. The possibility that rules of different content could be allowed to coexist alongside each other raises two contradictory fears. One is that the union-wide rule will be squeezed out of use as people prefer alternative rules. If this were to happen, the union's main activity would become sterile. The other, contradictory fear is that the advantages of making rules on a continent-wide basis will drive out all other rules, so that other jurisdictions with regulatory authority will become redundant. Member states and their regions will thus eventually do nothing, in what is becoming the most important area of government, other than exercise delegated powers necessary for implementing the common union-wide rules.

Thirdly, there is a need to ensure that the union's rules remain up-to date. In a large union, decision-taking will always be slow and cumbersome. There needs to be a means of finding out when union rules have to be changed and of knowing in what ways they have to be changed. If the system is not adaptable, then the principal function of a European system of government and the principal advantage it offers will be badly damaged. Europe will become a tangle of obsolete rules and regulations. In other words it will lead once again to exactly the situation that Tocqueville feared: where faults in one system of choice aggravate weaknesses in the other system.

Each of these key issues for Europe's framework is discussed below.

Defining the Union Role: Richness and Reach

Rules with Reach

The key to unlocking the regulatory role of a continent-wide union is to distinguish between rules with 'reach' and rules with 'richness'.[12] The rule-making role for which a European system of government is best suited is in providing rules with 'reach'.

Rules with 'reach' are those rules that offer sufficient common ground to be useful throughout a continent-wide union. By contrast, 'richness' stands for the variations around a common and general rule that different jurisdictions will want. Some will think that less detailed regulatory content will produce a richer rule; others will think that more detail will offer greater richness. 'Richness' therefore represents the difference in content that a local jurisdiction may still prefer to the general rule with reach.

Defining the inherent advantage of a European system of government in terms of the reach of rules and regulations that are observed across the continent should not be seen just as a means to exploit the advantage of geography. Reach means not just territorial reach but also social reach – in the sense of rules that connect individuals, groups and communities who may have only limited knowledge of each other and limited interchange. In a small community where people know each other, or have to interact with each other by virtue of proximity, formal rules and regulations may be quite unnecessary.[13] In a large political space such as Europe, where there is a lack of social familiarity, formal rules are needed.[14]

The Relationship between Reach and Richness

The key to distinguishing between rules with reach and rules with richness is to be found in the procedures of the regulatory process itself. It is this that provides the guide to identifying rules with sufficient common elements that they can reach across the continent.

In highly simplified terms (illustrated in the box at the end of this sub-section) the process involves three different types of judgement. The first involves the scientific evidence. In ideal circumstances this should be based on a standard science so that common agreement can be reached. There would be reason for rules to diverge only when differences in engineering or scientific appreciation are large. In practice, the scientific basis may well be in dispute and judgement will invariably be needed.

Even greater scope for subjective judgement arises in relation to the next two stages, where various sorts of public interest tests are applied (such as cost–benefit or risk analysis) and where public opinion itself also comes into play. Neither of these two stages offers the same prospects for common agreement. On the contrary, judgements about the public interest and expressions of public opinion are very likely to diverge. Different jurisdictions may have different weights they want to attach to the processes of measuring the costs and benefits of rules and they may have different approaches towards risk and assessing one risk against another. In addition, public attitudes may vary.

What this means in practice is that a 'trade-off' can arise between the reach of common rules and their 'richness' or variety. Rules with reach need to be of general content and applicability. When scientific opinion diverges, or when opinion differs about what is best at the public interest stage, or when public opinion goes in different directions in different jurisdictions, it may only be possible to reach a very general agreement at very broad and imprecise levels of principle. The aim will often be to find the common ground for a sufficient agreement rather than to try to reach a common assessment of 'the best'. The common standard judged to be sufficient may be more than a minimum standard but in some cases agreement may only be possible on the minimum. Rules with richness thus involve variations in the direction of more or less detail that may not be generally acceptable throughout Europe. If rules with richness are to be provided, they would have to be provided by those jurisdictions dissatisfied in one way or another with the common rule and put in place in their jurisdiction alongside the common rule.

The analogy in the marketplace is with products aimed at a mass market compared with products occupying a niche market. For example, in the case of fast-food outlets, McDonald's can offer a general product of a hamburger in a bun in many different markets. It taps a market through the convenience it offers to those who want a basic product and who wish to know exactly what they will get to eat even if they are in an unfamiliar town or location. The product is a good and satisfying one since otherwise there would be no McDonald's outlets. At the same time it is a product with limitations that does not appeal to all tastes.

In the case of rule-making, the union will be aiming at that same mass market for simple, predictable products for general consumption. They will be rules with sufficient common elements that they are usable all over the union. They too will have their drawbacks in not suiting every taste. In order to allow for rules with richness there is a need to allow jurisdictions to offer rules with variations in content alongside the common rule. The demand for these variations will arise wherever public interest determinations and public preferences arise that depart from the common assessment. In other words, in order to allow for variety, or for richness, in most markets the McDonald's product, or the union rule, will not be the only product.

The Components of Regulatory Judgements

Regulation and rule-making is sometimes thought of as a mainly technocratic activity. But it is not. The regulatory process typically involves three distinct types of judgement. First, there is a scientific or technical assessment. Secondly, there is a 'public interest' assessment. Thirdly, and increasingly important, there is a judgement passed by public opinion. What is significant for the rule-making process is that most rules and regulations will have to pass through each of these three stages of assessment. Each of these components in the rule-making process needs to be recognized in order to identify the role for a continent-wide union.

Technical Assessment

Science or scientific knowledge provides the starting point for much regulation. For example, the starting point of the evaluation of medicines for regulatory approval involves a scientific investigation of whether the claims behind a new medicine are scientifically well founded and whether there are unwanted side-effects. Similarly, regulations to improve aircraft safety will involve an engineering assessment, for example of the feasibility of a new form of cockpit warning system. Environmental regulation starts from a similar attempt at a scientific assessment. What is particularly difficult about environmental science is that it is not as securely grounded as some other fields, for example because of insufficient knowledge about oceans or the sun, and some of the science seems to be geared towards publicity and funding rather than accuracy. Economic regulation similarly starts from a basis of applied economics. Here, as in all social sciences, the knowledge base is much less secure. However, even in the case of more securely based science it has to be remembered that scientists can differ in their appreciation of the scientific evidence

Box (*Cont.*)

and, moreover, the evidence is often in the form of probabilities rather than certainties.

Public Interest Assessment

Following on the first step of scientific assessment, the next step in many regulatory processes is a broader 'public interest' assessment. This occurs even in the most science-based approaches to regulation. For example, in medicines evaluation a test of 'proportionality' may be involved that is essentially a judgement about social benefits. Hence a particular pharmaceutical product may have severe and adverse side-effects but, in the absence of alternative treatments, the risks may be judged 'acceptable'. The 'public interest' evaluation more typically focuses on whether the benefits of the regulation outweigh the costs. For example, by installing smoke hoods above passenger seats, it would be technically possible to reduce the risks that passengers involved in fire on board an aeroplane might die of smoke inhalation. But smoke hoods are in themselves costly and would add to the weight of the aircraft and lower its fuel efficiency. The benefits from saving relatively few lives have to be weighed against very substantial costs.

The public interest assessment has also come to be increasingly influenced by risk assessment techniques. Increasingly regulatory assessments involve weighing one type of risk against another. The reason for this is that the regulatory benefits in terms of risk reduction may be net benefits, or they may be offset or counterbalanced by increases in related risks. For example, measures to improve safety on a system of underground transport in large cities may raise the costs of travel and persuade some people that they are better off relying on road transportation. There the risks may be higher. Thus lives saved on the underground may be offset by a larger number of lives lost above ground.

This does not mean that underground systems should be left unsafe. But it is a guide to what types of safety measure make sense. The important point about risk is that there are few if any risks that can be treated as self-contained with self-contained remedies. The need to weigh one risk against the other is the norm.[15]

Risk assessment is also important for taking into account the severity of risks. For example, the regulations imposed on the beef industry in the wake of the BSE scare may have resulted in people eating more chickens as an alternative and thus exposing themselves to a much more frequent risk of salmonella poisoning. But while salmonella does, in fact, kill people from vulnerable groups, the generally less severe risks from salmonella and the greater familiarity in encountering it and treating it seem to have been outweighed, rightly or wrongly, by the fatal and unfamiliar risks of BSE-related disease.

The public interest assessment in the case of environmental risk is particularly difficult and contentious. This is partly because, as already mentioned, the scientific assessment may be based on incomplete information so that there is uncertainty about the problem. In addition, remedies may impose large costs. As a result the prevailing approach has emphasized the so-called 'precautionary principle', which can be taken to mean that the public interest warrants taking on small costs (even in the absence of secure knowledge) now so as to avoid much larger remedial costs later. A different principle applies to severe risk. Here 'irreversibility' seems to be the relevant criterion. Risks of irreversible damage – for example, species loss, or the loss of coral reefs – should be treated as a higher priority than other types of less certain risk. What is important about this second stage in the regulatory process of 'public interest' assessment is that it becomes less science- and technology-based and more behavioural science- and judgement-based. Behavioural sciences are inexact;

Box (*Cont.*)

judgements will predictably diverge. As a result, 'public interest' assessments of what is 'reasonable' will differ.

Public Opinion

The third component in regulatory judgements is public opinion itself. Even after a first-stage scientific assessment of a regulatory matter has been made, and even after a second-stage 'public interest' assessment of the costs and benefits, or a risk assessment, of a new rule or regulation, still at the third stage public opinion may have a different judgement to pass. In cases where this happens it may sometimes reflect a distrust of the regulatory authorities themselves. For example, in France a scandal over contaminated blood supplies has eroded public confidence in what the authorities say on health and safety issues. On other occasions it may reflect a different assessment of the public interest considerations: for example, a rejection of the cost–benefit assumptions or the risk assessment. Thus, public opinion in Germany is leading to the decommissioning of nuclear plants because the public wants a zero risk attached to such plants rather than relying on an economic assessment of the costs and benefits of generating electricity from one fuel versus another, coupled with a low probability of danger to the public. Or yet again it may reflect an opinion about social or moral values that should be taken into account. For example, in the wake of a train crash, public opinion may want to see rail safety improved regardless of any other consideration because the public may regard it as 'immoral' not to save lives where they can be saved.

The Scope for Rules with Reach

Given that the process of making regulatory judgements will suggest a place both for rules with reach and rules with richness of content, the question arises whether the scope for rules with reach can be predetermined in advance.

One approach to defining the scope for common rule-making by Europe's system of government is through a distinction between rules that can be seen as representing 'negative' integration and rules that represent 'positive' integration. For example, rules that remove market barriers between member states are rules that remove negative barriers and represent negative integration, while rules that put in place social or public interest concerns stand for 'positive' integration.[16]

What is suggested by this distinction is that rule-making in Europe with reach must cover enough areas of public policy in order to include common rules of both types: those that represent positive as well as negative integration. Thus, rules and regulations relating to market efficiency must be accompanied by rules relating to social and environmental conditions, health and safety, and so on. An additional attraction of this approach is that it appears to apply to particular rules as well as to rule-making in general. For example, it implies that a union-wide rule that removes a market barrier should be accompanied by a rule that relates to the social or public interest concern in the same area. Thus, a directive that opens up the electricity industry across the union to competition should include or be accompanied by a rule about social obligations such as connections in remote areas, or billing and payments procedures.

The language of positive and negative integration is unfortunate in the sense that it is value-biased. 'Positive' integration sounds better than 'negative' integration. But the distinction is unhelpful in more fundamental ways. It assumes that market opening measures would not at the same time carry social benefits – for example, in the form of lower prices, or better service standards – and it assumes that additional social content provided by the union would necessarily be needed.

It is indeed possible that areas of social concern may need to be addressed by common union-wide rules. But the more that the proposed rules of the union move into areas of social concern, the more difficult it is likely to be to find the basis for a union-wide agreement on a commonly acceptable measure. This is because the initial scientific, or evidence-based, assessment of the need for rules will be more debatable, because it is more likely that there will be disagreements over how to define the public interest in the second stage of the regulatory process, and because it may also be difficult to find the common factor in public opinion as so many member states have differences in the structure and traditions of social protection and their view of what is, or is not, in the public interest.

What the distinction between positive and negative integration does call attention to, however, is that it is very difficult to predetermine according to policy area where the three elements in a rule-making or regulatory decision will combine to produce common agreement on a rule with reach that is seen to be both desirable and attainable. Instead, the relevant tests are procedural.

The structure of the regulatory process itself suggests that the decisive procedural tests are as follows:

- Is there a common scientific or evidence-based foundation for a common rule?
- Is there a common appreciation of the public interest (based on cost and risk assessment)?
- Is there a common element in public opinion?

It is clear that there will be many cases where these different elements do not come together. In such circumstances there will either be an absence of a union-wide rule or regulation, or the union-wide rule will be set at a very high level of generality so as to obscure underlying differences of appreciation. Moreover, even when the different elements do all come together so as to provide the basis for a union rule with reach, it will likely remain the case that the common standard will not make all jurisdictions happy. For these reasons, the analogy with the market suggests that different jurisdictions should retain their own regulatory capacities and be able to put in place their own rules alongside the common union rule. In this way they can reflect their own appreciation of the public interest and public opinion in their own domain. In other words the McDonald's product can be accompanied by other offerings appealing to different palates.

Thus a continent-wide union focusing on the rule-making function could and likely would offer a combination of rules: a union rule based on a common denominator, or set of broad principles, that provides a common standard and a common passport for cross-border activities; and, at the same time, local rules and local regulations offering variations of the general rule. In such instances users would have a choice of which rule or regulation to use: the union rule or the local rule; in some cases the local rule would form an add-on requirement, in others a less onerous obligation. It also has to be accepted that in contentious areas of public policy it may not be possible to agree on rules with reach and that entirely local standards will prevail.

The Potential Dominance of Union-Wide Rule-Making

As has been noted, the idea that a continent-wide form of government for Europe could and should allow for the coexistence of both rules with reach and rules with richness leads to two quite contradictory fears. One fear is that the value of common continent-wide rules will be eroded. The other, opposite, fear is that union-wide rule-making will come to crowd out all other forms of rule-making.

The first fear stems from the view that the scope for union-wide rules will be squeezed from two sides. If a jurisdiction offers less onerous rules or regulations, they will be preferred to the union rule. If, on the other hand, a jurisdiction offers a rule with higher content, some people could also prefer that. The union rule will lose support from both sides. As a result, the advantages of having a known common standard will have been lost as people have to get acquainted with alternative standards in different jurisdictions.

The second fear arises from the view that the inherent advantages in union rule-making will lead to the elimination of variations in rule-making across Europe. Other jurisdictions will find that some of their most important powers will have been completely eroded. They will end up exercising only the delegated powers that the union chooses to pass on.

Of these two fears, the earlier analysis suggests that the second fear, that union-wide rule-making could come eventually to dominate, is more realistic over the long run, since, as has been suggested, rule-making at the union level offers governments increasing returns to scale.

One of the implications for classical economists of increasing returns was that it offered the prospect that a firm that exploited them might end up dominating the market. The limit on dominance was the limit of the market itself. Contemporary discussion suggests that specialization by itself is not necessarily anti-competitive.[17] Moreover, in the case of the market, competition from other companies will, in most cases, prevent a firm from exploiting its position. This is why the successors to the classical economists did not pursue the implications of increasing returns.[18] But in some cases, competition will not work to prevent the rise of a dominant firm, and at that point governments may step in. This is why governments have rules in place to enforce competition so that companies that emerge with excess market power over their rivals can be checked. The US government action against Microsoft provides an example.

In the case of the rule-making function of governments, there are incentives for the European rule-making authority to try to dominate the market, namely to reduce the costs of coordination with other rule-making jurisdictions and to reduce the costs and difficulties of enforcement.

The question which therefore arises is whether there are equally good reasons for systems of government to be organized in such a way as to prevent a particular jurisdiction emerging as a monopoly provider of rules and regulations. In the case of Europe this would mean organizing the system so that the inherent advantages of rule-making by the union, and the incentives for the union to suppress other rule-makers, do not eliminate every other jurisdiction over time.

There are two compelling types of reason why a jurisdictional monopoly for union-wide rules and regulations should be avoided. One is in order to provide a responsive system of political choice. In just the same way that a government will move against a monopolist in the market because it denies consumers a choice among products and services, so too systems of government need to offer a range of choices. If people in different jurisdictions within a continent-wide union have different views of the public interest, or if public opinion in different jurisdictions has divergent views about what is the acceptable content of rules or regulations, then, as a normative matter, it is desirable to allow for these differences to be expressed.

The other type of reason given why a system of European government should not aim to become the monopoly provider of rules within the continent is related to the knowledge base for government. In particular, a monopoly provider of rules is likely to ignore signals about the need for change and updating in the rules. In just the same way as a monopolist provider of goods and services will fail to innovate or keep abreast of what people really want, so too governments that become monopolist providers of rules and regulations will also become unresponsive. They will not pay attention to market developments that call for updated rules and, instead of listening to what people want, they will start to prescribe what they think people *should* want.

Either type of failing will be extremely costly for Europe's system of government. In the first case, 'Brussels' will be constantly accused of insensitive and intrusive regulation. In the second case, 'Brussels' will be seen as the reason why Europe lags behind market developments in other areas of the world and be accused of ignoring what people really want. The danger signs are already there in the case of the existing union. A mythology has grown up that 'Brussels' symbolizes irrational rules and regulations – a world of straight bananas. Most of the stories are indeed myth. But they point towards an underlying reality: that the existing union has not got its rule-making and regulatory role right.

Coexisting Regulatory Systems

The vital question for Europe is how to take advantage of the rule-making function of a continent-wide system of government without imposing an unresponsive and rigid regulatory system. The coexistence of rules with richness alongside rules with reach can be seen as a defence against the abuse of the regulatory role by a potentially dominant source of rule-making – the union itself. But, equally important, the coexistence of rules serves as a means to ensure that the rule-making system has an institutionalized way of keeping up to date. Rules suffer from being overtaken by events, and when markets and societies are rapidly changing they can quickly become obsolete. Most economic regulators have found themselves playing a game of 'catch-up' with their regulatees as change in the market has obliterated old industry boundaries and old ways of doing things. Regulatory 'lag' can be damaging enough in the context of a single sector. It becomes an enormous cost to society when it spreads across all activities.

Historically there have been two main sources of innovation. One is from outside a society. The other is from the benefits of the geographic periphery. The periphery has been able to innovate partly because distance has made it less subject to the control of the centre and partly because peripheral locations are often those that have been most exposed to outside influences. The question for the union is thus how to mimic in its own rule-setting procedures the advantages that once accrued to the periphery as a source of innovation.[19]

External Signals for Change

External pressures on the rule-making functions of a continent-wide union will occur through international trade and capital movements. This is because regulatory issues over the whole range of market, health and safety, labour, social and environmental rules are increasingly becoming a factor in international trade relations. The international market will therefore be one source of signals about the content of European regulations. In addition, international organizations such as the World Trade Organization are likely to play an increasing role in surveilling the interaction between different regulatory regimes. Thus the rule-making functions of Europe will also have to become increasingly integrated into those of the various international rule-making regimes.

The equivalent of signals from outside Europe can also come from a union's own members. This happens whenever a member is allowed to 'opt out' from a particular area of rule-making – whether it is in respect of social rules, environmental rules, the single currency or any other area of public policy. From this perspective it makes sense for the union itself to allow for members to opt out of a rule-making area precisely because the opted-out member will provide useful information on the success or otherwise of the rule being pursued by the other members of the union.

Internal Signals for Change: The Delaware and California Effects

In addition to those signals that may come from rule-making jurisdictions outside Europe, an internal source of information about change and innovation is provided when different jurisdictions inside Europe have the possibility of offering different standards. It is in respect of these internal processes that controversy arises because coexistence prompts the fear mentioned above that the availability of different rules will squeeze out or damage union-wide standards.

The coexistence of different rules alongside each other gives rise to an interplay between the two. One version of this interplay is sometimes termed the 'Delaware' effect. Its counterpart has been called the 'California' effect. What these terms refer to in this context is what can be expected to happen to rules when different options are available to choose from. The Delaware effect reflects the fact that in the United States companies incorporate in the state of Delaware because they anticipate that it will be cheaper than in their original state of incorporation. The Delaware effect thus stands for the expectation that, given a choice between different regulations or regulatory regimes, users would choose the cheapest rule and other rules would be undermined and effectively lapse. The California effect, by contrast, reflects the fact that automobile manufacturers have met higher environmental standards in the state of California rather than following cheaper federal standards. Thus, under the so-called California effect, a possibly more expensive rule would be chosen rather than the rule that is cheapest to observe.[20]

What this means in the case of Europe is that, if the Delaware effect operates, a union rule offering sufficient standards could be preferred to more onerous local rules offering higher standards. The higher standards of the local jurisdiction would in effect be undermined. Similarly, if the sufficient common rule offers a higher standard than the minimum and the local rule offers the minimum, the more onerous union rule could be undermined. Conversely, if the so-called California effect prevails and people prefer to follow the high standards of a particular jurisdiction, then the union rule with a sufficient common standard will fall into disuse.

The question that arises in the case of the California effect is whether a preference for a more expensive rule represents an isolated case, which requires a highly particular set of circumstances, or whether the circumstances are more generally applicable. If it is an isolated case, then cheaper rules can usually be expected to undermine the use of more expensive rules. If the case is generalizable, then it suggests that interrelationships between rules and regulations of different qualities involve a more complicated set of factors.

The circumstances where the California effect may occur seem to involve the following. First, the market where the more onerous variation occurs must be significant enough that producers accept the higher cost. As far as market weight is concerned, the wealth of a market may be more important than size because it is purchasing power that counts. In the case of California, it is of course both large and wealthy. In the case of Europe, it could mean that a more onerous regulation in a wealthy but relatively small state such as Sweden counts for as much or more than a rule or regulation in a large but relatively less well-off state such as Spain.

Secondly, the market must be influential in the system of political choice as well as market choice. Public opinion in California is seen to have a nation-wide impact on environmental issues because it is regarded as a leader in attitudes and an indicator of where public opinion in other markets may shift. The fact that California also carries important political weight in a more direct form – for example, its weight in the selection of presidents and consequent likely foreshadowing of federal approaches – is also a factor. At first sight, political weight appears to depend on size. But in the context of

Europe's political system the relationship is probably more accurately characterized as the size of coalition that any state can mobilize. If a small state can put together blocking minorities or supervening majorities in the Council of Ministers, it will have more political influence than size would indicate.

A third factor concerns the reputation and influence of the rule-making jurisdiction, not in the system of political choice but in the system of market choice. For example, a financial service company offering products across several different states with different regulatory standards may prefer to operate out of a jurisdiction with tough standards. This is because it may be easier subsequently for that company to get regulatory approval in other markets worldwide and because it may make it easier to sell the product concerned. Someone in Europe might, for example, prefer to buy a pension or insurance product from a financial company regulated in the Netherlands or the UK, where the markets are perceived to be well regulated, rather than from a market, such as Greece, where standards may be perceived to be less rigorous or less well enforced.

It is the so-called Delaware effect that tends to raise greater anxieties. This is where those who need to observe the rules and regulations choose the cheapest and least onerous rule. It paints a picture where higher standards will lapse and there is the proverbial 'race to the bottom'. In the case of the European Union, it holds out the possibility that if standards lower than the union standard are allowed in particular jurisdictions, they will create inequalities and consequently undermine the common standard.

However, the picture of 'a race to the bottom' is a misleading one. Delaware achieved its initial advantage as a state for incorporation through historical accident, but its success in maintaining its position has involved substantial investment. Companies that incorporate in Delaware are making use of the state's administrative expertise, a body of corporate case law and judicial expertise related to that law. [21]

What both the California effect and the Delaware effect therefore show is that a market in regulation can work in sophisticated ways as can any other market in goods or services. What coexistence between regulatory regimes does is to provide choice, a way of testing rules and an incentive to invest in and develop the most up-to-date practice. Regulatory differences should be seen as part of a normal market framework, as the following box demonstrates.

Choice between Regulatory Systems

Environmental Rules

Example: *Europe agrees on common rules for the cleanliness of public beaches. Jurisdiction A permits lower cost standards. Jurisdiction B insists on higher cost standards.*

Implications: Potential users among the public have a choice. They can go to the beaches that offer the cleanliness guarantees of the Europe standard or to beaches with higher or lower standards. Some will prefer the Europe standard or higher and be prepared to pay for the difference. Others will go for the cheaper option. If everybody prefers the cheaper option, or there is no significant attraction to the Europe standard or higher, then what is revealed is that the public does not place any value on the European standard (or the higher standard in Jurisdiction B) and it should be rethought. In practice, different markets for different beach standards are likely to develop.

A refinement of practice that offers different standards is through allowing for tradeable certificates between the different jurisdictions so as to ensure that on average throughout Europe the effect of a uniformly observed standard is met.

Health Rules

Example: *A European standard for abattoir practices is established. Jurisdiction A allows lower standards. Jurisdiction B insists on higher standards.*

Implications: Abattoir owners in Jurisdiction A cannot export products from their abattoir unless they meet the Europe standard. They therefore have a choice of meeting the Europe standard in their practice and marketing for export as well as for the local market or operating at the local standard just for the local jurisdiction.

Box (*Cont.*)

If local consumers only buy the product that meets the Europe standard, despite its higher cost, abattoirs operating to the local standard will have to upgrade to meet the Europe standard or go out of business. If consumers buy products meeting the local standard, abattoirs operating to the Europe standard, including exporters, will face a smaller market. Europe standard abattoirs will therefore have to market the advantages of the Europe standard or they may choose to set up in a jurisdiction for the local market.

Abattoir owners in Jurisdiction B will be able to offer their product anywhere in Europe. If, because of higher abattoir standards, they have to offer a higher cost product, they will be testing consumer demand for the higher standard. If there is insufficient demand, the signal suggests that the higher standard is not valued by the consumer. At the same time they will face competition in their own jurisdiction from abattoirs operating from other jurisdictions that meet the Europe standard. If the consumer accepts the lower Europe standard, then again the market is not valuing the higher standard. Local abattoirs will go out of business, or insist on a change in the local standard, or relocate in different jurisdictions.

Financial Risk

Example: *A Europe standard for the investment policy of pension funds is established that provides qualitative tests for whether a pension fund is being operated prudently. Jurisdiction A allows pension funds to operate at lower cost (by minimizing reporting requirements). Jurisdiction B insists on a quantitative measure of prudence that (by limiting investment possibilities) raises the cost of pension funds.*

Implications: Pension funds meeting the qualitative Europe standard can sell pension products Europewide. Pension funds in Jurisdiction A will have a competitive advantage in Europe unless their supervisory

Box (*Cont.*)

> standards are seen to be lax, in which case there will be consumer resistance. The pension funds may therefore move jurisdiction to a centre that is perceived to be well regulated. By contrast, pension funds in Jurisdiction B will be disadvantaged and will either have to convince pension buyers that they offer a safer standard or move out to a different jurisdiction. Because pension purchasers may have difficulty in evaluating pension safety (regulatory risk), the Europe standard is likely to be accompanied by some kind of brand labelling or kite marking to show that the pension company meets the Europe standard of regulation, or by the marketing of different regulatory centres.

The Implications of the Rule-Making Role

There are far-reaching implications from viewing the long-term comparative advantage of Europe's system of government as lying in its rule-making and regulatory role. First, a continent-wide system of government should not be seen as performing the same functions as a traditional government in an individual state. Europe's system of government does not need to perform a provisioning role.

Secondly, how to define the rule-making role itself becomes a matter of critical importance for the continent. If Europe gets it right, then it will have the basis for a responsive system of political choice and a well-functioning system of market choice. If it gets it wrong, both systems of choice will be clogged.[22]

Thirdly, the analysis suggests that, when thinking of a continent-wide system of government in a rule-making capacity, the union should be seen not as an exclusive rule-maker but as a source of generally applicable rules that coexist alongside the rules of other regulatory regimes of the localities, regions and states. What needs to be set up is a framework for coexisting regulatory regimes where rules with reach, provided by the union, coexist alongside rules with richness, provided by member states and their regions. If rules with richness are allowed alongside rules with reach, then people will have a choice between goods and services produced under different regulatory systems.

The existing union has never known quite whether choice would be a good or a bad thing. The original approach stressed the need for the harmonization of rules. The attraction of harmonization is that it suppresses entirely any rivalry between rules by establishing a single rule. This proved to be largely impractical because it was so difficult to get agreement on a single standard by member states with widely differing practices and traditions. The attention then switched towards 'mutual recognition', which meant that the rules and regulations in each member state could be recognized in other jurisdictions. This, however, does not seem to allow sufficient space for the advantages of union-wide rules and regulations. The result has been an uneasy tension between both approaches. The main fears on both sides have been left unresolved. Some fear that the current union remains a costly tangle of different rules and obligations. Others see union powers heading still in the direction of centralizing all key responsibilities.

When the dilemma is framed as a matter of the relationship between reach and richness, it suggests a less confrontational relationship between rules with different content. Variety in rules is seen as part of a normal marketplace. There are added costs from having more than a single common rule. But the benefits flow from a more responsive and a more up-to-date system of rule-making. In rapidly changing societies or markets, the savings from a single rule-maker are likely to be outweighed by the costs of regulatory lag. Rules with reach will offer an inbuilt advantage because they provide access to the largest market: Europe as a whole. At the same time, rules with richness alongside rules with reach should be seen not as 'displacing' rules with reach but as giving society a way constantly to monitor and improve their quality.[23]

Fourthly, the rule-making role of governments places an enormous weight on communication and information in both politics and the market. People want to know what the knowledge base is behind a rule or regulation and they want to know on what basis the public interest has been determined. Information about the assumptions and evidence underlying rules is essential to avoid conflict between rules and rule-makers.[24] Moreover, the rule-making functions of government also touch on many of the important social and moral values of communities. Europe's system of government must therefore be responsive to the manner in which people register their values in politics. Thus, in the same way as the market has become more responsive to what people want by redefining core products and using improved communications to customize products, so too Europe's system of government will not only have to focus on the core product, where it possesses comparative advantage, but it will, in addition, have to look at how best to take advantage of changing patterns of communication in politics. The next chapter therefore looks at the ways in which people signal what they want within systems of political choice.

5   Signals and Noise

The Role of Rights

After the idea of virtue, I know no higher principle than that of right ... There are no great nations – it may almost be added that there would be no society – without the notion of rights.
Alexis de Tocqueville, *Democracy in America*

The Focus of Rights

In a continent-wide union covering all of Europe it will be extremely difficult for people to signal what it is they want from politicians and equally difficult for politicians to pick out genuine messages from the noise of a multitude of different voices saying different things. Cutting through this clutter is the language of rights. Thus, in thinking about how Europe's system of government can provide a system of political choice that matches the responsiveness of market choice, the need is to take into account not just the traditional mechanisms of the ballot box, but also the new ways in which the language of rights is used. The critical issue for Europe's system of government is how political expression based on votes relates to political expression based on claims about rights.

This chapter explores this fundamental issue. It argues that the key to organizing Europe's framework for rights-based politics in relation to vote-based politics is to distinguish between two completely distinct and different constitutional uses of rights. The first is their use as a way of defining those values that lay down the preconditions for systems of political and market choice. They establish the ground rules without which the system will not work. The second is their use in talking about important public policy values *within* systems of political choice. In this second role, rights help to debate social choices within a political system. This second use involves a much wider use of the language of rights in order to be able to talk over the whole range of public policy.

In both cases it is possible to talk about 'basic' or 'fundamental' rights. But the rights are basic in different ways and in different contexts. Rights that are 'basic' to a system of political choice are those rights, such as freedom of expression, without which the system will not function at all. By contrast, those rights that may be singled out as 'basic' for the purpose of guiding policy priorities within systems of choice are rights, such as those to protect against social discrimination or social exclusion, that reflect our highest social concerns. They are 'basic' in the sense that they provide a starting point for a discussion of the principles that guide many of the most important public policies in society.

In considering how best to build rights into Europe's system of governance, these distinctions, and the other distinct ways in which rights are used, must be observed. Otherwise, rights that are of the greatest importance in one context become misused in another. In constitutional terms they have to be treated differently, each placed in its own context.

The focus on these two aspects of rights in this chapter is not intended to downplay the other uses of the language of rights. In particular the use of rights in debates about the legitimation of political systems remains highly important in Europe. Europeans no longer have to argue against hereditary systems of government that demanded allegiance simply because of the laws of succession. On the other hand, for compelling historical reasons in Europe there still needs to be a way to reason about such questions as the relation between a legitimate system of government and a society's highest moral values. The questions relating to legitimacy are, however, taken up in chapter 9.

It is extraordinarily important that Europe's system of governance gets the constitutional framework for rights specified in the correct way. In Europe the question of how to ensure respect for the basic preconditions of democratic and market choice cannot be taken for granted. In a continent-wide union, democratic habits and a market economy will be a relatively new experience in historical terms for a majority of states. At the time of the formation of the American system of government, Madison could be confident that the American people knew what their rights were and would take action if their new system of government were to infringe them. After all, the American people had just thrown out unrepresentative colonial rulers. In Europe, unfortunately, democracy is not so firmly established.

It is equally important that the constitutional framework is correctly specified for the way in which rights are recognized as a means to talk about policy priorities within Europe's system of political choice. The language of rights lends itself to those who feel very strongly about an issue of public policy even if they are in a minority. In most voting systems, by contrast, it is the simple majority that counts. The risk is that there will be tension between inflamed minorities claiming rights and normally 'silent' majorities expressing a backlash through the ballot box. If the relationship between vote-based politics and rights-based politics becomes imbalanced, there are two dangers. One is that dedicated minorities, even with the most high-minded motives, can abuse systems of democratic choice. The other, connected danger is of populist reaction. Europe cannot run either risk.

The discussion in this chapter suggests that, in order to get Europe's framework correctly specified, the key constitutional question centres on where rights claims should be adjudicated and legislated on. The analysis suggests that rights concerning the preconditions of systems of choice should be handled in the constitutional provisions related to the conditions of membership of the continent-wide union. By contrast, rights claims that are about priorities within politics should be recognized on a decentralized basis. This is because decentralized recognition makes the best use of rights as guides to 'right reason' and offers the best setting through which democratic societies can resolve potential tensions between minority and majority opinion.

The Dominance of Rights

Over their long history the use of rights has come and gone, propelled by different historical exigencies at different times. In their medieval origin, rights seem to have emerged as a result of an assertion of group interests (barons versus kings) and because of a need to express a clearer relationship between church law and secular law. They re-emerged again in the seventeenth and eighteenth centuries as a language to talk about the legitimacy of systems of government – as doctrines such as the divine right of kings lost their potency and government had to find a source of authority that did not rely on inheritance. Famously, a Bill of Rights was added to the American Constitution as a way of making clear what this new constitution stood for. Their prominence in the second half of the twentieth century, symbolized by the United Nations Universal Declaration of Human Rights (1948) and the European Convention on Human Rights of the Council of Europe (1950), came in reaction to the atrocities of the Second World War in Asia and Europe.[1]

Throughout this history, rights have given us the means to talk about the fundamentals of a political system: the basic rules and conditions for choice. However, the massive extension of rights as the more general language for talking about priorities within systems of political choice is relatively recent.[2]

There are three extremely important classes of reasons why the language of rights has become the predominant way in which people talk about priorities within politics. The first is that rights provide people with a versatile and flexible language for talking about values in public policy across the whole range of individual and social policy preferences. The second is that the language of rights provides a way of communicating people's preferences in a very direct form – thus counteracting the indirectness of a system of representative democracy. The third is that affiliation based on rights provides a means to reduce or circumvent the costs of political expression in traditional forms – particularly, rights provide a way to get round the high entry costs of traditional politics.

Rights and Social Choices

The versatility of the language of rights makes it possible to express and debate some of the most important social and moral values in society over the entire range of subjects that may come up for choice:

- Rights can be used to talk about a huge range of social issues, from questions of social exclusion affecting the rights of impoverished groups in society, or questions of social prejudice affecting the rights of ethnic minorities, to such questions as the protection of the environment or standards of animal welfare. Rights cover subjects as diverse as the right to housing and shelter, or the right of access to walk across privately owned land.

- Rights can be used to discuss questions affecting the largest groups in society, such as the rights of women or the rights of the elderly, or questions affecting relatively smaller groups, such as the rights of the disabled, through to questions of the rights of individuals.
- Rights can be used to tackle some of the most sensitive moral issues in society, such as those associated with abortion or euthanasia, or sensitive social issues such as the rights of immigrants, and at the same time they can be used to talk about the mundane, such as the level of service to be expected from transport, health care systems or telecommunications or other service-providers.
- Rights can address the public sector – for example, through rights for information from government departments or agencies – and they can also address the private sector – for example, through the right of privacy for personal or confidential information supplied over the internet.
- Rights can refer to old and venerable social issues, such as property rights, and they can also refer to the new, such as the right to be informed whether foods contain genetically modified products, or the right to privacy for information on one's own genetic code.

Some observers have deplored what they refer to as a 'proliferation' of rights because they feel it devalues their worth if there are too many rights asserted. There is a fear that the more the language of rights is used, the more rights will confuse different types of claims and the more that different claims will be in conflict. Moreover, it is pointed out that when rights clash, the conflict is not at the level of abstract debate but can be one that contributes to actual tensions between different groups in societies. For example, when universities give special preference to admit minorities, they will, if the total intake is limited, have to exclude non-minority applicants. Debates about affirmative action in this and other settings, such as the job market, thus are far from theoretical; they affect people directly and can set one group in society off against another.[3]

Such criticisms have not halted the extraordinary growth in the use of the language of rights, or their extension into ever-widening areas of social debate. In any event it is difficult to know how their use could be limited. There is neither a fixed supply of rights, nor are there fixed limits to their use. It is precisely the flexibility of the language of rights, their suitability for talking about values and the wide scope of their potential application that makes them so useful for discussing a multitude of social issues.

It is this versatility of rights in talking about an enormous range of social choices that makes them particularly the language through which people can talk about rules and regulations in society. Indeed many rules and regulations are the direct product of claims about rights. For example, equal rights claims that age should not be the basis for discrimination in employment policies might lead to legislation against mandatory retirement ages, or rules and regulations against age bias in job advertising.

Another reason why the language of rights is particularly well suited to the rule-making functions of governments is that, like rules, rights claims can be either general or particular. For example, a claim about women's rights might be used in a particular case to change the rules of membership for an exclusive club in order to open it up for women's membership, or, in more general circumstances, to change the regulations so as to open up a profession to women, or, in even wider circumstances still, to argue for a change in regulations affecting the job market in general (for example, part-time working provisions) in order for women to find jobs more easily.

Yet a further reason why rights are particularly well suited to the rule-making functions of government is that they provide an extremely useful way to talk about the content of rules and regulations. For example, it might be decided to protect public service broadcasting so as to safeguard the rights of those who speak a minority language or who belong to a minority ethnic group. Similarly, it might be decided to tighten up the rules governing food labelling in order to protect the rights of consumers to know the origin and content of a product, or to regulate transport systems or other services so as to offer customer rights in terms of the standards of service that users have a right to expect.

As the European Union increasingly becomes a union with common rules and regulations, the common political language used to talk about them will be the language of rights. It is this language that helps to decide whether rules and regulations are needed in the first place, what their scope and objectives should be and what their content should include. It is the language that helps to explain the trade-off between rules with reach and rules with richness, and why it is that rules with different degrees of richness may be desired in different jurisdictions.

Rights as Correctives

The second enormously important characteristic of rights is that, as a means of communication and as a way of signalling, they help correct for those weaknesses that relate to the indirectness of representative democracy.[4]

First, elected representatives can be told what is wanted from them only through votes at election times, and once elected they have a large discretion as to what they do. By contrast, rights claims give people a basis for exerting continuous pressure for action. Instead of elected representatives telling people what is good for them, by insisting on their rights, people can tell their elected representatives what they are expected to do.

Secondly, when people vote at elections, they face a choice between parties offering very general political platforms that may not possess much specific appeal. Rights cannot be classified in party-political terms since the issues they address cut across party-political lines and can be appealed to by all shades of the political spectrum. But what rights can do is to provide society with groupings that are more attractive affiliation groups than political parties. They are more attractive because they consist of the like-minded, address what really interests and motivates people and can try to exert pressure in a focused way.[5]

Thirdly, rights groups can also mobilize more effectively across boundaries. Political parties not only have to offer general platforms with appeal to a wide electorate but they also have to organize their activities on a constituency or regional basis. The organizational infrastructure of political parties in Europe is cumbersome both because it is historically tied into the nation state and because it has to be territorially extensive. Even if Europe's system of government sees the growth of political parties organized across state boundaries, the parties will still remain tied to territory. By contrast, rights groups, which bring together the like-minded to press particular values, have flexibility as to how they organize. The mobile phone – not territorial coverage – is the key to organization.

Fourthly, the traditional territorial boundaries of the nation state limit in a more general way the extent to which political parties can organize opinion across member state boundaries in Europe. Territory stands for differences in political cultures as well as actual organizational cost barriers. Rights are not limited in the same way by territory. They measure value distance not territorial distance. The language of rights crosses boundaries and provides a way of identifying values that are relevant and salient to other like-minded people across Europe.[6]

Finally, rights have another advantage as ways of getting what people want out of systems of choice: they can exploit judicial channels for action as an alternative to politics. Judicial channels not only can force an issue towards resolution while politicians might prefer to stall for time, but in addition the law also provides an instrument that can be used against politicians if they do not themselves act.

These various ways in which rights can be used to correct deficiencies in the indirectness of representative democracy are extraordinarily useful in the case of a continent-wide union. Any Europe-wide system of governance will encounter problems arising from the very indirect way in which representative forms of democracy reflect people's preferences and the difficulties inherent in trying to connect political systems across traditional territorial boundaries. These difficulties are acute for Europe because any continent-wide system of government will be large and seen to be remote and difficult to influence. Individual voters will typically feel powerless, even groups may feel excluded. Politicians, on the other hand, can be counted on to remain arrogant and to proclaim that they know what is best for people. If rights can help to overcome these barriers, as they can, then Europe's political system needs to take maximum advantage of them.

A Cost Perspective

Thirdly, the advantages of the language of rights can be expressed in terms of the earlier discussion about the opportunity costs of using systems of market choice compared with using systems of political choice.[7] It was argued that the external setting for governance has given systems of market choice a boost as the system through which people can get what they want while, by contrast, systems of political choice have lost ground. It was suggested that part of the reason for this is that changes in the setting have enabled systems of market choice to take advantage of lower entry costs and lower information costs. This has meant that people can communicate more directly what they want, as well as receive goods and services more precisely tailored to their needs from businesses that have been forced to rethink what they provide and the way in which they provide it.

For systems of political choice, the advantage of the language of rights is that it provides a potent way to lower entry costs and information costs in politics. The earlier discussion about some of the ways in which the language of rights helps to correct for the indirectness of representative democracy can also be framed in terms of the ways in which rights reduce entry costs in politics. For example, forming groups of the like-minded, clustered around rights claims, is far easier and far lower in terms of entry costs than is establishing political parties, with the territorial infrastructure that the latter entails.

Many of the other advantages of rights can be seen as providing ways of reducing information and particularly communication costs. For example, it was pointed out that rights groups lower the costs of expressing people's preferences and values compared with traditional parties by providing a much more tightly focused and continuous message instead of the episodic and general messages involved in party-political platforms in electoral campaigns. Claims about rights also provide a hugely important way of communicating across borders from the local level to the global level. In systems of political choice there are no political parties operating from the global level to the local but instead there is the language of rights.[8]

The versatility of rights as a way of expressing values over the range of individual and social choices that arise in politics can also be expressed in terms of information savings. Claims about rights provide a way of identifying salient values and of bringing together and organizing the relevant information people need to arrive at a decision.

These three features of rights – their versatility, their directness, the assistance they give in reducing the costs of getting views across in politics – each help explain how important it is to consider how the language of rights can best be built into a system of governance for a continent-wide union. However much some observers may deplore the growing use of the language of rights, the reasons why rights have risen to prominence as a means of signalling what people want are not going to disappear. Historically, there have been times when the language of rights has fallen into disuse. But in today's setting for government, the language of rights provides one of the few ways in which systems of political choice can start to match the cost reductions of making choices through the market.

What is a legitimate cause for concern is that the extension of the use of the language of rights has led to a blurring of the very different uses to which rights are now put in systems of government. In order to organize Europe's system of government so as to make best use of the language of rights, these different uses must be distinguished.

Rights as Preconditions

The first step in thinking about how the language of rights and Europe's system of governance fit together is to clarify the different purposes to which the language of rights is put. In particular there is a need to distinguish between the growth in the use of the language of rights for talking about priorities within politics and the use of the language of rights for talking about the basic rules of a system of political choice.[9]

The Different Uses and Purposes of Rights

The language of rights serves four related but distinct purposes. They are arrayed below, not in the order of their intrinsic importance, but starting with those that are about practical concerns in people's lives and ending with those that are the most abstract.

A first use of the language of rights is to enable people to talk about important values that are the subject of social choice within the rules of politics. For example, when it is said that public transport systems should be designed and operated so that they do not discriminate against the rights of the disabled, then a value judgement is being made about the kinds of social choices people should be making within politics. Similarly, when a right to a good-quality environment is asserted, the right is about the public policies that groups may want adopted by governments within the system of political choice. As described above, it is in this area of political choice that the language of rights has expanded particularly rapidly in recent decades.

A second use of the language of rights is as the language of adjustment and correction to the rules of political choice. For example, if it is claimed that women have a right to be equally represented in legislatures and in the lists of party candidates for legislative office, a debate is being prompted about the choice between different rules for democratic systems. The language of rights is being used to press for revisions or corrections to the rules.

A third purpose of rights is to provide a way of talking about the preconditions for systems of political choice. For example, appeals to the right of free expression, or the right of freedom of association, are assertions about the preconditions that make it possible for a democratic system of political choice to work at all. If a political system is deficient in some basic way – for example if it disallows freedom of expression – an appeal to rights is a way of highlighting the preconditions that must be observed in order for a society to be able to make its choices through a system of democratic politics. If people cannot express their political views freely, then politicians have no way of knowing what people want, the people have no way of telling politicians what they want and they have no way of debating their concerns among themselves.

The fourth purpose of the language of rights is to provide a way of talking about what it is that legitimates or justifies a system of political choice. For example, when it is argued that rights that reflect social solidarity are a necessary component of a system of political choice, the view is being advanced that, unless a system of government provides social justice, it is a system that is difficult or impossible to justify. Everybody has to accept the system of government into which he or she is born, but the language of rights offers a way of talking about this acceptance and, if need be, a means of questioning it. To put it more bluntly in the European context, Europe needs a language to talk about the legitimacy of a European system of government when the system is taking shape against a historical background where a large majority of people acquiesced in the evils of fascism and communism.[10]

These different purposes are related and sometimes rights claims in a particular area may fulfil more than one purpose. For example, claims about women's rights have involved claims about the preconditions for political choice (when women were excluded from voting), about the rules (when they discriminate against women representatives in legislatures) and about social values affecting women – (for example, the right of women to equal pay for equal work). Similarly, a right to social assistance may be seen as a right that is both about the legitimacy of a system of government and about the choices to be made within politics.

Nevertheless, these different purposes of rights remain distinct. For example, it is possible to want to take decisions within a system of political choice that recognize the rights of otherwise disadvantaged groups within society without necessarily arguing in favour of a link between rights to social justice and the justification or legitimacy of the system. One reason for rejecting such a link is because even authoritarian forms of government claim to be benevolent and acting in the best interests of their peoples. Thus, in putting forward reasons that justify democratic forms of government, it can be argued that something is needed other than a claim of social benevolence.

Similarly, it is possible to employ rights as a means to define the preconditions for a system of political choice, for example through asserting the right to free expression, without necessarily implying one way or the other what social values citizens should aim for in exercising choice under the system. Thus, within the system of political choice people may wish to use freedom of expression to argue in favour of measures that protect the rights of disadvantaged groups such as the elderly, but they may not. Instead, they may wish to argue in favour of placing the responsibility on families or voluntary groups in society, or in favour of helping people to make their own provision for themselves before they reach old age. On whichever side of the argument rights are used when debating social choices, none of those choices would be available without the precondition of freedom to debate and express opinions.

Each of the different uses of rights has its own importance. But for the purposes of talking about the European constitutional framework in which rights must be placed, it is the use of the language of rights to talk about the preconditions for the system of government and about policy priorities within the system of political choice that is the focus of attention in the rest of this chapter.

Absolute Values

It is possibly tempting to think that these distinctions can be ignored by trying to identify rights that are, in some sense or another, 'basic' or 'absolute'. The sense in which rights can be seen to express basic values can be described in various forms:

- *Universal truths*: Rights are often presented as universal truths that apply to all people everywhere. For example, the United Nations Universal Declaration of Human Rights was put forward in this spirit.[11]
- *Irreducible truths about human dignity*: Fundamental rights are sometimes defined as those values that are essential to human dignity. The advantage of this type of definition is that it can

embrace traditional rights, such as the right to life, but can readily be extended to new areas where rights are asserted, for example to include values related to genetic biology.[12]

- *Pre-emptive values*: Rights are also sometimes seen as 'pre-emptive' in terms of establishing values that subsequently ought not to be violated by political or legal systems. For example, the right to liberty and security of the person can be seen as a right that any political or judicial system must respect.[13]

- *Higher-order values*: Rights can also be represented more broadly as those values of society that must be respected above all other values. For example, the right to education might be regarded as a value underpinning personal freedom that must be preserved at all costs.[14]

None of these different ways of trying to define rights that, in one sense or another, are 'absolutes' or 'fundamental' is without challenge. Thus the United Nations Declaration is sometimes criticized for reflecting 'western values' rather than universal values. Moreover, each of these ways of trying to define which rights are basic or fundamental can lead to different listings of what should be included. For example, people may have different views about what should be included in order to safeguard human 'dignity'. There are, however, three more compelling objections.

A first difficulty is that from a general moral or philosophical perspective it is very hard to argue that there are any absolute rights at all – 'absolute' in the sense of rights that cannot be qualified or challenged. For example, the right to life is one that is typically qualified by allowing for one person to take the life of another when acting in self-defence. Similarly, the right to free speech is often qualified by excluding incitements to violence or racial hatred.[15]

Secondly, the search for absolutes that cannot be challenged is itself a dubious one. Societies need to keep their most important values alive through reason and debate and not just by assertion. If they find it useful to list their fundamental values, this should not be for the purpose of curtailing reasoned debate.[16]

Thirdly, even if it is admitted that some rights cannot readily be challenged, such as a prohibition against torture or slavery, and even if some values are regarded as beyond debate because they are accepted by all reasonable people – for example, the right to a fair trial – it remains the case that a proper use of the language of basic rights cannot be made unless the different contexts in which they are used, and the different purposes to which they are put, are respected.

What this means is that when thinking about the rules of Europe's system of government, the different ways in which rights can be held to be 'basic' have to be identified and each treated in its own context in the system of government. Those rights that are basic in the sense that the system of political choice could not work without them have to be isolated and treated in a way suited to this purpose. At the same time those rights that are basic in the sense that they provide principles about choices within politics also have to be identified and reflected in the most fitting way in the system of government. The same treatment will not be appropriate for each type of right, however 'basic' the right may seem in a particular context.[17]

Rights That Are Basic to the Framework for Choice

Rights that are basic to the framework of a democratic system of government are those that can be identified as a precondition of democratic political choice. For example, unless there is freedom of expression and freedom of association, democratic politics is not possible. On the other hand, the right to paid maternity leave is a social objective that can be debated as desirable or not within a system of political choice. The system of choice itself does not depend on it. By classifying rights in this way it is possible to arrive at a list of rights that can reasonably be held to be 'basic' enough for a system of democratic political choice to work at all.

If the search is widened to include rights that are basic to market choice as well as to political choice, then it would be reasonable to include the right to private property and the right to freedom of contract. Those rights that are 'basic' and 'fundamental' in this context are those that set the preconditions for the two systems of choice.

It remains the case that such rights are not 'absolute' in any philosophical sense. There is still room for differences in interpretation and for qualification even for rights that provide the foundation for systems of choice. For example, the right to private property, which is a precondition of market choice, is not an absolute right. Similarly the right to freedom of expression makes it possible to talk about freedom of opinion and where the limits to it lie. Nevertheless, even if not 'absolute' in any deeper philosophical sense, the language of rights provides a language with which to talk about the basic framework of political choice.

The question remains about how to make operative in practice those rights that are preconditions of political and market choice – while allowing for the fact that there can be scope for differences of opinion about how precisely to interpret or qualify them. The simplest constitutional form this could take in the case of a continent-wide union would be for such rights to be made a condition of membership of the union. Any country that had not established the conditions for democratic political choice or for a market economy would therefore not be allowed membership. Correspondingly, if such freedoms were lost after the country became a member, then suspension of membership could be triggered. The treaty of the existing union refers to such conditions of membership in truncated terms and experience is demonstrating the need to spell them out.

When in Europe the need for rights to address the preconditions of political choice is considered, there can be no disputing that many of the old battles about pre-democratic forms of government have been won. There is no longer any need to argue about rights that limit the powers of kings or about the right to vote. Nevertheless, Europe needs to remain vigilant about the preconditions of democracy because democratic norms and market rules are not always respected. In Germany, Chancellor Kohl demonstrated a disregard for democratic norms in his methods of political financing; and in Austria, Jörg Haider has demonstrated an even greater disregard by not putting a distance between his Freedom Party and the pre-war Nazis.

Once the preconditions of the system of democratic political choice have been established, the next task in thinking about the setting for rights is to define the way in which the language of rights can best be exploited to guide priorities within that system.

Rights within Politics

It was described earlier how the language of rights brings within its compass a huge range of social and moral values that help people to discuss, within a system of government, questions of individual and social choice from the most sensitive to the most mundane. In this context of policy choice within a system of government, there are two aspects of the use of rights as the dominant language of social choice that seem particularly important. The first is the role that rights play in helping social debate to move from established social values to new areas of public concern. The second is the use of rights to reflect intensity of belief and feeling.

Exploring Values

Claims about rights now provide the principal means through which the extension of commonly accepted values is explored in new areas of social or moral concern. Exploration works in the reverse direction too. If commonly accepted values do not help deal with new areas of concern, then values that hitherto have been commonly accepted are likely to be revised. This is an extraordinarily important function when societies are under pressure to change quickly.[18]

The exploratory role of rights is illustrated in the example given in the box below. The case illustrated involves an imaginary rule or regulation by the European Union that all public bus transportation systems across the continent should provide buses that enable the disabled to have access to them. This entirely theoretical illustration is not intended to provide a discussion about the substance of the rule: that is to say, it does not attempt to show whether or not the proposed rule or regulation is a good regulation. What it does attempt to do is to illustrate the logical features of a rights claim in the area of social choice. Although claims about the rights of the disabled are not as new as rights claims about certain types of bio- or medical ethics, nevertheless it is relatively recently that society has begun to appreciate the many ways in which the disabled are disadvantaged and to remove those disadvantages. The illustration is therefore intended to show how a rights claim is used to explore new applications of our social values in a relatively uncontroversial area.

The Logic of a Rights Claim

The Illustrative Claim

All public transport buses should provide wheelchair access so that the disabled can exercise their right to use public transport.

(**Counter-claim:** *The disabled have a right to transport but it is up to the authorities to decide in which form or mode to provide it as long as it is equally efficient and removes their disadvantage.*)

Box (*Cont.*)

The Reference Value

The right of equal treatment/opportunity.

(**Counter-value:** *The right to equal respect.*)

The Connection Claim

The commonly accepted principle of equal treatment of all people extends to providing the disabled with exactly the same access to public services as is extended to the able-bodied. The disabled have this as a 'right'.

(**The connection challenge:** *In giving equal respect to the disabled, we can recognize their right to public transport but are free to provide it in the form which best recognizes their different needs.*)

Other Relevant Values

The cost of the changes (see below) will disadvantage a different group, the poor, who rely on public transport and will have to pay higher ticket prices while the better-off continue to use their cars.

Higher ticket prices will cause a switch to other transport modes (notably the car), which will lead to extra air pollution and damage the environment.

Greater use of cars in crowded streets will increase the accident/mortality rate.

(**Contested relevance:** *These effects can be avoided if the costs are met out of general taxation and not out of higher ticket fares/reduced services.*)

Relevant Facts

All buses will have to be expensively modified or replaced. The bus system will be bankrupted or ticket prices will need to be raised substantially.

Box (*Cont.*)

> Service on some bus routes will be reduced or eliminated as a further cost-saving measure. It would be cheaper to provide the disabled with subsidized taxi coupons whenever they need transport.

Multiple values   The first point illustrated by the example is that a typical rights claim involves several values and not just one. This is because the starting point of the rights claim may itself involve more than one value (in this case, the right of equal treatment and the right of equal opportunity). In addition, other values are brought into the discussion as the claim is further explored. In this example environmental values are introduced and the rights of the very poor. What the initial rights claim has achieved is to provide a common starting point for a discussion of this particular issue and a lead in identifying other relevant values.

Costs   The second important point illustrated by the example is that rights involve resource costs. These are costs in a literal sense. All rights claims involve costs to implement and to enforce and they may be substantial. In this particular case the costs are those associated with the renewal of bus fleets. But other examples could be given. Thus property rights may require police forces and courts to enforce, or a right to clean water might necessitate investment in an expensive water treatment plant.[19]

Costs are important in themselves because, if large enough, they may result in the rights claim being denied. But they also signal a different aspect of a rights claim and that is that a social benefit for one group may come at the expense of another. Costs are often the mechanism that draws in other affected groups in society and other related values. In this particular example, where the illustration postulates that tickets will have to rise in price in order to pay for new fleets, low-income groups may be adversely affected, and there may be further knock-on effects if better-off passengers switch to using their own cars rather than pay higher ticket prices.

It is possible to mitigate the effects on other specific groups if the costs associated with a rights claim are passed on to society as a whole. This can be done either through general taxation, or through the passing on of costs to consumers or citizens in general rather than to a particular group. In this example, it would be possible for governments or government regulators to tell bus companies to hold their ticket prices steady and to offer them subsidies, from general taxpayer funds, to re-equip their fleets. However, at the end of the day someone will have had to pay. The more that governments turn to rule-making because they have reached the limits of acceptable tax burdens, the more likely it is that the costs will be borne by particular groups directly affected by the rights claim.

Contestability not trumps   The third important point that arises from the illustration is that each aspect of the logical thread – from the beginning assertion of a rights claim that a commonly accepted value is applicable in a new area, to the final points about the factual context of the claim – is open to contest, challenge and counter-challenge. Rights claims are inherently contestable.

In this particular example, the starting point can be contested because there is more than one commonly accepted rights claim that potentially provides a basis for the debate; the factual context can be challenged because the financial consequences of adapting bus fleets may be questioned; and, along with any questioning of the factual context, there may be questioning of related values such as the extent of any adverse environmental impact. Even if there are potential adverse side-effects, for example on low-income bus-riders, there can still be debate about how best to mitigate them.

In one well-known account of rights it has been suggested that rights are 'trumps', and this is often repeated without much thought.[20] If claims about rights were indeed trumps, then it would be very convenient because a claim could be asserted and further debate shut down. What this example of contestability demonstrates is that claims about rights do not curtail further debate. This does not mean that a claim is without purpose. But what it does mean is that the use of a rights claim is in giving a starting point to a debate – sometimes an uncontested starting point – and provides the further framework in which can be assembled other relevant facts and values and within which debate can be organized. The analogy with card-playing suggests that an appeal to a right will trump appeals to other facts and values in the case. The example demonstrates that this is not so. What the initial rights claim does do in terms of the card-playing analogy is to provide a 'bidding convention' where people can declare their values and start a process through which information on other relevant facts and values can be exchanged until agreement (or a contract) is reached.

The essential lesson that emerges from this discussion of rights as aids to the making of social choices within politics is that the rules need to provide a framework in which the exploration can take place. This means that they have to allow for the expression of multiple values, for different costs, for different balancings of costs and values, and they have to allow for contestability.

Intensity of Preferences

The second extraordinarily useful role of rights claims within politics is to bring together those who feel very strongly about a matter of public policy with those who feel less strongly or even feel indifferent. In other words, rights can bring together strongly committed minorities with the proverbial 'silent majority'. This is important, for two main reasons. First, democracy does not give any special place to strength of feeling. Each person's vote is counted equally. Thus there is a need for a mechanism that can somehow, within the rules of democracy, take account of different strengths of commitment. Secondly, the relationship between strongly committed minorities and the silent majority is one that is important to get right, for very practical reasons, because when the silent majority does awake from its slumber in response to the assertion of a right by a dedicated minority, it may feel that the right has been asserted at its expense and at the cost of its own interest. Rights claims can therefore become a frequent source of social and political friction and engender a political backlash. The task thus is to be able to use the language of rights for registering intensity of feelings on important issues in society, without at the same time provoking backlashes that at best reflect friction and, at worst, can take populist and anti-democratic forms.

In an extreme case a failure to communicate between committed minorities and the silent majority can threaten democracy itself. When democratic government first became the norm, the main concern of observers was that majorities, often assumed to be uneducated and ignorant, would trample on minorities – often assumed to be those with more discerning views and refined tastes. This concern reflected the fears of a minority, educated elite. But more importantly it was a fundamental misdiagnosis. In Europe in the twentieth century democratic practices proved to be much more at risk from committed minorities than from tyrannical majorities. The problem with majorities was their passivity. Europe thus has to guard against two different but related dangers: the abuse of political choice by minorities taking advantage of passive majorities; and the risks of popular backlashes when passive majorities are stirred to react.

The key to specifying how a system of government can best make use of the way in which society uses rights to explore new social issues and to register differences in the intensity of feelings is to decide where in a political system claims about rights are best 'recognized'.

Rules of Recognition: The Largest Unit?

Faction and the Common Good

In the discussion that follows, the phrase 'rules of recognition' refers to the most important location in a system of government where rights are to be the subject of legislation or adjudication. In the United States the most important location is Congress for legislation and the Supreme Court for adjudication. Effectively, therefore, the United States has centralized rules of recognition – in part a result of the incorporation doctrine of the Supreme Court rather than of original design. For Europe's system of government the question is how far the central institutions of the union should have the responsibility to legislate and adjudicate on rights claims and how far such matters should be left to the member states and their regions. In the current union the existing system is a muddle. Some rights are recognized by union institutions and procedures while others are not. Justiciability can involve the national courts of member states, the European Court of Justice (European Union) or the Court of Human Rights (Council of Europe). Reason has not guided this situation; power-plays between the institutions have.

One way of presenting the issue of where rights claims should be recognized is to see it in terms of a potential conflict between the 'common good' of the union as a whole and the powers of vested interests at the state and regional levels. This way of looking at the issue has a long history. When Madison discussed in the Federalist papers (No. X) the advantages of the proposed American federal system, he followed David Hume in suggesting that the larger federal stage provided the way to arrive at the common good because 'faction' at the state level could no longer block action and because more diverse interests would be represented in the union as a whole.

In the contemporary setting of Europe, the logical force of the proposition that the common good is more easily attainable within the largest political unit can be seen at work in the quite different context of European monetary union. For example, the fact that member states such as Italy that wished to join the common currency had to rein in their budget deficits meant that the logjam against reforms provided by vested interests within the state had to be broken (and was in fact broken) by the force of incentives to join others in the larger club. In other words, a sense of wanting to belong to the larger common good prevailed over the power of factions within the member state. Thus, the implication of posing the issue as one of the common good against faction is that the common good can best be realized on the larger union stage.

When Madison talked about 'faction', it is not at all clear that he had in mind claims based on rights. His illustrations referred to competing commercial interest groups in society. But his argument is often extended to rights. The reason for this is that it is tempting to identify basic rights with definitions of the common good. After all, a statement of basic rights is intended to reflect those values that are the most important for a society.[21]

What the juxtaposition of faction against the common good means in more practical terms in the context of rights is that those who claim a right may find it easier to gain acceptance of that claim at the federal or central level, rather than at the state level. This is because, on the larger stage, claimants will find additional allies who share their interpretation of a rights claim, and, at the same time, claimants will have broken away from any entrenched opposition at the state level.

Centralized recognition also seems to be called for if rights are looked on as providing ways to make strong, generally valid and applicable claims across territorial boundaries. The reduction in entry and information costs, associated with using the language of rights as a means of directly signalling what like-minded people want across Europe, seems to be nullified if the claims are only recognized at the state or regional level.

Before Europe follows the American example of putting in place a centralized system of rules for recognizing rights claims that are about choices within politics, the notion of the 'common good' and its relationship to rights needs closer examination. The reason for this is that rights draw attention to two different ways in which the 'common good' can be approached:

- '*Right allocation*': From this perspective a claim about a right is a claim about how a society should allocate resources.

- *'Right reason'*: From this perspective a rights claim provides guidance to the way reasoned debate should be conducted in order to realize the most important values in society.

What this distinction means is that when thinking about where in a system of political choice claims about rights should be recognized, there is a need to decide about how and where claims about allocation are best recognized and also about how and where right reasoning is best conducted. There is also a need to think about which claim has priority.

Rights as 'Right Allocation'

The relationship between claims made about rights and the allocation of a society's resources could be seen in a very immediate way, for example, in the illustration about affirmative action – to enable a minority group to achieve more numerous representation in a workforce or in an educational system. If the number of jobs is limited in that work setting, or the number of places limited in that educational setting, then it follows that if the claim to greater representation is recognized, someone from a non-minority group will be displaced. A different and less obvious example was also illustrated earlier in looking at a hypothetical claim for the disabled to have access to public bus transport. The claim would involve the bus companies investing in new buses and that investment would be found either at the cost of cutting back on some other service or by finding someone else to pay (from the bus-riders to the general taxpayer). Regardless of who in the end pays, the claim about the disabled states that society should devote more of its resources to them at the expense of some other priorities.

The reason why the allocation dimension to rights claims cannot be ducked was mentioned earlier. All rights have costs. Someone, somewhere in society, whether a specific group or the general taxpayer, has to meet the costs of any rights claim, and this inescapably affects the allocation of resources in society. Even if a right is expressed in the negative – for example, that a society should not undertake research on genetically modified crops, or on human cloning – a statement is being made about how resources should be allocated. It was mentioned earlier that governments have difficulty in moving away from universal provision in their tax and spend policies. But they are moving toward targeted allocation in a different way through their rights-based rule-making and regulatory activities.

When rights are seen as about allocation, then what is being asserted in a rights claim is that the common good is best represented if the resources of society are allocated in a way that, for example, enables the disabled to use public transport, or socially excluded groups to be recognized in affirmative action programmes.

When rights are viewed in this way as priority claims on the allocation of resources in society, there are two negative points that can immediately be made. The first is that those who claim rights, or speak on behalf of claimants, can themselves be seen as 'faction' – in other words as special interests. Their particular causes may be worthy, but their claims have to be treated with no less caution than those of any other special interest in politics.[22] The second point is that centralized institutions, particularly legislatures, have shown themselves no less vulnerable to special interests than have state institutions. Indeed it is a perennial criticism of the US Congress that it is far too beholden to special interests. In other words, the proposition that the larger political stage enables society to escape from faction is untenable. The change of setting changes the stage on which faction works. It may also change the balance of power between different factions. But there is no clear basis for saying that the common good is better represented by this shift. Faction is ever-present.

To safeguard against the misallocation of resources in society by faction, wherever in the political system faction operates, democratic procedures within the system of government have to provide a setting where rules of right reason can be observed and the claims about what is right allocation can themselves be justified. For example, in the case of the US Congress, there are certain safeguards that limit the powers of powerful committees that might be prone to fall into the hands of vested interests. Thus procedures have been designed so as to make sure that before final decisions are taken, debate is taken out of committee onto the floor of the house as a whole, so that the deliberations of the committee can be exposed to a wider scrutiny and a space is provided where a wider range of views can be expressed.[23]

What this boils down to is that when scrutinizing claims about rights within politics, it is critical that this should take place in a setting that provides for 'right reason'. Claims about right allocation have no special status for legislative or judicial action unless they can be justified by right reason. The procedures to help establish right reason have thus to be followed.

Rights as 'Right Reason'

Treating rights as guides to 'right reason' in political choice returns us to a very old conception of rights being derived from reason.[24] What it means in a contemporary setting is that those rights that are selected as 'basic' in social choice are to be seen as principles that help to get policy priorities right when making political choices and that lead democratic debate in a reasoned way towards a conclusion that serves the common interest. In other words, rights claims provide the signposts that can help social groups reason through to arrive at the common interest. As described earlier, rights provide starting points, help marshal other salient values and help organize and identify relevant facts.[25]

In recent years when political scientists have turned their attention to the role of right reason in politics they have focused their gaze on the shortcomings of electoral politics as a source of reasoned debate about the common good. There has been a wave of ruminations on 'deliberative democracy'. This has not led to any consensus on how to improve the quality of debate through democratic politics: some have concluded in favour of a new style of 'town hall' democracy, others in favour of more direct democracy, and yet others in favour of reorganizing the way legislatures go about their work.[26] More unfortunate perhaps is that most of the discussion has been cast in terms of electoral politics rather than considering the role of rights in political debate. Consequently, almost the entire discussion of deliberative democracy has overlooked the main way in which social priorities are debated in politics. It has, moreover, missed the relationship between rights-based politics and vote-based politics.[27]

When the priority use of rights is seen to be about 'right reason', it then becomes clear, in the light of the earlier discussion, that the key to where rights should be recognized within a system of political choice is provided by their role in helping a society to explore the application of values in new areas of concern and their role in expressing different intensities of feeling and commitment. What this means is that the setting that can most make use of the language of rights as the language of 'right reason' is the one that allows them the fullest range as mechanisms to explore how to interpret the fundamental values in a society and that provides the best way of bringing together committed minorities and the silent majority.

Exploration and Right Reason   A centralized setting for exploration can be provided both by legislatures and by the law. For example, if a central court is the location where ultimately all rights claims are finally adjudicated, the procedure of judicial review allows for the initial claim to be refined and honed through a succession of courts until the crux of the matter reaches the final court (the Supreme Court in the case of the US). The process of adjudication and appeal is itself an exploration process. In addition, while the court of final review decides on that particular case, that does not end the exploration of how best to interpret the value concerned. Claimants can come back to the courts with a slightly different claim, or legislatures may pass slightly different laws that they think may pass through judicial review in the light of the court ruling. This is one way of exploring values in society. At the same time it is a lengthy process and allows for only one authoritative interpretation of any one particular point. The alternative is to allow for courts in different legal jurisdictions to offer different, and possibly conflicting, legal interpretations.

Turning to the political process, where rights claims may be the subject of legislation and law-making, it is fairly evident that legislatures in different jurisdictions are likely to place different interpretations on rights claims. They will be considering claims against different backgrounds, may weigh values together in different ways, public opinion may well diverge in different jurisdictions, and resource priorities may be seen in different ways in different circumstances.

The recognition of rights in different jurisdictions through either the judicial or legislative process will therefore lead to an enormous variety of interpretation. Thus, if societies want to use rights claims as ways to explore their most important values, rather than to impose a uniform interpretation, everything points toward encouraging rights claims to be under the aegis of decentralized authority. The 'common good' is to be equated not with uniform outcomes but with a common language to explore a society's most important values.

Feeling and Right Reason   In looking at the setting that best can mediate between different intensities of feeling about a society's highest values, what is key is to get the relationship right between the procedures of vote-based democratic politics and rights-based politics. As discussed above, rights provide a language to express principles – sometimes strongly held ones – more directly than is possible through the electoral process. It is the language that brings together, in a potentially reasoned way, minorities who may feel very impassioned about a cause with those who feel indifferent. By contrast, democratic vote-based politics disregards strength of commitment and treats everybody's vote as equal. Differences in strength of feeling are registered only obliquely by differences in voter turnout. If a political system does not get the relationship right between the two systems of expression, then politics can take an ugly turn.

The relationship can be illustrated by experience from the United States. It is not coincidental that in the United States, alongside the growth in the use of the language of rights, has come a growth in other forms of direct political expression – in particular the use of the referendum or popular initiative. The rise of the use of referenda represents in part the voice of the silent majority, the sound of backlash, the sign of those who feel that the allocation of resources is being turned against them. In the United States the forces of populism have historically been contained. In Europe they have not. It is therefore vital for Europe to avoid the risks of getting the relationship wrong between rights-based politics and vote-based politics.

The key to this is to recognize that all rights claims are inherently contestable and that, if right reason is to prevail, context is all-important. Context is decisive for the fundamental reason that it is crucial for deciding on the aptness of a claim. Aptness is not about the justification of an underlying value, for example whether it is justified to say that everybody has a right to equal treatment; it is about the judgement over its application.[28]

Even common standards cannot be reasonably applied outside an apt context. Differences in context can lead to reasoned differences in interpretation of even the highest values held by a society.[29] The issue is illustrated again by the example of adapting buses to carry the disabled. It is quite possible that one jurisdiction will decide that the costs are so high that the changeover is not in the general interest and that the transport needs of the disabled can be better met in other ways, while other jurisdictions will re-equip their bus fleets. It is very difficult to argue that these possible different outcomes are undesirable. On the contrary, the differences may be valid reflections of differences in circumstance (for example, cost differences or differences in the way other user groups are affected), or they may simply reflect the fact that on such matters where typically more than one value is involved, different people in different circumstances may reasonably arrive at different conclusions.

This example illustrates again that, when rights are viewed as guides to 'right reason', what is important is not so much arriving at the same outcome as having a framework within which to be able to discuss the applicability of a common starting point and the reasons for differences in interpretation and application. In other words, in order to make best use of the language of rights in Europe, rights claims should be viewed as a way to provide a check for reasonable differences of judgement rather than as a way to guarantee a uniform result. This attribute is hugely helpful when applied to rule-making in Europe. It suggests how rights can help both in establishing common standards and in talking in a reasoned way about variations from them.

In theory it would be possible for a centralized system for recognizing rights to appreciate differences in context and aptness of application. In practice, central courts and central legislatures are more likely to stress what is uniform rather than what is different, and lean against recognizing differences in context.

What this means is that rights claims in Europe should be recognized on a decentralized basis, on two fundamental grounds: first, this allows for a greater use of the language of rights as the language of exploration; and, secondly, this allows for a greater use of the language of rights as the language of moral judgement.

If the language of rights is used and respected in this way, then the chances that there will be a collision between vote-based politics and rights-based politics, between minorities and majorities, are much reduced. Taking full account of local context and allowing for a range of interpretation means that values important to a community are not seen to be values imposed from outside. Nor does a central authority become the object of protest. A clash within a decentralized jurisdiction between expression based on rights and expression at the ballot box is still possible, and indeed likely, but such conflicts will be localized.

Being able to recognize the importance of rights as the language of exploration and of judgement in context and to provide for this by allowing for different interpretations of a society's highest values is thus a hugely important way in which differences between minorities and majorities can be mediated. If rights are centrally recognized, then one form of political expression – the vote – is likely to end up in collision with the other form of expression – the rights claim.

In the final analysis there is only one important objection that can be made to decentralized procedures for the interpretation of rights claims within politics – namely that a coherent legal and political framework necessitates a uniform and singular source of interpretation of our most fundamental values. At a mundane level of practical politics this proposition is difficult to sustain, for the reasons discussed above. At a much more theoretical level the issue is about whether uniform interpretation of a society's most important values is an essential requirement for any political and legal system to be 'coherent'. This abstract issue is discussed in chapter 8. All that need be said at this point is that debate about what makes a political system 'coherent' leads some observers in the direction of viewing rights as a way to put limits on different interpretations of important values.[30] Whether this is the correct way to approach 'coherence' in a pluralist society is, however, a very different matter.

Decentralized Reasoning – Decentralized Rule-Making   In their different ways, both rule-making and the best use of rights in political systems involve decentralization. In the case of rule-making, decentralization is needed not only to provide for a rule-making system that receives reliable information about when changes to a common standard are needed, but also in order to allow for different views about the content of rules. In the case of rights that are about priorities within politics, decentralized rules of recognition are also needed. How to approach the organization of a continent-wide system of government that is decentralized in these ways is discussed in the next chapter.

6   Networks and Nexus

Nothing is more pitiful than the arrogant disdain of most of our contemporaries for questions of form; for the smallest questions of form have acquired in our time an importance which they never had before: many of the greatest interests of mankind depend upon them.

Alexis de Tocqueville, *Democracy in America*

Something Old, Something New, Something Borrowed

The new setting for governance has not yet produced new and convincing theories as to how systems of political choice should be reorganized. Systems of market choice connect from the global to the local. Systems of political choice do not. In thinking about how best to reorganize systems of political choice, some cling to the belief that public policy functions can be clearly divided up by territory so that it would be easy to distinguish among those best managed at the global level, by a continent-wide union as a whole or by the member states and their regions. Others believe that coping in the modern world is just a question of size and that we should think of Europe as a scaled-up version of a traditional nation state. Still others recognize the shortcomings in both these responses and, in looking for new forms of organization, turn to business models for inspiration. Business, however, is not the same as government. Questions of form in a democratic society are different both in kind and in importance compared with questions of form in a business corporation.[1]

When politicians enter the debate, the terms they use do not help in clarifying what is really at stake for the citizen. When they refer to a 'United States of Europe', they are really referring to the advantages of scale. If they refer to 'Network Europe', they are drawing on a business model and suggesting that Europe has to find a fast-moving style of government. When British politicians suggest that the United Kingdom should be at 'the heart' of Europe, or, conversely, that Britain is in 'mid-Atlantic', they are referring to a tension between the fading importance of geographical location in the modern world and the rising importance of rules for international behaviour that override geography. But the underlying meaning of the metaphors is rarely spelt out for the public and few, if any, politicians have thought them through. More often, Europe's politicians are drawing on their old stock-in-trade: playing on the fears of the public of the world outside and suggesting that, given power and discretion, they, the politicians, can be trusted to sort it all out.

Alternative Perspectives

This chapter starts by examining the oldest and most frequent response given to questions of organization, which is that in the modern world what is needed is to upsize systems of government. Much of the conventional thinking about a system of government for Europe is based on exactly the proposition that the best response to the new setting is to scale up the size of governmental units in Europe from the generally small nation state to a union that can replicate their functions on a much larger scale.

The discussion then turns to look at one proposed borrowing from business organization: the currently fashionable idea of the 'network' organization. Those who are attracted to this model suggest that what is actually happening in Europe and should be encouraged further is the emergence of a new type of governmental network organization analogous to business networks.

The general idea that, in thinking about forms of government in the contemporary world, there may be something to be drawn from business is a useful one. If systems of market choice have been able greatly to improve their responsiveness in providing what people want – in part through adopting new models of business organization –

then perhaps government should reorganize itself along the new business lines. But the network suggestion fails because it does not recognize that form matters in politics in ways that do not matter in business. Politicians may sometimes be attracted to the network model, but it is for the worst of reasons: they see it as a way to escape the constraints of democratic form, or as an excuse to think no further about the shape of a continent-wide union because it is already a 'network'.

The discussion therefore turns next to look at a different business model: the idea that firms are best viewed as 'nexus' organizations. This approach looks at the firm as a nexus of contracts or treaties. Analogously, 'Brussels' could be viewed as a nexus of contracts or treaties. This model arrives much closer to questions of form that are crucial in systems of government. It suggests in particular that there is a need to distinguish between questions relating to the organization of government for dealing with public policies within Europe and questions that relate to how Europe conducts its relations with the outside world. It also provides an approach to defining the span of authority needed by a continent-wide union in both situations.

The analysis brings together these different ways of looking at the organization of government with the earlier argument that the function of European government needs to focus on rule-making. It suggests that the task of organizing Europe's system of government should be looked at in a very different way from organizing government in a traditional state.

A Question of Scale?

The idea that the traditional democratic state could be scaled up in size was one of the earliest responses to recognizing the disconnection between the boundaries of public policy and the territorial boundaries of traditional states. It remains the most common response. It seems an utterly straightforward proposition to assert that, in today's world, the small nation state belongs to the past and that size matters. Because one nation – the United States – wields so much more power in the world in so many different areas of influence, it seems self-evident that the small and mid-sized states of Europe are better off combining as one much larger unit.

The outward plausibility of this assertion is challenged by a curious fact: that nation states continue to exist, their number has grown substantially over the last fifty years and continues to grow. One explanation for this phenomenon is that there is a tension between the advantages of larger size and the disadvantages of trying to hold together, both effectively and amicably, a very diverse society.[2] Thus, while some states are trying to combine, as in Europe, other multi-state combinations are dissolving, as in the former Soviet Union. This explanation is sometimes popularized in terms of a conflict between globalization and localism.[3]

Democratic theory has recognized that the transition from a small democratic state to being part of a larger democratic system can indeed be a mixed blessing. But it has been suggested that if the move away from a small democratic system were to involve some losses in democratic values, any such losses could be offset by gains somewhere else in the larger system. It has been suggested further that any democratic losses that arose from scaling up could be offset by gains below the level of the nation state. In this way any potential tension between localism and the larger unit could be avoided.[4]

The scaling-up response seems directly applicable to Europe. There has been an attempt within the structures of the existing union to offer democratic safeguards in a larger setting. Also, there have indeed been gains at levels below the nation state. Underneath the broad umbrella provided by membership of the larger union, it has been possible for some communities to reassert their own particular identities. As a result, a number of countries in Europe have decentralized and devolved previously centralized powers. The security provided by a large union has helped an important decentralizing dynamic that is revitalizing local and regional government within a number of hitherto centralized states such as Spain or the United Kingdom. This can have destabilizing effects, however. At the extreme, it has called into question the very existence of Belgium.

At the same time, actual experience with political unification in Europe has also shown the limitations of scaling up. First, the nation states in Europe have different myths, histories and structures and to try to reproduce any one model on a larger European scale does not seem credible. Furthermore, there is no agreement on what the one model should be. The constraints imposed by diversity seem to bite at an earlier stage in the scaling-up process than democratic theory has wanted to recognize.

Secondly, the calculation of trying to balance democratic losses against democratic gains in Europe is not reassuring. Member states of the existing union have seen a loss in the grip of the traditional mechanisms of democratic control within their own systems of government, but the gains from control by the union as a whole are unconvincing. On the contrary, there is a widespread perception that governments have gained in the discretionary powers they enjoy. In other words, the traditional checks and balances in each member state have not been replaced by new ones with comparable effect in the larger union.

Thirdly, the gains at the level of regional and local government are difficult to capture on a European scale. Because the forms, powers and structures of devolved government across Europe differ so widely, a stronger devolved voice within a particular state does not translate into a strong European voice of devolved authority. Indeed, some units of regional government, such as the states within Germany, feel that they have lost power and authority in the process of European unification.

Finally, any response along orthodox lines based on the traditional state remains wedded to the past. In one way or another, the assumption behind scaling up is that it is only the size of past forms of governance that needs to be adjusted to fit the new setting. There is no recognition of either the magnitude or variety of ways in which the world has changed for governments.

The inadequate and unconvincing explanations of traditional political science that the answer to modern problems of government can be solved by increasing the scale of the unit of government have led observers to look elsewhere for their models. Because business has been enormously successful in adapting to the new setting, it is to this that some observers have turned. In particular it has been suggested that the 'network' model can be borrowed by government from business. We are told that 'the network state' is the characteristic response of political systems to the 'information age'. Europe, it is suggested, can already begin to be seen as a new form of state: a 'network state'.[5]

Networks

The sources of the network model lie in thinking about the way in which biological systems adapt, about sociological connections, and about the way in which business is adapting to the modern world. It is the business example that is the main source of inspiration for trying to apply the model to politics.

The Network Model

The idea of 'network' government has four main components. First, authority within the system is shared and traditional hierarchies of authority are dispensed with. Secondly, the network is based on its 'nodes' or units rather than relying on a dominant centre. Thirdly, it is possible and likely that these different nodes or units will be of different sizes, carry unequal political weight, and have different types of relationships between each other. Finally, the units are 'interdependent', so that no single node can ignore another in decision-making.[6]

At first sight this kind of description appears to fit the existing European union quite well. There is power-sharing between governments within the highest organ of the union, the European Council, and between the Council, the Commission and the European Parliament. The different states or units of the union are indeed of different sizes and carry unequal clout in decision-making. At the same time, the Council, in particular, tries to take the most important decisions by consensus so that no member's vital interest is overlooked or ignored in a key decision.

The strength of the network model is that it highlights certain key qualities of modern business organization that have helped make business so responsive in providing what people want. They are qualities that systems of government must also try to emulate. The weakness of the model is that it does not give guidance in those questions about form that may not be so important in the business world but that are critically important in systems of government. Form is important in systems of government because key characteristics of democracy – such as the need for those with authority to be accountable to the people – depend on it.

Network Qualities

Expressed in the most general terms, the extremely important message from network theory to government is that, in today's world, systems of government have to be as fast on their feet as business and equally able as business to organize flexibly to deal with rapidly changing circumstances. Networks are part of the business response to a much more competitive market setting. They are associated with a rethinking of management chains of command and with a willingness to break away from long-established corporate boundaries: in addition, businesses have learnt to be open-minded and open-ended about where market opportunities may next appear. Sociologists have added further to the story from business by drawing attention to how formalized organizational stereotypes have given way to more flexible types of association. They have emphasized the additional quality that, in today's world, informal networks play a much larger role – both in the market and in politics – than they did in the past.

Reorganizing Chains of Command   In business many firms have flattened their chains of command. The offices of CEOs have been slimmed and layers of management have been cut out. In some areas of activity, authority has been delegated from the centre to outlying operating units, and in others, authority has actually been handed over from the centre of a firm to its component units or affiliates.

There is a debate about how far this process has gone. CEOs, or managing committees of one sort or another, still exercise a central authority in areas they consider to be key. The debate is about distinguishing between those changes that are about the range of authority wielded by central management (the 'span of control'), and the way in which powers have been reorganized (the flattening of hierarchies).[7] Managements still need to manage, but they may exercise their span of control in different ways, or they may have to adapt it. Thus, some firms seem to combine elements of horizontal organization with elements of central hierarchy – the so-called 'duality principle'. For example, within many Japanese companies personnel functions may be centralized and organized hierarchically, but operational functions may be decentralized and organized horizontally. Conversely, within many American companies, personnel decisions may be decentralized and strategic decisions controlled centrally and hierarchically. Even taking account of such qualifications, the message from business to systems of government remains one of the need to rethink chains of authority, and in particular to reduce hierarchy.[8]

Connecting across Traditional Organizational Boundaries   A second message from business to government arising from network theory is the importance of being able to break out of traditional organizational boundaries. An example in the business world is provided by so-called 'business-to-business' (B2B) networks. Thus, a number of major oil companies have set up a new network to achieve economies in purchases of equipment that they all needed but had been ordering separately. Airlines and other businesses are setting up similar organizations. What these business-to-business organizations aim to do is to exploit efficiencies that could not be achieved within standard company boundaries, but that can be achieved if a cross-boundary organization pulls together activities previously dispersed among several separate and competing businesses.

Open-Ended Purposes   A third message to government from the network model of business is about the impossibility of predicting consumer preferences and the need to be open-minded about the uses to which a product or service may be put. There are many dramatic illustrations from the past, including the failure to foresee the mass use of the telephone, or the failure to foresee the use of computers by the general public. Even now, businesses are having to gamble billions on the way consumers may use the mobile phone compared with the TV screen, lap-top computer or individual 'smart' products, and having to prepare themselves for unwelcome surprises if they judge consumer preferences wrongly.

The importance of being open-ended is perhaps best illustrated by the internet itself. The networks created through the internet are made possible because the internet protocol performs two very precise functions. It provides an addressing plan and a service model for sending messages. With only a twenty-page protocol in the middle, a 'soup' of applications is possible at one end and a 'soup' of technology is possible at the other. The design of the internet has thus been oriented to connections, not to specific purposes. Indeed, the whole intent has been to allow for a myriad of uses at one end and a diversity of technologies at the other. The design of the internet in this format may now be about to change as a result of challenges both from governments and from a new breed of internet service providers. But it remains important as an illustration of the value of organizing in ways that allow for a multitude of uses that cannot be foreseen at the time of original design.

The Importance of the Informal   A fourth and final lesson from network theory is about the importance of informal networks for getting things done and for influencing the way things are done. Striking examples of the strength of informal networks can in fact be drawn from politics. The power of voluntary groups to come together to help block agreement on a treaty on international investment under the auspices of the OECD, and to help derail discussions of a new round of international trade talks under the auspices of the

World Trade Organization, is evidence enough of the new power of informal networks. In both cases they were far from the only or the most important factor. And in both cases governments had probably set their negotiating targets too high and had bitten off more than they could chew. Nevertheless, it is a valid lesson for government that policy-making circles are not just those defined by officialdom and by politicians but include other, external actors.[9]

The Shortcomings Concerning Form

The qualities of network organizations provide insights that are important for systems of government to absorb. However, they do not justify the breathless jump to the conclusion that systems of government must now be organized as networks, let alone the conclusion that the existing European union has discovered in its own workings that it has miraculously stumbled on a new and perfect form of governmental system: the network state. Those politicians who claim that the existing union should be seen as a network are in practice often doing nothing more than disguising, under a conveniently trendy label, the fact that they want to keep the present organization in its current inchoate form and that they have not the slightest idea how a continent-wide union might work.

The reason why network theory cannot be transposed lock, stock and barrel to systems of government is that it does not integrate the qualities of a network described above with questions of form that are of the utmost importance in thinking about the design of systems of government. There are highly important questions about the form that democratic systems of government should adopt that are not concerns – or not in the same way – in business. In the business world, companies may not need to worry too much about how they may be organized in the more distant future, or whether the current form of organization is intended to be a lasting one. Flexibility to respond to rapidly changing market circumstances and to deliver shareholder value is more important. If they cannot respond quickly to changing circumstances, they will be swallowed up by the competition or go out of business. By contrast, in the world of democratic systems of government, form matters vitally.

Chains of Command and Lines of Accountability The purported 'lesson' from network theory that chains of command need to be rethought so as to reduce hierarchical decision-taking is an odd one to be delivering to systems of government. It is odd because the whole premise of democratic theory involved a decisive historical break with the idea of organizing political systems on a hierarchical basis. Instead democracy enshrined the principle of replacing commands from the top down (from kings or emperors) with a system that tried to ensure that power flowed up from the people.

In practice it has been extraordinarily difficult to articulate the democratic principle that the line of authority flows from the people to their rulers. There are two basic reasons for this. The first is that the democratic principle is expressed through representative government – where the representatives have a good deal of discretion in what they do. Experience has shown unfortunately that representatives have a boundless appetite for abusing their discretionary powers. Yet, at the same time, framing the rules that will constrain their behaviour is enormously difficult. The second problem area is in harnessing the dynamics of systems of government. The size of the problem can be seen by looking at the American experience. The description of a system of government with a weak centre and powerful but disparate individual units, which is now applied by network theorists to the existing European union, could have been applied to the early United States. That has not stopped America developing into an essentially unified state. Some deplore the degree of centralization; others have welcomed it. But the dynamics were not foreseen.[10]

The lesson from network theory that businesses are having to experiment with different ways of organizing authority therefore does not translate into insights into the way authority is best organized in systems of political choice. The perennial problem of politics remains: those who are accorded authority have a persistent and alarming tendency to abuse it. Moreover, in many ways the plea from the example of networks that authority should be allowed to be exercised in flexible ways is a dangerous one in politics. It is tantamount to those with political authority asking for more discretionary powers. When politicians say that they like the idea of 'Network Europe', what they are saying is that they like the idea of more discretionary powers to act in whatever way they want. Politicians might well find that thought agreeable. However, it does not support the democratic principle that those with authority must be responsive to the people.

Organizational Boundaries: Fixity and Free Form   The lesson from network theory that businesses need to be able to break out of old corporate patterns to allow for the crossing of old demarcation lines and to set up new forms of company is also one with dangerous resonances in systems of political choice. In agreeing to the institutions and rules of procedure in politics, people intend that certain of these institutions and rules should be settled and lasting. In cases where the rules allow for an intentional dynamic, they wish that dynamic to be respected so that changes do not lead to unexpected destinations. The reason is that democratic politics calls for politicians to be accountable. Accountability requires in turn that certain forms and procedures should be fixed, and where flexibility is called for, it needs to be defined.

Businesses are also accountable – to their shareholders and large institutional investors – and here too certain rules are enforced. For example, if a company wishes to dilute the interest of existing shareholders by issuing more shares, the rules require such a decision to be ratified by the existing shareholders. The key, both in business and in politics, is to decide on what is fixed and what is flexible. Network theory does not provide a guide to this for politics.

Anxieties in democratic politics about which organizational and procedural arrangements are fixed and which are flexible can be illustrated by the existing European union. Many of the concerns about the existing union centre precisely on the feeling that present arrangements do not provide a settled form of government and that the dynamics are leading to a very unclear and possibly undesirable destination. Thus the message from network theory that systems of government must be structured in their form to respond flexibly to a changing world does not translate in any straightforward way into government. In democratic systems, the principles of accountability require definition of what is to be fixed and what is to be floating.

Open-Endedness of Purpose and Defining Where Authority Is Needed   The need for democratic forms of government to be held accountable and within certain defined boundaries is also why the third lesson from the network model – that businesses need to be open-minded and open-ended about market preferences – equally does not translate in any straightforward manner into systems of political choice. In systems of democratic political choice, the design of the powers of institutions and the rules of procedure that govern them should be informed by a view about the authority that is needed and how it should be circumscribed. In certain areas, flexibility about the uses to which political authority is put may well be desirable. But this means making a distinction between the functions of government that are core and those where flexibility is appropriate.

There are limits to what is open-ended in business too. Thus central management may retain control over strategic decisions even though operational decisions can become more decentralized. In the case of the internet, the design features of the internet protocol were also very precisely specified and maintained. What this means is that, while it would indeed be helpful in Europe's system of government to decide on what is a core set of functions and what is not, and to link this with its design, the network model itself does not provide guidance as to how to make this connection.

The Informal and the Transparent   The final lesson from the network model, that informal networks are important for modern democratic politics, is well taken. In looking at the present union it is interest groups that are in many ways better organized for European politics than are political parties. Interest groups already play, and will continue to play, an important role in building a public opinion that crosses national boundaries and that can be called 'European'.

At the same time, networks can be beneficial for an organization or they can be damaging. We can all think of examples in organizations we have worked for, or in communities in which we have lived, where informal networks of power, influence, information or simply gossip have been enormously destructive.

In democratic politics what this means is that in order to capture what is good in networks and to filter out what is bad, their activities have to be placed within a broader democratic structure. Thus the rules of democratic government call for such activities to be placed within a framework that tries to ensure that the views of interest groups are exposed to a wider debate and their claims to be representative are tested against a wider range of public opinion. In this way, as discussed earlier, interest group views about what is 'right allocation' or the right application of principles in public policy can be subjected to procedural checks.

What these different shortcomings in the attempted transposition of the network model to systems of government add up to is that, if borrowings are to be made from business theory, they must come closer to addressing the questions of form that are important for democratic forms of government. They must link the qualities that make business networks responsive to the new market setting to questions of form that are essential to democratic systems of political choice. This link is not made by the network model.

Nexus

A model of business organization that does achieve a much closer proximity to questions of form that arise in political organization is that of the firm as a 'nexus'. This model looks at the firm as representing a nexus of contracts or a nexus of treaties.[11] In a highly simplified analogy it suggests that, in at least certain respects, Europe's system of government should be looked upon in the same way. There is a superficial plausibility to such an analogy because the existing European union is indeed based upon treaties. When popular sentiment refers indiscriminately to the various institutions of the existing union as 'Brussels', it is also drawing attention to the fact that many threads of what is done in the name of the union come together in the nexus of Brussels. But the relevance of the nexus model does not depend on this analogy. Looking at the firm as 'nexus' seems to offer a closer analogy with systems of government than the analogy of 'network' because it gets closer to the questions of form that must be answered in discussing political systems.

The view of the firm as 'nexus' arises from examining the question of why it is that the firm is the dominant form of organization in the market. It means looking at the reasons behind the cost savings that can be achieved by the firm in gathering information and in organizing and coordinating the direction of resources.[12] This approach gives an account of where authority needs to be formalized and where it can be left flexible. The efficient boundary of the firm is defined by the core activities that offer cost advantages.

The nexus model is valuable for a further reason, in that it suggests approaching the two questions of how to define where formal authority is needed and where to draw the boundaries of the core organization by distinguishing between the different way in which a firm organizes itself internally compared with the manner in which it organizes relationships with the outside world. Thus, in the business world, for example, the internal organization of the firm may be built around directing core skills, while its external organization may be geared to making alliances work with other organizations with complementary skills.[13] Similarly, in the world of political systems, governments may be able to exert authority in a core area of domestic policy but in dealing with the outside world they are dealing with relationships which may have to be handled in different ways.

This distinction between the internal and the external is thus followed below in looking further at the organization of Europe's system of government.

Organization and Authority within Europe

When applied to the internal organization of a continent-wide union, the nexus model suggests linking the core organization with the comparative advantage that the union has as a system of government. In other words, the suggestion is that if the comparative advantage of a continent-wide union is in developing rules with reach, its core organization should be built around this activity. Other activities can be free-form. The nexus model also offers guidance about where the span of authority needs to be formalized and where it is that informal structures and procedures are likely to work well. It is in order to reduce uncertainty in the application of rules with intended reach that lines of formal authority are needed.

Defining the Core Organization

Systems of government were examined in chapter 2 to see where it is that they still have a comparative advantage as a system of choice. That discussion identified rule-making as the area where, in general, systems of government have comparative advantage. Rule-making not only takes full advantage of governments as rule-enforcers but, in addition, provides systems of government with the possibility of increasing returns to scale while the traditional role of provisioning is up against diminishing returns. Thus it was argued that in order to offer people a higher-value bundle of services from systems of political choice, governments should focus on their rule-making role. It was further argued that the particular area of rule-making where a continent-wide union possessed comparative advantage was in developing and applying rules with reach.

According to the nexus model, it is these advantages that define the efficient boundaries of the union's core organization. In other words, the core of the union's institutions and procedures should be defined as those necessary for its role of making rules with reach. Conversely, in other areas of activity where the union has no comparative advantage as a system of choice, there can be flexibility in the institutional arrangements and procedures to be used. Thus when member states of the union discuss their common interests as providers of welfare, where the union has no comparative advantage, the manner in which they organize such discussions can be left quite open.

An example can be given with the Common Agricultural Policy in the existing union. When it comes to establishing a union-wide regulation, for example that livestock infected with foot and mouth disease should not be exported across borders, the union is acting in an area where it has comparative advantage. On the other hand, when it comes to trying to direct income support to poor farmers, the union is not well placed to make the judgements necessary. As a result of the union acting in an area where it does not have comparative advantage, the policy has misused the regulatory function to tie farming up in increasingly onerous regulatory requirements without being able to ensure that income support reaches those who may deserve it, while at the same time channelling a large amount to wealthy farmers who do not need it.

The nexus model defines efficient organizational boundaries by relating them to cost advantage.[14] The union can economize on the costs of acquiring, using and disseminating knowledge in the making of rules with reach. For example:

- Governments can make savings in the costs of acquiring information needed for rule-making and regulation. Governments are not typically the original source of the needed information and more usually will rely on the market. However, they have two advantages: they are not constrained by competitive considerations that will prevent firms from voluntarily divulging information; and they have the power to enforce the release of information.
- Governments may also have an advantage in maintaining rule-related information and acquire specialized expertise in organizing, evaluating information and building up specialized expertise in regulation more generally. Firms may not invest in institutional memories; governments and agencies can.
- Governments provide a low-cost way of communicating between the specialists who have acquired and evaluated information and the mass of non-specialists – the public who depend on it. A pronouncement from an agency such as the Food and Drug Administration in the United States is regarded as authoritative.

- Finally governments have the traditional advantage of superior powers of enforcement.

These cost advantages of government can be abused, as the example of the Common Agricultural Policy illustrates. But the answer to regulatory abuse is to put in place procedures that filter out inappropriate rule-making from what may be necessary.

Defining the Span of Formalized Authority

Formalizing lines of authority involves costs and rigidities. Thus any organization, whether business or government, is better off where informal incentives can replace formal chains of command. The discussion so far has suggested that the core of the union should be organized around its specialized advantages in rule-making and regulation needed to establish rules with reach. What is needed, therefore, is to relate the formal lines of authority required to this activity.

When it comes to rule-making and regulation, informality can in certain circumstances work well. If an industry can be self-regulating, it can keep compliance costs down. If neighbours can settle differences amicably, they can avoid the costs of law suits. The nexus model views the question as one of incentives. If there are sufficient incentives for the member states to make it possible to establish, operate and enforce the rule-making role of the union without formal lines of authority, then formal lines of authority should be avoided.

The limits to voluntary compliance essentially arise from distance, and a lack of frequent and repeated contact. In a continent-wide union, members will want to be assured that rules and regulations that are intended to have reach are in fact in place and being complied with. For these reasons, they will look for the degree of assurance that formal lines of authority provide. Thus the union will need the formal authority to gather, to evaluate, to disseminate, to apply and to enforce the knowledge base that lies behind rules with reach. This does not mean that member states should give up their own regulatory authorities or rule-making expertise. They will need their own expertise in order to contribute to the substance of rule-making in the union, in order to retain and justify variations in standards, and because many of the responsibilities for applying rules with reach within the union may best be delegated. But it does mean that the union will need to bring together regulatory authorities to formulate, oversee and enforce rules with reach.

By contrast, no formal lines of authority will be required outside the core area of making rules with reach. There are many incentives for the different government units at different levels, whether national, regional or local, to get together to discuss common problems and common interests. Informal arrangements allow for much greater adaptability of groupings and modes of procedure.

In short, the span of authority needed by a continent-wide union is defined by its specialized advantage in rule-making and regulation. It needs this authority for the purpose of devising and enforcing rules with reach that offer sufficient common standards. In this area formal lines of authority are needed. Outside this area, informality should be the norm. The many incentives that exist to cooperate within Europe will result in forms of cooperation most suited to the particular subject being addressed.

In the case of the existing union, it is often asserted that because the union exercises authority in a certain policy area within the union, it should exercise similar authority in related areas outside the union. Thus, for example, it is argued that because the union manages the rules of the internal market, it should also take responsibility for the way international rules on trade and capital and money are developed. The two, however, do not necessarily follow. The nexus model points to why this connection is not automatic.

External Connections: Classes of Relationship

In turning to the way a continent-wide union should organize its relationship with the outside world, the key question is the way the internal rule-making function relates to global rule-making. If the span of authority of Europe's government inside its borders is defined by the rule-making function, the crucial question is whether this means that Europe should exercise a similar authority in dealing with rule-making authorities outside its borders. In other words, the question is whether the individual units within the continent-wide system – the member states – should accept that the union should gradually replace them at the table of the international organizations that operate global regimes and in dealing with other states on rule-making matters.

At first sight the answer seems straightforward: the union should indeed become Europe's authority for global rule-making. This would mean, for example, that a representative of the continent would combine the constituencies of individual member countries in the IMF and other international organizations and replace Britain and France as a permanent member of the UN Security Council. What this answer does not take into account, however, is that different types of international rules and rule-making involve different types of relationship.

The world outside the union shows two remarkable features. One, already mentioned, is the persistence of the so-called 'nation state'. In 1945 there were 51 original members of the United Nations. By the year 2000 this number had grown to 189. The other feature is the gradual development of global rules and rule-making, not organized through an entity that can be called a global government, but built instead around different multilateral regimes with different methods of persuasion and enforcement.[15]

These two features have led to a divide among specialists in international relations. Some have emphasized the continuing role of states and how much globalization is itself a creation of the states themselves.[16] Others emphasize how much states are part of an interdependent system.[17] Situated somewhere between these two sides is a third perspective provided by those international relations specialists who analyse global governance in terms of the various 'regimes'. They point to what lies behind the growth of international rule-making: the increasing acceptance of common principles for ordering relations between states (including ethical principles); the growth in the number and variety of subject areas now accepted as a matter for global concern; the growth in the number and types of organizations to deal with these matters of global concern; and a more general growth in reciprocity between states. International regimes constrain states, but they cannot be viewed as making up an integrated global system.[18]

All sides to the debate accept that it is premature to talk of cosmopolitanism in terms of a global public opinion or a global government. As far as an institutional focus for global government is concerned, the hopes of some that the United Nations might take on such a role seem far from reality.[19] Insofar as there is any overall institutionalized coordination of a global public policy agenda that identifies priorities, allocates tasks, monitors developments and oversees the different regimes, it takes place through such groupings as the heads of government of the seven wealthiest states in the world, the G7, and more recently through a broader grouping including some of the less well-off countries, the G20. The variety of international regimes, the

proliferation of international bodies and the use of informal groupings such as the G7 all make it difficult for public opinion to engage in
matters of international concern. But the increasing international
activity of non-governmental organizations such as Oxfam or Green-
peace and related networks is a first symptom of what might develop
as global opinion.[20]

The nexus model suggests that this traditional debate among specialists in international relations does not get to the heart of the
relationship questions that can help define the connection between
the rule-making function of Europe's system of government and the
growth in global rule-making outside Europe's borders. Therefore in
examining further the different types of relationship involved, another
type of distinction is followed, one about the qualitative character of
international relationships and the way they differ according to the
area of activity.[21]

The distinction is between:

- relationships that involve threats;
- relationships that are about exchange; and
- relationships that are about identity.

Differences in External Relations

Threat Relations

Threat relations are those involved in defence and security matters. They are also involved when it comes to any
enforcement of international rules of behaviour that
involves suasion or the use of force – such as the intervention in the Gulf to remove Iraq from Kuwait, or in
Kosovo to separate ethnic Serbs from ethnic Albanians.
The model is one of threat and counter-threat, action
and reaction.

The threat model seems to lead directly to the conclusion that bigger is better. This is because in order to be
credible a threat has to be capable of being carried out.
That means that if the use of force is threatened it must
consist of a clearly superior force, with actual capacity to
project and deliver superior force. What this has meant

Box (*Cont.*)

in practice is that very few states stand alone. For their forces to have credibility, either as a defensive force or as part of a mission to enforce international rules of behaviour, most states will seek allies – either through long-term alliances such as NATO or in the form of *ad hoc* coalitions such as fought in the Gulf War. What it also has meant in the past is that whenever significant firepower needs to be mobilized and brought to bear, the United States has needed to be involved. Indeed, over the last fifty years America has been the bedrock of alliances and the habitual convenor of *ad hoc* coalitions. Even in the case of methods of suasion, which fall short of the use of force, the maxim 'the bigger the better' still applies. Thus, a policy of trade sanctions is likely to have more effect the more states that try to apply it.

Exchange Relations

Exchange relations essentially involve trade relations and capital movements. The defining characteristic of such relationships is that free exchange is mutually advantageous and that it is possible to obtain advantages from exchange regardless of whether one is a small or a large society, rich or poor, and regardless of whether the benefits are reciprocated or not.

In addition, there are certain categories of relationship that seem to fall between threat relations and exchange relations. The movement of people falls into this category. So too do environmental questions. In both cases exchange can be helpful. The free movement of people is a way of matching on a worldwide basis the aspirations of people with the opportunities available. In the case of environmental concerns, exchange can also be useful. For example, trading in pollution certificates can help combat fears about global warming. Authorized trade in ivory can help eliminate illegal poaching and provide financial resources to support endangered species.

Box (*Cont.*)

The difficulty with such in-between cases is that exchange needs to be regulated. For example, in the absence of regulation, the movement of people can be seen by countries on the receiving end of migration as threats to their social order. Similarly, in the absence of a regulated framework, the trading of pollution certificates will not work.

The important feature of exchange relationships, including the 'in-between' cases of regulated exchange, is that advantage does not depend on size. All can benefit.[22]

Identity Relations: The Reputation of the Union

The third category of relationship revolves around questions of identity. The distinction is that communities may come together not for exchange or the ability to exert or ward off a threat, but just because they share a common identity and it is this that they want to project in establishing outside relations.

The most familiar examples involve national identity but others have also been asserted in the past. For example, in the Middle East, an assertion of pan-Arab identity has sometimes been made, with varying degrees of success. A sense of European identity is another example. If one follows this line of logic, the case for Europe's system of government to handle external relations rests on the belief that there is a common European identity that should be asserted.

In crude form this approach is unattractive. Sometimes the identity being asserted is bogus and artificial. But it is also unattractive as a means for approaching the world outside any community, for a different reason. To say that identity should be given primacy is equivalent to the old saying 'my country right or wrong'. In wartime such an attitude may be justified. As a guide to handling relationships in less dire circumstances, it is not.

Box (*Cont.*)

The point about identity can, however, be expressed in a different and much more persuasive form in terms of 'reputation'. Such theories draw attention to the way in which entities such as firms or alliances build up 'reputations' as a result of the way they behave. This becomes apparent in situations of repeated contact. The more frequent the contact, the more that behaviour is predictable and the more that it can be relied upon, or not.[23]

The concept of 'reputation' can be applied in a straightforward way to the question of whether Europe's system of government should handle external relations on behalf of the continent. The members of the union will acquire increasing knowledge of the behaviour of other members, and how the membership as a whole reacts, because of repeated contacts with each other on an enormous range of topics and through the use of a huge variety of means for joint consultations, coordination and decision-taking. In the light of this experience, all members will normally prefer to take decisions in the context of the union rather than in the context of other, less familiar alliances or external settings.[24] Europe's government should therefore become the preferred vehicle for dealing with the outside world. Alternatively, if there is a lack of trust or confidence after prolonged experience, either the member does not belong or Europe will have to recast its reputation by changing its behaviour.

The reason why the nexus model emphasizes the importance of the different qualities of relationship is precisely that their different characteristics lead to quite different conclusions about the authority of Europe's government in dealing with the outside world:

- Viewing relationships in terms of identity provides a strong reason to look to Europe to have similar authority over external rule-making relationships as it does over rule-making inside the union. Members should feel comfortable in formulating common positions, the world outside will find a continent speaking with one voice more predictable and more consistent to deal with, and, in turn, the member states will find that their collective voice is more effective than their voices as individual countries.

- Viewing relationships in terms of threat suggests, however, that the more that the states of Europe can continue to tie into the largest groupings, such as NATO, and act together with the US, the better. The credibility of threats is going to be greater the more force that an alliance can bring to bear. Even the United States, which alone among nations can in many cases still act unilaterally, prefers to act with allies and within the umbrella of a United Nations Security Council resolution.
- Finally, when relationships are about exchange, all can benefit, both large and small. Even the smallest states can go it alone.

The nexus model suggests that when external relations pose different management questions from those inside a company, they have to be handled in different ways. It thus suggests that even though a European government can define its internal authority around the core activity of rule-making within its borders, this authority should not necessarily extend to rule-making in the world outside. Any attempt to disregard the different types of relationship, or to treat them all as one, will lead to real damage. This is because any attempt to characterize all relationships in the same terms will result in the misrepresentation of the external world. Thus exchange relations, or mixed categories of relations such as the movement of people, will be misrepresented as falling into a pure threat relationship category. The terminology of trade 'wars' to refer to trade disputes, the apocalyptic language of environmental 'threats' or immigration 'invasions', use the language of threat relations to mis-describe relations where exchange is beneficial.[25]

The practical importance of keeping the language and the relationships of threat, identity and exchange clearly distinct can be seen in a different example. Many of those who make the case for the existing European union to develop its own security and defence capacity are really talking about identity rather than about threat relationships. The case may be presented as about developing Europe's own capacity to meet external threats to its security, but if it were about superior threat capacity, the emphasis would remain on NATO. Instead, what is really being asserted is that the union is likely to develop different criteria for interventions, and different perceptions of when it is in the interest of union states to bring force to bear, compared with when individual European states operate in the context of US-led alliances in NATO or in the UN Security Council. Thus, for some European politicians, the perceived advantages of the union in building up its international authority is that it may have different ideas about what constitute acceptable rules of international behaviour compared with the United States, which is now the predominant player. It is not actually about superior threat capacity at all.[26] If it were about defence capabilities, politicians would be telling citizens that Europe had to spend much more money on its armed forces. That is not what they are doing.

Politicians may find it convenient to dress up an identity issue in the clothing of threats. But such confusions can come at enormous cost to citizens. They can disrupt alliances and leave Europe exposed and unprepared when a threat does need to be made or to be countered.

Geographical Proximity and Issue Proximity

The Importance of Right Rules

The clearest way of interpreting the message from the nexus model about the handling of external relations is to say that it points to the primary importance of aligning the span of authority of an organization with the overriding need to get the rules of international behaviour 'right'. Right rules are of primary importance because:

- a European political union, no matter how large, will itself increasingly find its behaviour limited by the development of international rules;
- failure to distinguish between the different character of relationships can have enormously important practical implications for Europe and its citizens; and
- mistaken approaches to international rules of behaviour will be just as costly to countries that are members of a union as they will be if they were outside that union. Membership as such does not provide protection against the consequences of error.

Thus what is important about whether or not Europe's system of government should handle external relations for the continent is not size, or the ability to make threats or counter-threats. It is about whether or not it is the right vehicle for the formation of right rules of international behaviour.[27]

The case that the union is the right vehicle to manage external relations so as to support and help enforce right rules can be examined in two quite different ways. One way is to look at it, as economists, in terms of the costs and benefits of the union as a way of reaching agreement on right rules. The other way is to look at it in more traditional political terms – as a trade-off between geographical proximity and policy proximity.

Economizing on the Costs of Agreement

When the question is framed as about costs and benefits, the relevant costs and the relevant benefits are those involved in the making of agreements. In other words the question is to weigh the costs and benefits of the continent handling different types of external relations to see whether the overall balance 'economizes on the costs of agreement'.

The benefits of the continent handling external relations are that it can carry more clout in negotiating rules and rule changes. A single message voiced through a single spokesperson can be delivered more clearly than can a grouping of messages from individual member states.

The costs are that views within the continent will often diverge. This will lead to difficulties in formulating a common position and in implementing policy. Even threat relationships are rarely a matter of a single action followed by a single reaction. The process is very much less clear-cut, and so any difficulties in presenting a common view will be magnified enormously in implementation.[28] There will also be costs to any individual member state whose preferred position is forgone in the process of arriving at the common position. Another type of cost comes when a continent-wide view, or the assertion of bloc interests, comes at the expense of reaching agreement on the rules of a global regime.

Geographical Proximity

The costs and benefits can be viewed in more traditional political terms by seeing the question of union authority as involving a weighing of the importance of geographical proximity in relationships against 'issue proximity'.[29] What this means is that the process of arriving at right rules of international behaviour is no longer dictated by geographical closeness. In the past, if neighbouring countries strongly disagreed on rules of behaviour, even rules of exchange, it could lead to catastrophic consequences for their own relationship.[30] However, when everybody is constrained in their behaviour by international regimes of one sort or another, and when all countries, large or small, can benefit from regimes that encourage exchange, sheer geographical proximity counts for much less. An individual state can voice its own views about what it considers right rules without fear of adverse consequences, and it can form alliances or coalitions with other like-minded countries on a global basis. The consequence for a European country of staying out of a continent-wide system of government in the making of international rules is not isolation; it is the possibility of working with other coalitions with closer perceptions of what the rules should be.[31]

The tension between geography and policy in Europe is best illustrated by the case of the UK. Geographical proximity pulls it in the direction of working with its European neighbours, yet its perceptions of what are right rules of behaviour often lead it to feel closer to the USA on issues. Thus its preferred position is sometimes referred to as a 'mid-Atlantic' one. In other words, 'issue proximity' with America pulls it away from its geographical moorings in Europe.

These two different approaches – of the economist and of the practical politician – do not yield clear answers. It is not easy to tell what would best economize on the costs of agreement, or how to weigh the advantages of acting with one's immediate neighbour as compared with acting with a state that is more distant but that shares more of the same viewpoint on the content of international regimes. Successive British governments have sat on the fence and tried to have the best of both worlds.

Incentives

The nexus model suggests that in order to arrive at a solution for authority on matters of the external policy of Europe, what is essential is to get the incentives right within the system of government. What this means is that there is a need for the individual member states of a continent-wide government to institutionalize incentives for right behaviour by the union. The incentives must encourage Europe to support right rules of international behaviour, to build its reputation as a reliable and consistent actor and to formulate its own internal rule-making in ways compatible with, and supportive of, global rules.

The overriding importance of getting incentives right argues against Europe having an exclusive authority for dealing with matters of external relations. Providing the system of government with a monopoly power over external relations does not provide any incentive. In fact it works in the opposite direction: monopolists exploit their position to ignore what people want. Instead, incentives can be provided in two ways:

- through member states maintaining independent relations with international regimes and external alliances; and
- through the ability of member states to opt out of common positions in particular areas of external policy such as a common foreign policy, common defence policy or common trade policy.

These two possibilities offer different but mutually supportive incentives. If a member state simply opts out of a common position, it sends an alternative message to the outside world that what is being presented as a common front may not in fact be so. As a result the union message is weakened. The members of a union have therefore an incentive to formulate the message in a way that will bring the opt-out country back into the fold. In the case of countries maintaining their independent relations with international regimes, the signal is that the member state can form alliances elsewhere in order to get international rules of behaviour it believes to be right. If acted upon, the action does more than simply challenge the message; it challenges the composition of the union. In this way the possibility of maintaining independent relations with international organizations and alliances can be viewed as a limited right of secession in a particular part of international relations.[32]

Taken together, the two types of procedure would provide powerful incentives for a continent-wide system of government to make sure that it does fully reflect what its members consider to be the right rules of international behaviour and does not involve, for example, a projection of identity for the sake of identity. If the incentives work in the way they should, the result is a paradox. Member states will retain their own relationships with international organizations. But, at the same time, precisely because the continent will take care to reflect the views of all its members, it will be more likely, rather than less likely, that European institutions will provide the normal vehicle for dealing with the outside world.[33]

The nexus model thus allows for Europe to develop as the usual vehicle through which member states deal with the different international regimes. But it suggests that incentives must be maintained that ensure that the benefits from acting together outweigh the costs, and that the fading importance of geography does not outweigh the growing importance of getting the content of international rules right.

* * * * *

In order for Europe to get the organization of its system of government right, we need to discard the erroneous notion of seeing the union as a way to scale up the size of the nation state. A more promising alternative is the network model, which points to lessons that the union can usefully absorb from the ways in which business has been able to respond flexibly to what people want. The nexus model goes further in addressing questions of form that are important in systems of government because it gives guidance for what should be fixed and what left to a more open form of architecture. In addition this model draws a valid distinction between the authority of the union over internal matters and its authority over external relationships. But in the end, no model of business organization can be transferred directly to systems of government. The worlds are different in too many respects. The next chapter therefore brings the lessons that can be learnt from this review of the organization of authority in a continent-wide government together with the earlier chapters and places them foursquare in the world of systems of government.

7 Simplicity

Thus ... did this new account of things render the appearances of the heavens more completely coherent than had been done by any of the former systems. It did this, too, by a more simple and intelligible, as well as more beautiful machinery.

Adam Smith, *Essays on Philosophical Subjects*

Introduction: Complexity Signals Collapse

The ambition to form a continent-wide European union confronts Europe's politicians with a fundamental decision. They can put in place a new system of government designed to bring the best out of the system of both political choice and market choice in Europe, or they can continue along the path established by the existing union, which is delivering an increasingly over-complicated system, damaging to the mechanisms of both political choice and market choice. The choice is between increasing complexity of the old system or something new.

Systems of market choice have adapted in recent years to provide customized products, to connect efficiently from the global to the local, and to respond quickly to signals from people about what they want. The continent needs a framework for government that allows people to signal what they want through their system of political choice with equal ease. In this way, people can obtain the best out of both systems of choice. Achieving this combination requires a radical rethinking of the shape of European government. The

analysis of previous chapters suggests that the new shape of a continent-wide system of government should be as simple as possible.

When, over two hundred years ago, Adam Smith turned his attention from economic explanation to scientific explanation, he placed
particular emphasis on the virtue of simplicity. Looking at the history
of scientific explanation in the field of astronomy, he noted that, when
a theory had difficulty in incorporating new observations and facts, it
often became more complicated. According to him, such increasing
complexity was not a sign of the robustness of the theory. On the
contrary, it was a sign of its imminent collapse. It would be replaced
by a new theory that could contain all the observed facts within a new
and simple explanation.

When attention turns to modern-day Europe, the current framework of the existing union is becoming more and more complicated as
member states struggle to adapt to the new facts posed by enlargement and by fast-moving markets. The current union can proceed by
becoming even more complicated and even less intelligible. Alternatively, the existing union can be replaced by a new and simple structure for the continent as a whole. The analysis of the earlier chapters
suggests that a simple democratic system of government for Europe
will be a better system. Only in this way can market choice and
political choice operate together across the continent so that people
get the best of each. This chapter spells out what 'simplicity' would
mean.

What Simplicity Means

'Simplicity' means that Europe's system of government must simplify:

- what it does, so that it focuses on the provision of rules with reach;
- the way in which it works, so that its span of authority is defined
  by the rule-making role;
- the task of communication across the continent, so that it respects
  the limitations of what can be communicated on a continent-wide
  basis through the ballot box or through rights claims; and
- the role of its institutions, so that they focus on the functions
  where the union has a comparative advantage and do not try to
  replicate the institutions of the member states.

Simplifying What the Union Does

The purpose of simplifying what a continent-wide union in Europe does is to enable the union to respond to the changing functions of systems of government, to focus on what the union can do best, and to do what only a continent-wide union can do.

As has been noted above, where a continent-wide union can most add value for people is in providing rules with reach. This does not mean that a continent-wide union should try to cover Europe with a mass of detailed and prescriptive regulations. Instead it means that a system of government for a continent-wide union should focus select-ively on providing rules with the reach that makes them appropriate for adoption across the union as a whole.

One key implication of the rule-making role is that the continent-wide union will be defined by the type of activity it carries out, and not by its responsibilities for particular subject areas of public policy. What this means is that a continent-wide union should not try to divide up subject areas of public policy according to territory – between union, member state and member state regions. In today's world, where public policy boundaries do not align with territorial boundaries, territory is an arbitrary base for dividing up policy re-sponsibilities. Instead the focus should be on the type of activity where a continent-wide union has comparative advantage.

A second implication of 'simplicity' is that a system of government for a continent-wide union should remain focused on the rule-making and regulatory function. Most scenarios for the future of the union see it evolving along the lines of systems of government in the member states and eventually carrying out a similar, extensive range of func-tions. A focus on what a continent-wide union can do best suggests otherwise. It should not try to replicate the functions of a state. It should not go down the provisioning path of governments. It has no need for a budget at all.

A third implication of concentrating the activity of the new contin-ent-wide union on rules with reach is that the procedures that justify those rules have to be given much greater prominence and importance. The fear aroused by a continent-wide union that focuses on rule-making is that it will borrow its approach to rule-making from the regulatory pattern established by the existing union. The existing union has encouraged unnecessary and over-detailed rule-making. A union that works in this way stifles choice in both politics and the market.

The source of the problem of unnecessary and over-detailed regulation in the existing union is that those tests that can help decide whether a regulation or rule is justified or not are often regarded by each of its institutions as no more than inconveniences to be got around. In addition, its judicial system has developed legal doctrines and practices that have encouraged an indiscriminate spread of union law-making.

Constitutional experts have grown accustomed to thinking of constitutional rules in areas that define, for example, central banking and monetary arrangements, or fiscal powers and budget-making. With the shift in the function of systems of government away from the taxing and spending function towards the rule-making function, much greater constitutional prominence has to be given to those provisions that set out the procedures for rule-making. They must place a much more rigorous burden of proof on the justification of union rules and regulations.

Simplifying How the Union Works

Simplifying how a continent-wide union works means defining the span of authority needed by the union in relation to its core activity of providing rules with reach. The core activity defines both where the union needs authority and what kind of authority it needs. It defines the boundaries of what should be fixed and what can be left flexible.

In cases where rules with reach are appropriate, the union will need firm authority to implement and enforce them. In some cases, such authority may be delegated. But the union will still need to be able to exercise authority over the powers delegated and the bodies involved.

In certain cases, common standards will not be well suited to hard rules. This applies, for example, in areas of economic management, where precise rules are difficult to draw up and where judgements about the circumstances may lead to differences in application. In such areas the union should not seek firm authority but needs to adopt softer styles.

In its dealings with the world outside Europe, the union needs conditional authority. That is to say, in dealing with international trade, financial, foreign policy, security and defence matters, the members of the union may increasingly wish to act as one and build common institutions and procedures for this purpose. However, the union's authority should be conditioned on respect for international rules and the different types of relationship involved. In order to achieve this respect, member states will still need to be able to conduct their own relationships with the outside world. This is the most effective way in which member states can help ensure that the union adds content to international rule-making and does not undermine the development of international rules.

The core activities of the union also define where it does not need to exercise authority. A continent-wide union has no need to look for authority in the many areas outside the making of rules with reach where cooperation between units of governments will take place in the union. There will be examples of area cooperation between member states or their regions – for example, in the Baltic or Mediterranean or North Sea – or regional cooperation between units of regional government that share common problems, that require no union authority.

Similarly a continent-wide union has no need to intervene in how the governments of member states carry out their traditional roles as providers, or how fast they scale down that activity. It has no need to intervene in the tax policies of members. It should not be involved in their financial reallocation efforts or in their income redistribution activities. It has no need for tax authority of its own.

Simplifying What People Need to Communicate About

Communications in modern democratic political systems take place in two ways. One is through the electoral process. The other, nowadays the most important, is through the uses of the language of rights. A continent-wide union will have difficulty in respect of both. This difficulty has to be recognized in what people need to communicate about across Europe.

The electoral approach has basic weaknesses in Europe. It involves extremely high entry costs involved in building up the infrastructure of political parties with pan-European networks and branches; it means putting together common platforms and disseminating common political programmes. Little of this has actually taken place. The existing European assembly provides a forum where national parties, not pan-European parties, come together. The groupings inside the assembly primarily reflect their need to command influence and position within the parliament's own structure – particularly the committee structure – and not the need to fight pan-European electoral campaigns.

The union is also disadvantaged when it comes to making the best use of the language of rights. Centralized systems of recognition do not make best use of rights, either as the language through which to explore values, or as the means for bringing together passionate minorities with silent majorities.

These shortcomings of a continent-wide union as a forum for communication have to be recognized. The assembly should not be treated as though it were representative when it is not. The language of rights for helping to determine priorities within politics should not be applied out of the public contexts where they can most help as signposts to right allocation and right reason.

The remedy for the shortcomings of a continent-wide union as a space for electoral politics or for communication based on rights is to keep simple what needs to be communicated about in the union. In this way the difficulties in communicating across an extensive political space are reduced and the advantage offered by the union-wide context can be taken advantage of.

The advantage of a European union for communication is that it facilitates extensive exchanges of views across the union. This is entirely appropriate for communicating about the content of rules with reach because their content is general. The focus is on rules with sufficient content to be useful everywhere. They will not be rich in content. They will not offer maximum standards. Indeed, they may only identify minimum standards.

The recognition of where the union offers advantages for communication, and of where, conversely, it has disadvantages, means that its decision-making will remain closer to public opinion. It does not place unsupportable burdens on the weakly representative quality of a European assembly. Nor does it involve using rights claims out of context. The union is not the arena where rights that are about priorities within a system of political choice should be legislated or adjudicated upon. Any attempt to do so will result in an imbalance between vote-based politics and rights-based politics.

Rules with reach suited to general and extensive communication across the continent can be viewed as a 'McDonald's' product. Their content is not sophisticated and there is space alongside in the market for products that are more or less specialized. But the McDonald's label is not one to be belittled. Rules that make it easier for people to get what they want across the union, to know and to be assured about what exactly they are getting in otherwise unfamiliar places and circumstances, are enormously helpful for them in their lives. People will continue to satisfy more particular preferences in their states and regions, but the union will have added a valuable new dimension to their range of choice. It is a function that only a union can carry out. Elites may sneer at McDonald's but part of the problem of the existing union is precisely that it is seen to represent the interests of an elite. That same elite should stop sneering and start thinking about how to respond to what people really want.

Simplifying Institutional Roles

The existing European union has taken a very traditional approach to thinking about the roles of the institutions. Typically, they view themselves as though they must become the replicas and counterparts of the institutions in the individual member states. Thus, the parliament of the existing union tends to see itself as needing to perform the tasks undertaken by national parliaments; the Commission aspires to become the 'government' of the union in the way that member states have governments; and the Court of Justice of the existing union aspires to become a constitutional court, in the way that many member states have constitutional courts.

The message of simplification is that institutional roles should not be thought about in these terms. The tasks of the institutions of a continent-wide union will not mimic those of the member states.

The clearest illustration is provided by the Commission. If it were to act as a government in the traditional sense, its task would be to take initiatives in all areas of European public policy, manage the economy, react to foreign policy and security exigencies, steer legislation through parliament, and manage the civil service and agencies of government. It would be largely separate from the judicial branch and semi-detached from quasi-judicial functions. In its composition the Commission would need to reflect the way in which people have voted for parties to form a government or to be part of it.

By contrast to the sweeping political functions of a government, the Commission's role in a continent-wide union will be quite different. It will need to scrutinize the proposals for union-wide rules that come from individual governments of member states against a background of the Commission's own comparative knowledge about the applicability of the proposals across the union. It can provide an expert setting in which the specialized knowledge of the member states in that area of rule-making can be evaluated and compared across the range of membership. It will also have its own knowledge to help identify if a common rule is required and what a sufficient content would be. Where common rules are adopted across the union, it will need to help oversee that they are implemented and managed effectively. It will need the ability to seek judicial remedies where rules and regulations are not implemented. It may itself handle some judicial or quasi-judicial functions. It will essentially be a multi-purpose regulatory body.

The representative assembly for a continent-wide union will similarly perform different kinds of functions compared with the popular assembly in a member state. If there is an analogy to be drawn with the assemblies of the member states, it is more properly drawn with second chambers because, in a number of member states, it is second chambers that provide for more substantive review of the content of legislative proposals.

An assembly for a continent-wide union will gravitate towards an active review role of proposals for rules with reach. It will receive proposals for rules and regulations for general application across the union that will have emerged from a process of intensive bargaining between member states, mediated by the Commission and the Council secretariat. In this process, national parliaments will already have been involved. The parties in the European assembly will not necessarily feel obliged to support, nor necessarily expected to oppose, the proposals emerging from this process. The assembly will typically seek to amend proposals because, unless it adds a view of its own, there would be no reason for anyone to pay any attention to it. By contrast, in national parliaments, the parties that form the government will typically command a majority in the popular assembly and it will be incumbent on the majority to support their government and pass its proposals. Thus, in many ways, the European assembly will be more like a second chamber in national systems, which also may be more potent sources of legislative review than the first chambers. Like them, its ability to block and delay may need to be a qualified one.

When it comes to scrutinizing the quality of administration, popular assemblies in member states are also constrained by their need to provide support for the government. By contrast, a continent-wide assembly will have an incentive to scrutinize because it is an attention-getting device. The only time when the parliament of the existing union has commanded headlines across Europe was when it forced the resignation of the Santer Commission. A European assembly will therefore have an incentive to watch over the performance of union agencies, including the European Central Bank and the Commission. But the ability to force resignations is not the instrument of everyday oversight, and even where the power exists, it is a weapon of last resort. Moreover, the assembly's zeal to scrutinize will be diluted by its desire to expand what the union and its institutions do and by a reluctance to point out what the union does not do well. Thus other bodies will need to develop a scrutinizing role too.

The Court of Justice should also be seen as playing a limited role. It has an essential function in adjudicating on disputes about the content of union-wide rules and on whether due process has been observed in their formation. It should not, however, be adjudicating on broader matters in which a central court is not a neutral arbiter. In the existing union the court has pursued a certain 'idea of Europe' leading it to extend the powers of the union when it could, and to beat tactical retreats when the outside political climate made retreat prudent. The member states themselves, or their institutions, must retain the role of guardianship of the overall framework of a continent-wide union.

The message that a good continent-wide system of government requires a simple framework therefore has radical implications. It means that such a union should be focusing its activities on what it can do best and on what it alone can do – the making of rules with reach – and should shun the provisioning role of traditional governments. It means that its span of authority should be defined in relation to this reassessment of the core activity of the union and complete flexibility of association should be allowed in all other areas. It means accepting that the union cannot provide a context for communications involving complex signals about what people want. Instead, it must realize that a context of extensive communications is consistent with rule-making that offers general applicability, providing a minimum and sufficient content to be useful across the continent. It means accepting that the union is not the place where rights claims should be legislated or adjudicated upon. Finally, it means readjusting the aspirations of the institutions to highly important, but limited, tasks that are adapted to the particular circumstances of the union and that are not replicas of the roles performed by institutions in the member states.

Simplicity and Conventional Futures

This vision of Europe's future is fundamentally different from the conventional scenarios so firmly locked in the past that were described earlier (in chapter 3). A comparison with the model of 'simplicity' reveals that the basic flaw in the conventional models is that, in one way or another, each misrepresents key aspects of relationships in a continent-wide union. Departing from a wrong starting point, they lead thinking about a continent-wide union in completely the wrong direction.

Superpower Europe: Misrepresenting External Relationships

The vision of 'Superpower Europe' makes the aim of success and power in the wider world the starting point for thinking about the design of the union. The union's internal arrangements follow from what is judged necessary to achieve this success beyond Europe's borders. By contrast, the message from 'simplicity' is that if Europe gets the best out of both political choice and market choice, it will become a highly successful society and one that will, as a result, carry great influence in world affairs. In other words, success in the world will be a product and outcome of success within the union.

Approaching a system of government as a question of building from the outside to the inside is fundamentally flawed because the temptation is to misrepresent the outside world. The incentive is to treat all relations with the outside world as 'threat' relations. In this way the model of 'Superpower Europe' misrepresents the nature of Europe's relations with the outside world. The damage affects all external relationships.

First, it is damaging when it comes to handling relations that are essentially about exchange, such as the rules governing trade and capital movements. It means that any trade dispute, even with the closest of trade partners, risks being treated as a test of strength rather than something to be resolved according to international dispute settlement rules.

Similarly, it means that the standards needed to underpin world capital flows also get viewed through a distorting prism of state rivalries. For example, technical difficulties in the method of achieving accepted international accounting standards for businesses no longer get treated as a matter of professional standards but are regarded as a contest between the United States and Europe. Likewise, the creation and adoption of the euro as an international currency is not seen in its primary role of providing the global economy with a new unit of account and store of value, but is described in terms of displacing the dollar, as a blow against the United States.

Thirdly, it is also damaging to treat as primarily threat relations those relations that were referred to earlier as 'mixed'. Immigration starts to be seen as a security problem and countries that are sources of pollution begin to be seen as committing the equivalent of hostile acts. Neither way of responding is likely to be conducive to solutions because solutions require a willingness to cooperate on both ends of the problem.

Finally, if all relations are essentially viewed as threat or potentially threat relations, this will also end by damaging the union's ability to manage security, defence and international rule-keeping relations, which actually do involve threat relations. The key to handling such threat relations is through the maintenance of allies and alliances. It is most unlikely that standing alliances such as NATO, or *ad hoc* alliances such as those organized in the Gulf, will remain unimpaired if precisely the same countries that the union may wish to treat as allies have been regarded in other contexts as a source of threats.

The frame of mind underlying the idea of a European superpower is one that sees the answer to the problems of governance as mainly ones of scale. Individual member states can no longer act as global powers. The answer is to create a larger state. This completely fails to understand the nature of the challenges facing modern systems of governance.

A system of government that tries to reproduce the traditional functions of the state and thinks of a system of European governance as one that differs just in scale is not going to be receptive to the idea that possibly the functions of the union do not consist in trying to do everything the traditional state did, or that the union has to be organized differently, or that its institutions might perform different functions. Such resistance to change will condemn Europe's system of government to act as an inferior system of choice. It will result in politicians trying to shift their responsibility and blame the market, thus triggering exactly the kind of behaviour that will set Europe to handicap the system of market choice. Europe will end up with neither system of choice working properly.

Eco-social Europe: Misrepresenting the Relationship between Market Choice and Political Choice

The flaws in the vision of 'Superpower Europe' start from a misrepresentation of the outside world. The flaws in the vision of 'Eco-social Europe' start from a misrepresentation of the relationship between government and the market. The role of the market in delivering social benefits is ignored; instead it is seen as the source of social failures. Conversely, the role of government as a source of social failure is downplayed; instead it is seen as the automatic way of correcting failure.

By contrast with the 'Eco-social' model, the starting point of 'simplicity' is that, in today's world, one cannot begin from a predisposition as to which system of choice is superior in which circumstance. Getting the connections between the two systems of choice right means looking much harder at where the comparative advantages of each really lie and how they relate. Otherwise the weaknesses in one can aggravate the weaknesses of the other.

The predispositions behind the 'Eco-social Europe' model mean that it fails to recognize that the functions of government are changing. The vision is still of the state as provider. The many reasons why the limits of this role have been reached and probably exceeded in Europe are not recognized. In addition, the model fails to appreciate that even if individual member states can continue to try to offer traditional forms of social provision, the comparative advantage of a continent-wide union does not lie down this route.

The failure of the 'Eco-social Europe' model to look more closely at the way in which systems of market choice and systems of political choice interact in the modern world will lead the union into difficulties by failing to limit its rule-making role to rules with reach. The model has an inbuilt tendency towards over-regulation and the use of political power to handicap market choice. It will be unreceptive to the constitutional safeguards needed to constrain the regulatory role of modern systems of government. Once again, Europe will end with a system of governance where neither the system of political choice nor that of market choice will work.

An Order of States: Misrepresenting Relationships between the Units of the Union

The vision of an 'Order of States' misrepresents relationships in yet a different way. The flawed starting point is to think about the functions of government in terms of territory, for, in today's world, the disconnection between the boundaries of public policy and the boundaries of political territory means that the latter cannot serve as the basis for dividing up power and authority in Europe. By contrast, the model of 'simplicity' emphasizes the importance of trying to define the type of activity where a continent-wide system of government will have a comparative advantage in relation to the system of market choice.

The consequence of trying to divide powers according to territory is that most functions of government will be shared between states and the union in an arbitrary and haphazard way. This in turn will lead to difficulty in defining authority and responsibility. People will have no redress when things go wrong – they will not know whom to blame – and the states will increasingly act as a cartel to deflect criticism and censure. The failure to distinguish where the comparative advantage of Europe's system of government lies means that neither European government nor the governments of member states will be able to deliver what people want. The system of political choice will look less and less attractive in relation to market choice and increasingly be dismissed as irrelevant.

Thinking about the future of the union in terms of an 'Order of States' is not only unhelpful in terms of trying to define functions – who does what and why – it is also unhelpful when thinking about the tasks of union institutions. Union institutions and the institutions of their member states will increasingly find themselves in overlapping roles. Their distinctive but complementary roles will become blurred.

Because those who espouse the vision of an 'Order of States' cannot offer a model that engages either with the modern functions of government, the way in which we communicate, or the way in which units of government inside and outside the union can best be connected, the vision damages its own cause. Some have rushed to embrace the idea of 'network' government as a way of rationalizing an 'Order of States'. But it fails to provide the guide to form that Europe needs. The states and their regions have a continuing future in a simple system of government for a continent-wide union, but this is for different reasons and has different organizational implications.

In the context of a simple model, the states and their regions will provide a means for making sure that there is a way of measuring when union rules need to be changed and updated and that there is a means of responding to people's desires for different standards alongside rules offering a commonly available sufficient standard. States and their regions can also provide the context for a decentralized means of recognizing claims about rights. They can, in addition, provide a check on how the union exercises its external rule-making authority. However, the model of the union of states does not help define these potential roles. By clinging to territory, it too provides a model that will handicap Europe's systems of choice.

Jurists' Europe: Misrepresenting the Relationship between Legal Systems and Political Systems

The concept of 'Jurists' Europe' misrepresents relationships in a quite different way again. The faulty starting point is to confuse legal relationships in Europe with political relationships. This triggers a misleading chain of logic: European law is viewed as an instrument of integration → all integration is good → since all integration should be integration under the law, the more that law pervades all activities, the more that the union's good is secured.

The confusion of legal relationships with political relationships leads to very unfortunate results. It undermines respect for the law since European law comes to be seen as serving a political agenda. It sees all authority exercised by the union as 'good' and the union's span of authority as one where the limits are always to be stretched. It also leads to a misrepresentation of the way power is organized. In law there are some laws more important than others and courts are often organized in hierarchical form. From this point of departure, the jurists' view misrepresents political relationships as hierarchy in the same way as legal form is hierarchy.

By contrast, the starting point behind the model of 'simplicity' is to treat the definition of authority and the way powers are to be organized as questions about the system of political choice in relation to the system of market choice. This makes it possible to distinguish where authority is needed in a European system of government and where it is not, as well as how powers are best organized to respect the boundaries of what the union will be good at. Hierarchy as a model of organization for democratic politics is rejected. Democracy is about powers flowing up and not coming down.

Simplicity and Democratic Values

Compared with the conventional models for Europe's future, a simple framework will provide a superior model because it focuses on how to get the best out of Europe's system of political choice in relation to the system of market choice. At the same time, the processes of European government are not just about efficiency, or even mainly so. They are more importantly about democratic values. What has been said about simplifying Europe's system of government is also very germane to essential democratic processes in Europe.

Democracies offer three – and only three – ways of reaching decisions:[1]

- *Argument, debate and deliberation*: Through debate people can persuade and be persuaded until the point is reached where there is a consensus.
- *Bargaining and exchange*: In other words it may not be necessary to win arguments, or to convince those of a different view through debate, but, instead, agreements can be reached or outcomes arrived at where each party gains enough to be content.
- *Voting*: People agree on a decision procedure which they can accept in advance – even if they disagree with the arguments underlying a decision and fail to gain any bargaining advantage from it.

In practice, all three methods are often used together. For example, in the case of the existing European union, the Council of Ministers does not normally vote, but it is the forum for intensive bargaining. In the European Parliament, votes are usually taken and the parliament is also a focus for further bargaining and more debate.

The model of 'simplicity' has something valuable to contribute to the way each of these methods applies in the context of a continent-wide system of government.

Argument, Debate and Deliberation

In recent writings on democracy it has been the first aspect of democratic processes – the deliberative qualities, or their absence – that has been the subject of particular attention. As mentioned earlier, the focus has been on electoral politics and their shortcomings. This attention is partly in reaction to how far away modern electoral practice seems to have strayed from providing for reasoned debate among citizens. It also recognizes how far electoral politics falls short of being able to aggregate preferences in any clear way. It tries to provide an account of how societies can make more acceptable and representative social choices. It is also a reaction against viewing politics in terms of exchange and bargaining, which seems to legitimize some of the most disagreeable aspects of contemporary government: the activities of lobbyists, the privileged access of special interest groups and the influence of money.

Accounts of deliberative democracy draw attention to two aspects of systems of political choice:

- the theoretical form of debate in politics; and
- the actual setting in which debates can be resolved.

'Simplicity' adds to both accounts. It provides both a different view of the nature of political debate and a different perspective on the settings for democratic debate.

The logical form of debate set out in conventional accounts of deliberative democracy is that of 'reflective equilibrium'. The idea is that people can reflect in a calm and dispassionate manner on their fundamental values, listen and persuade and eventually arrive at some agreed concept of the common good.[2] By contrast, the attention that 'simplicity' places on rights as signalling methods characterizes the more usual form of democratic debate as one where the views of those with strong convictions, possibly minorities, have to be weighed against the views of majorities with less strongly felt opinions: the so-called 'silent majority'.

A rights claim provides a debating tool to pass between the views of inert majorities and those with more committed views. The rights claim points to the commonly accepted value – in other words, the majority view – and offers a logical thread to the new rights claim or new policy application, which may be espoused only by a minority.

Those who signal what they want through rights claims are far from the calm, dispassionate citizen, open to persuasion. On the contrary, they are committed and dedicated to their cause. The connection between their cause and the common good is asserted in the rights claim itself. Political choice is seen therefore as not just about reason; it is about reason coupled with desire. Debate is not founded on 'reflective equilibrium'.[3]

As also mentioned earlier, conventional accounts of deliberative democracy have not achieved any consensus on how to improve the setting for debate through electoral processes. Some accounts stress the role of direct democracy; another well-known account emphasizes the possibilities for a new kind of 'town hall' debate; others stress reforming traditional representative assemblies or their committees or privileging under-represented groups; still others stress the substantive aims of politics.[4]

By contrast, by focusing not just on electoral process but on the way in which people communicate through rights and how the two systems relate, 'simplicity' draws attention to a different dimension of the setting. It focuses on the need to provide the proper context for the use of the language of rights as the language of both 'right allocation' and 'right reason'. It involves looking much more closely at what the language of rights is bringing to political debate and how the language of exploration can best be fitted within a political system.

Bargaining and Exchange

When democratic politics is viewed as about bargaining and exchange, the emphasis tends to be placed on providing neutral rules for the political framework within which the bargaining can be done. The rules are set in ways that do not bias or predispose the outcomes of bargaining or that favour particular groups. For example, the rule in favour of freedom of expression allows for all opinions to be expressed. Similarly, the most common voting rule is that the majority prevails. This gives equal weight to doing something as to not doing something, and is the only voting rule where minorities are not put in a privileged position to block or to carry legislation.[5]

Neutrality in this conventional sense has long been attacked on the grounds that it overlooks the importance of norms such as equality and fairness in the rules for political choice. It is suggested instead that the rules and institutions for political choice should promote such norms.

The arguments in favour of a simple form of government for a continent-wide union have attempted to sidestep this ancient debate by looking at neutrality in a rather different way. Neutrality is viewed as about arranging the rules of governance so that it is possible for individuals and groups to make the best out of each of the two systems of choice: politics and the market. Simplifying Europe's system of government so that it focuses on the rule-making role, on rights and on a formal span of authority in core areas is a way of making Europe's system of political choice as attractive to use for what it can do best as the system of market choice is for what the market can do best.

The rules of a simple system of government are not value-free because, for one thing, they respect democratic values. It is the participant who is neutral in the sense of starting from a position of being prepared to use whichever system of choice is most responsive to delivering what they want.

Looking at the relationship between political choice and market choice in this way also warns against viewing bargaining and exchange in political systems in terms of equality and fairness by dividing up a fixed sum of benefits. The relationship between the two systems of choice is not of this nature. When the two bring out the best in each other, then individuals and groups can all get more of what they want; when the two systems of choice work in ways that are damaging to each, everybody gets less of what they want.

Voting

Voting has a special place in democratic theory because it is the instrument through which people can get rid of those who hold political office and wield political power. It remains essential for this purpose. However, as discussed earlier, more emphasis has been placed on the vote than is accurate or realistic. The model of 'simplicity' rectifies this imbalance. The emphasis on rights as the principal means through which people communicate preferences about public policies is a way of recognizing a different signalling system in politics without removing the essential and necessary device of the vote as a way to remove politicians.

The model of 'simplicity' not only suggests that in thinking about deliberation in politics there is a need to look more widely at the way in which the language of rights is used, but it also points to the connection between claims about rights and vote-centred politics. The risk of not treating intensity of desire explicitly in the design of political systems is that relationships between minorities and majorities can go badly wrong in ways that are to the detriment of the standing both of claims based on rights and of politics based on the vote.

By looking at these three benchmarks for the way decisions are taken in democratically organized politics, it can be seen, therefore, that the model of a simple system of government for a continent-wide European union is contributing something important to each:

- It approaches the deliberative quality of democratic procedures by trying to be more realistic about the way in which political differences are debated and by pointing to the role of the language of rights as the language both of desire and of right reason.
- It approaches the question of the bargaining framework by trying to provide a framework for political choice that will match the ease with which people can make choices in the market.
- It continues to honour the importance of the vote but does not accord it a role it cannot fulfil, and points to the importance of relating vote-centred politics to rights-based politics.

Therefore a simple model for European governance has virtues in comparison with more conventional models, and draws attention to aspects of democratic practices that are sometimes not given sufficient importance. However, we need to address a fundamental question about 'simplicity': is there some inherent virtue in trying to make the organization of systems of political choice 'simple'?

Why Simplicity?

When it comes to trying to explain the world around us, it has long been held that a simpler explanation is preferable to a complicated one. When Adam Smith speculated about the virtues of simplicity in scientific explanation, he joined a long line of philosophers who have drawn a connection between simplicity and good scientific reasoning. The connection continues to interest philosophers today. The analogous question for political science is whether there are some intrinsic virtues in the idea of simple systems of democratic government.

One type of intrinsic virtue is that it possibly forces people to consider the basic foundations of a system of government for Europe. Once Europe has got this foundation right, then the door is open for a more complicated and sophisticated system to emerge over time. Law is sometimes approached in this way.[6] Given the challenges Europe faces in building a continent-wide system, there are advantages in trying to identify what are the fundamental components needed.

A different way of viewing simplicity in connection with empirical observation is to suggest that simplicity helps as a method of reasoning. What is suggested is not that simplicity is itself a test for truth,[7] but that simple explanations help distinguish between rational and irrational choices and between justified and unjustified beliefs. Just why this should be so is a matter of debate. Among the reasons given are that simple hypotheses may be more efficient to work with, while, in contrast, complexities incur greater risk of error. A simple device has less that can go wrong with it. Simplicity is itself a form of efficiency.[8]

There is no direct analogy to be drawn between the methods of scientific reasoning and the organization of the arrangements that societies make for individual and social choices. When it comes to systems for making social choices, the normative element is just too large. Nevertheless, even if direct analogies are inappropriate, it may still be the case that greater attention should be paid to the virtues of simplicity when it comes to the design of the procedures and institutions of governance in Europe. In the same way that simplicity is seen to be more than the product and fall-out of good theorizing in the physical or social sciences and rather as something to take into account as input into scientific method, so too perhaps Europe should build simplicity into its processes of government. In other words, possibly there should be a deliberate attempt to capture the virtues of simplicity in the design of the processes of social choice. Possibly, within a democratic framework, there should be a deliberate search for rules and procedures that favour simplicity.

If there are reasons to favour simplicity deliberately in the design of democratic systems of political choice, the justification lies in method. If a simple system of government can provide a guide to good method in politics in the way that it is sometimes claimed that simplicity is a guide to good science, then this is something that should be valued. If a simple system of government for Europe can provide a framework that is less prone to error than is a complicated one, can offer better adaptive qualities and can help distinguish between rational and irrational social choices and rational and irrational social beliefs, these would be virtues indeed.

The idea that Europe should deliberately try to put in place a simple structure of governance for a continent-wide union will offend all those who think of European government as needing to offer the same range of functions as the traditional nation state, with the same procedures for mobilizing public opinion, and the same institutional arrangements, with the only difference being the scale of operations. It will give equal offence to those who do not wish to see a new continent-wide system of government but who just want to extend what is already in place. The purpose of subsequent discussion in this book is not to go over again the reasons why 'simpler is better' but instead to discuss two lines of objection to the idea that a simple form of government for Europe could have intrinsic virtues.

There are two important criticisms which can be levelled at a simple system of government for Europe. One is that a system of government with a limited span of authority, which relies on decentralized rules of recognition for many of society's most important political principles and which focuses on a limited task of implementing and enforcing rules with reach, will not provide Europe with a 'coherent' system. Too many of the conventional tasks of government will be left out; too much inconsistency can arise between the component parts of the union, and it will lack the necessary range of authority.

The other criticism is that these same characteristics of a limited and decentralized form of government for the union will prevent Europe from developing the values across the continent that express its special character and that will enable it to realize its highest aspirations. Underlying this criticism is the view that unless Europe's form of government is designed to implement the highest moral values held by a society, ultimately the system will lack legitimacy.

The way in which a simple system of government for Europe relates to these two important issues of coherence and legitimation is therefore discussed in the next two chapters of this book.

8 Coherence

> *The very next notion to that of a sole and central power, which presents itself to the minds of men in the ages of equality, is the notion of uniformity of legislation.*
>
> Alexis de Tocqueville, *Democracy in America*

Defining Coherence in Politics

Coherence and Reasonableness in Politics

'Coherence' is about identifying the qualities that make a system of government a good one. What it is exactly that would make a European system of government 'coherent' is not an esoteric issue of interest only to political theorists; it is of the greatest practical importance. The reason for this is that some very common traditional assumptions about coherence – for example, that the system of government has to offer consistency and uniformity in the way that policies are applied and in the way that institutions and procedures work across the continent – collide headlong with one of the most striking features of contemporary societies: their pluralism. Within any large-scale society, and certainly within a continent-wide union, how the system of government deals with a plurality of beliefs, values and attitudes is a central issue – possibly *the* central issue – in the organization of the system of political choice. Pluralism argues for a political system to provide for variety. The virtues of uniformity and consistency argue against this. Thus the approach to coherence will be critical for the qualities of government and society in Europe.

The practical consequences for Europe's framework for government of different approaches to coherence are underlined in this chapter. It argues that the framework must offer an explicit treatment of the requirements for tolerance across Europe and should not attempt to impose values beyond the requirements for entry and membership in the union.

One way of identifying the issues surrounding 'coherence' is to equate coherent government with the notion of a 'well-ordered' system of government.[1] Unfortunately, this is not a definition that helps in any way at all. Almost anything one wishes to choose can be read into the phrase 'well-ordered'. A better starting point is provided by the connotations of the word 'coherence' itself. Its use is closely connected with the processes of reasoning – thus in everyday discussion people may be inclined to dismiss arguments that strike them as 'incoherent'.[2] In the context of a democratic system of government, the issue of 'coherence' can therefore be approached as trying to identify the qualities that make a democratic system of government 'reasonable'.

'Reasonable' is not the first word that springs to mind when one listens to Europe's politicians speak, or to the sound of a crowd demonstrating in a Brussels street. So much goes on in democratic politics, and in the expression of political opinions, that is not rational that it would seem any search for coherence defined in terms of what is reasonable will be predestined for failure. As discussed earlier, the essence of democratic politics is the combination of reason and passion. However, irrationality in politics makes the framework even more important. What it means is that a democratic framework has to provide a way of processing and containing irrational as well as rational expression. Coherence in a system of government is thus essentially about the reasonableness of the political structure in the sense of a framework for politics that is reasonable, given that it has to contain both rational and irrational behaviour by groups and individuals.[3]

Alternative Approaches to Coherence

This chapter examines three traditional approaches about how to make Europe's framework of government reasonable before comparing them with what the model of 'simplicity' has to say about coherence:

- '*Uniformity*': According to this approach, the union will not be coherent unless policies are uniformly applied across the entire European political space. For a policy to be applied in one part of the union and not in another fails the test of what is reasonable in a framework of government.
- '*Consistency*': This is a less rigorous test than is uniformity for what makes a system coherent because it just requires the framework to provide for policies and procedures that are mutually consistent. They can be consistent without necessarily being the same everywhere.
- '*Core values*': This approach essentially rejects the tests of uniformity and consistency on the grounds that they demand too much of a system of government that has to provide a framework for pluralism of values and beliefs in society. It suggests instead the identification of those areas where there are 'overlapping values' on which everybody agrees. The framework should be coherent in the more limited sense of its approach to these core values.

Each of these approaches has practical consequences for the way in which Europe's system of government will be built. 'Uniformity' encourages the view that the political system is more coherent the more that the same rules and regulations apply everywhere. It is therefore hardly surprising that the model of 'Jurists' Europe' prizes uniformity as a key quality to be promoted by the spread of European law into as many areas as possible. By contrast, the test of 'consistency' is attractive to those who take a holistic approach to public policy, and thus appeals to the model of an 'Eco-social Europe'. This is because 'consistency' encourages the view that Europe's system of political choice must allow for as complete a set of public policies as possible to be pursued across Europe since this is the best way of ensuring an integrated approach to public policy. Moving away both from the test of uniformity and the test of consistency, an emphasis on 'core values' takes a more limited approach to what the political system should concern itself with. It is more compatible with the idea of Europe as an 'Order of States' because the idea of overlapping values is closely related to the idea of separate but overlapping identities.

The approach to coherence offered by 'simplicity' differs from each of these traditional approaches. Instead, it suggests that in a pluralist society a reasonable framework for politics has to focus on the design for 'tolerance'. Even in societies where, at some high level of generality, core values are indeed shared or overlap, people may still reasonably differ on how to balance, interpret and apply them. The approach thus identifies tolerance as the key to making a system of political choice reasonable in today's world. It justifies tolerance as the quality to be sought in a reasonable system of government for Europe. Among the different approaches to coherence, a simple system of government will offer by far the greatest degree of tolerance.

Practical Consequences

The differences in the ways in which the issue of coherence can be approached are not trivial; they have a practical importance for the way in which Europe's system of government actually evolves. For example, within the existing union an exercise took place in 2000 to draw up a Charter of Fundamental Rights. This exercise has appealed, among others, to those who would like the union to define its core values as a way of making the powers and responsibilities of the union and its institutions more coherent. It does not appeal in the same way to those who value tolerance because such a charter can lead to the imposition of a centrally determined interpretation of important values. It can become a way of limiting pluralism. A debate is now underway as to whether the charter should, or should not be, incorporated as part of the basic law of the existing union.

A completely different example of a much more insidious kind of practical issue in the existing union is given by the new provision for the funding out of the Community budget of political parties represented in the European Parliament. The funding is not to be used to fund political parties at the national level.

At first sight this provision seems eminently reasonable. It addresses real problems for representative government in Europe: the current lack of pan-European parties and high entry costs. In addition, it addresses an equally genuine problem in that there are some political parties at the national level in Europe that have their roots in an anti-democratic past of communism or fascism and that endorse views that are morally repugnant to many. If the view is taken that Europe's system of government must be based on implementing core principles uniformly and consistently across Europe, then such provisions seem reasonable because they encourage one set of principles – which most people would agree with – and they discourage another. In other words, the provision about how the framework for politics is to be set up in Europe can pass three of the tests of what makes a system of government coherent: uniformity, consistency and conformity with core values. The test that questions the provision is that of 'tolerance', because the provision sets limits to the toleration of unpalatable and undemocratic views.

The test of tolerance forces further reflection on official funding for approved European parties. Possibly the preferable way to deal with parties espousing anti-democratic and morally repugnant views is to expose their arguments to counter-facts and to alternative values. If the electoral system is deliberately loaded against them, then their contempt for democratic procedures may simply be accentuated; their view that European political union is a conspiracy could even be given some plausibility in fact. Looking further at the other side of the equation, a number of democratic parties that would receive funding under the terms of the resolution have their origins in religious affiliation – that of Christian democracy. Since Europe's system of government has to represent non-Christian views as well as Christian, it is not at all clear that public funding of parties with a religious background – even an attenuated one – would be desirable in a multi-belief society. Moreover, a number of policy areas – for example, those that relate to family values – may set those whose moral views stem from religious precepts against those who look at such issues from a secular perspective. Public funding of parties with a religious background may be seen as tilting the terms of the debate.

In short, the provision helps entrench the main parties now represented in the European Parliament and takes an approach to the arrangements for a European system of government that is in conformity with some views of what it takes for a system of government to be 'coherent', but in potential conflict with one of them. The outcome of this and other debates about Europe's system of government cannot be a matter of indifference and may be of very great practical importance to the kind of system that eventually emerges.

The Two Sides of Coherence

There are two sides to what can be said to make systems of government coherent or reasonable. One way is to look for the system to be substantively coherent. That is to say, its reasonableness is judged by what it does. The other way is to look for the system to be procedurely coherent. That is to say, the system must be reasonable in the way it approaches the democratic formation of public policy.

For the system to be rational from a substantive point of view, there must be an idea of the kind of society the political system is intended to promote and the kinds of beliefs and the kinds of public policies it is to foster. The political system is seen as not just about compromise and living together, but also about implementing common principles. The institutions and procedures of a coherent system of government are seen in terms of providing the means to the end of achieving substantive principles and goals.

Procedural rationality looks instead to procedural values for the important qualities in a political system. For example, one is provided by the democratic ideal itself. According to the democratic ideal, the institutions and procedures of the political system should aim to produce policies and priorities generally in line with what people want. What the actual substance of those choices might be can be left open. It is accepted that people can want many different things over time and that their wants may change.

Each of the different approaches to coherence tries to give an account that addresses both aspects of the reasonableness of a system of political choice for Europe. In other words, each account tries to explain what coherence involves in terms of the substance of European politics as well as explaining what coherence means in terms of the procedures of Europe's system of government. The different ways in which they try to meet both these objectives are described below.

Uniformity

'Uniformity' as a measure of the coherence of a system of government starts from the premise that a political system such as Europe's stands for some overall concept of justice and fairness. The system of politics must uphold the integrity of the communities that have come together in a union and treat people in that new community equally, fairly and according to a substantive conception of what equality and fairness are all about. According to this view, concepts such as social inclusion and social solidarity can help give shape and substance to notions of justice and fairness and help anchor a system of government for Europe.

Uniformity is a powerful procedural criterion for coherence because it is a way of putting substance into practice and making principle real. As a procedural measure of coherence, the criterion of uniformity holds that the institutions and procedures of the union should concern themselves with implementing the overall concept of justice and fairness in a uniform way. By contrast, a patchwork approach to rules, legislation and adjudication seems intrinsically undesirable. It can encourage arbitrary choices by those with political power because no common principles need to be invoked. It can lead to people being treated differently when there is no principle to justify different treatment. It can lead to inequality before the law. Thus it is uniform law, uniformly applied, that ensures the coherence and integrity of the system with the overall concept of justice and fairness.[4]

In practical terms, the appeal of uniformity is one of the driving forces behind the idea that more and more powers and competences should belong to the current union. It is only through the extension of competences that the uniform and equal treatment of everybody throughout the union can be ensured. The debate about uniformity is also very much alive in the difficulties the existing union confronts with enlargement. On one side are those who stress the need for new members to accept and apply the rules of the existing members on a uniform basis so that the union does not become a patchwork quilt of different obligations. On the other side are those who argue that the union must have the flexibility to allow different members to do different things around a fixed core of common obligations.

There are two main weaknesses in the account of coherence given by uniformity. One is the need to know more about the substance to be applied. The idea that there is a common conception of justice and fairness to be applied uniformly is too vague. The criterion becomes open to abuse as an instrument to apply unclear substantive ideas and principles uniformly. Thus the treaties of the existing union are sometimes criticized for not setting out powers and responsibilities clearly and thereby allowing too much scope for expansive legal interpretations of what needs to be uniformly treated.

Within the existing European union, in practical terms, it is also this vagueness that leads many lawyers to wish to see the union have its own charter of fundamental rights. A charter is seen to provide a way of making clear what justice and fairness are all about and what the mandate of the legal system is. This, however, leads to the second source of weakness in uniformity as a measure of coherence.

This second weakness is that it fails as a procedural criterion. If uniformity is a virtue, then it is tempting to conclude that the more there is uniformity, the better. This bias gives a misleading and possibly dangerous guide to authority in a political system. Since it treats uniformity as a 'good', it takes an indiscriminate view of the range of authority needed by the political system. It tends to treat any extension of central authority as good because that will promote uniform treatment throughout a union. Such an attitude towards authority in a political system is far too permissive. Efforts to define where authority is required and to maintain the checks and balances needed on the exercise of authority are placed under constant pressure or go out of the window entirely.

Consistency

'Consistency' is a less demanding test for the coherence of a political system than is uniformity because it does not insist that everything should be the same everywhere. At the same time, the idea that consistency should be sought in the arrangements for a system of political choice is an attractive one at first sight. It provides the image of a European people who know what their main belief systems and values are and what they want to accomplish through political choice.[5]

As a measure of the substantive coherence of a political system, consistency lends itself to a holistic view of politics and the sense that the range of policies to be pursued must be 'integrated'. The goals of political union are seen not in terms of separate and possibly disconnected objectives, such as the pursuit of a common defence policy and the pursuit of the free movement of people, but as an integrated set of goals that reflect a coherent overall set of beliefs and values. If these goals and belief systems are thought of in holistic terms, then the political system should provide the legislative framework in which an overall body of beliefs can hang together. The legal system is similarly seen as providing for a morally coherent total set of laws. From a holistic perspective, both the political system and the legal system should try to avoid conflicting sub-systems.

There are a number of political viewpoints represented in the debate about the future of a continent-wide union that espouse a holistic perspective on principles and policies. The holism of green parties is one of the sources of their appeal. For those who adopt a holistic approach to politics, a coherent system of government for

Europe will be one that is judged in large part by the consistency with which the framework makes possible the pursuit of a holistic view of European society.

As a procedural test, consistency provides a powerful rationale for implementing a complete range of policies. It suggests that a coherent system of political choice in Europe must offer the kind of institutional and procedural framework needed so as to ensure consistency between the integrated political ends to be pursued and the political means that can be mobilized. The more complete the range of policies to be pursued, the more the system must work to achieve consistency.

In practice, the assumption that Europe should aim for 'completeness' is one of the driving forces behind the desire of some to extend the existing union into all areas of activity, together with ever more accompanying detail. If the view is that a continent-wide union is about putting in place an eco-friendly social market, then the political system for Europe must have an integrated set of powers, instruments and institutions to pursue this vision in all its ramifications: from an 'ethical' foreign and defence policy, to a green farming policy, to a sustainable energy policy and to the attainment of high social standards in the workplace. For many, this is an attractive vision. Politicians too fall for putting all the attributes that might be considered desirable in society into the objectives of European political union because, in this way, they can appeal to everyone and offend no one. However, it is not a way to build a coherent system of political choice.

The flaw in looking at systems of political choice in terms of consistency and completeness is that it runs counter to some important practical ways in which the substance and procedures of political and social choice are actually approached.

First, in respect of the substance of politics, it overstates the importance of the need for an integrated set of beliefs.[6] On the contrary, political systems have to allow for the situation where people may be able to reach agreement in particular circumstances on the basis of rather narrowly defined principles but may not be able to agree on the more general principles. For example, many cases in law are settled on the basis of the facts of a particular case, leaving the general principles to emerge, if at all, from a body of related cases. Even in the case of very important values, it may be possible to act without a general set of beliefs. For example, people may be able to decide what constitutes discrimination against certain groups in society, even if they are less certain about its application to other groups and have no general theory of what constitutes discrimination or not. It is possibly dangerous for society if its political system is set up to implement all-embracing ideologies rather than practical solutions to practical problems.[7]

Secondly, and relatedly, the demand for consistency over a set of beliefs does not appear to correspond to the way people actually approach the taking of decisions. The main accounts of rational choice have the common feature that, in one way or another, people seem to take decisions not against the background of a consistent and integrated view of their values and priorities, but following a more selective procedure of what is most relevant to them and by limiting their focus of attention. It seems that in everyday life people do not have complete systems of norms, or do not know quite what weight they attach to particular values. Instead, they approach their choices in ways that save time and attention by, for example, following conventions or rules of thumb.[8] Thus to look for completeness in a system of political choice is over-demanding. Instead, a system is needed that is salient to people's concerns – a much more selective criterion. Europe thus should not attempt to do everything but, instead, do only what is salient and only that part of salient policy-making that it is well suited for.[9]

Thirdly, from a procedural perspective, the demand for consistency overlooks one highly important feature of democratic politics: that, in democracies, power alternates. As a result, the policies that are pursued in a democratic system over time may well not be consistent at all. Moreover, what sustains faith in a democratic system is that precisely those people who may be excluded from power at one point feel nevertheless that their time may yet come at a future point. At that future point they may wish to reverse policies or take them in a quite different direction. From this perspective, it is inconsistency that is the hallmark of a democratic system of choice. To look for the system to promote consistency is fundamentally undemocratic.[10]

Finally, some of the most well-established procedures for trying to reach agreement in societies represent agreements that are deliberately left incomplete. For example, people might be able to accept a very general principle but not be able to agree on particular applications. Thus it is not uncommon for constitutional arrangements to set down general descriptions of institutional roles or important principles, such as the right to vote, but to leave the detail to evolve in practice.[11] The Constitution of the United States, famous for its brevity, is a leading example. Europe too has to think carefully where in its system of government it wants fixity and definition and where it wants flexibility and open-endedness.

The idea that coherence can be approached through the test of either uniformity or consistency is thus undermined. Each tries to be too comprehensive in its approach to what constitutes substantive coherence and too demanding in its treatment of procedural coherence. As a result they provide misleading and possibly dangerous accounts of both substantive and procedural coherence. Europe should discard each of these approaches to defining what would make its system of government coherent and reasonable.

An approach that is much less vulnerable to these defects, however, is the idea that in order to achieve coherence in a system of political choice, coherence need be sought only in a limited sense – coherence can be found by defining the core values in the system. This looks a much more promising approach for Europe. It suggests that, across a highly diversified continent, coherence need be sought only in terms of the most important values that are shared throughout.

Core Values

Defining the reasonableness of a system of political choice in terms of its coherence around a set of 'core values' stresses the need for agreement on beliefs and principles in only a limited area. According to this view, in today's pluralist world, coherence is given to a system of government not by a comprehensive agreement on moral or philosophical beliefs but instead through political agreement on a limited set of 'overlapping' values to which all subscribe and which can give stability to a constitutional system of political choice. It is an account of coherence that therefore decisively rejects the view that a system of politics is needed that applies a holistic view of the substance of politics in a uniform and consistent way across a political union such as Europe. On the contrary, the suggestion is that the need is to focus on the characteristics of a system of political choice independent of comprehensive religious, moral or philosophical doctrines because comprehensive beliefs will not be shared in a pluralist society.[12]

The idea that the coherence of a political system is to be found through agreement on a limited set of values is targeted at a central feature of all large contemporary systems of government, one that is crucial to the future of a continent-wide union: the pluralism of modern societies. A continent-wide union will contain a multiplicity of different belief and value systems and many different views on how to interpret even those values that seem to be held in common. The diversity of Europe is not reflected in the villages of Bavaria; it is reflected on the streets of London. In London, it has been estimated that about one quarter of the total seven million population represents ethnic minorities of one sort or another. If the qualities of Europe's system of government are not defined in a way that responds to this pluralism, the continent will never arrive at a system of government based on the consent and respect of its peoples and communities.

Coherence defined as centring the political system on core values steers a path through the confusion of the many different substantive values in a pluralist society by identifying the area in such a society where core values overlap. In substantive terms, 'the core' consists of those values that relate to basic questions of justice.

From the perspective of procedural coherence, the idea that the political system should be looked at independently of religious, moral or philosophical doctrines does not mean that political arrangements are being viewed just as practical working arrangements – a grand *modus vivendi*. The approach also offers a set of constitutional values. It suggests that constitutionalism should be valued in itself as a means to tie a political union together. It suggests also that consensus should be valued. In addition, underlying both the constitutional norm and the valuing of a consensus, is a third value judgement: that there is a benefit from stability in a system of political choice. Stability is to be valued because it reduces the uncertainty in people's relationships in the union.

Despite the enormous merit of trying to define coherence in Europe's system of government in a way that places pluralism at the centre of its concerns, there are, nevertheless, three types of objection to this particular approach to pluralism. The first is that there is no clear guide to what makes up the necessary core substantive values. A basic conception of justice can include almost anything.

A second objection is that the existence of a consensus around a core set of values is not a test of the rightness of that consensus or of those values. There can be a social consensus that is later seen to be clearly wrong. Philosophers express this thought by saying that social communities do not have epistemic authority in themselves. That is to say, that because a social community says that something is the case, or that something is right or wrong, does not necessarily mean that it is so. Instead, epistemic authority lies in the justifying evidence possessed by a social community. In other words, the assertions of the community must be supported by valid reasons.[13] Another way of questioning the value of a consensus is to say that even if one looks for agreement in a limited area, there still remains a need to look at the adaptive and learning qualities of any system of government. Better, or more recent, knowledge may change the consensus or improve its quality. Consensus by itself is thus not necessarily a good measure of the coherence of a system of government because it may be built around faulty values or values that will change. At best it can only be one element in judgement.[14]

There is, in addition, a third reason why the idea of an overlapping consensus does not help in defining the coherence of a continent-wide system of government. The weakness is that it fails in its own terms. It does not provide the guidance needed to address the political organization of a pluralist and multicultural society. In order to do this, there is a need to look specifically at how systems of government treat the issue of tolerance. Approaching pluralism as a matter of defining and implementing core values provides for a greater degree of tolerance than do approaches that define coherence in a system of government in terms of uniformity and consistency. But the system of government could, and likely would, see it to be its duty and obligation to promote those core values – even if they lend themselves to many interpretations and combinations. Thus tolerance for the differences in a pluralist society could still remain greatly restricted.[15]

Thus each of the traditional approaches to defining what would make Europe's system of government 'coherent' is flawed. The criteria of uniformity and consistency ignore the problem of what kind of system would be best suited to a pluralist society such as Europe. The idea of viewing coherence around the implementation of core values also does not get to grips with pluralism because it fudges the key question of how and to what extent a coherent system of government should reflect the quality of tolerance, or, instead, impose values.

Tolerance in a Political System

As a matter of logic, the fact that a society holds plural values does not mean that it necessarily has to make arrangements to tolerate those differences.[16] However, the essence of a democratic society is that it provides safeguards against the suppression of alternative views about what is right or wrong or good or bad. In the final analysis a majority may decide – but that too is subject to safeguards. Thus, as a practical matter, the arrangements for tolerance are of central importance for a democratic system of government in Europe. They provide a means of focusing on the question of how far a system of government in a pluralist society should expect to have to handle divergent opinions, even on important values that seem to be held in common; a means of examining what the constitutional arrangements for handling those differences should be; how far they should extend; and what the underlying justification for such techniques would be. Each of the hitherto discussed approaches to what would make Europe's system of government coherent suggests that the toleration of differences should be limited. By contrast, a simple framework provides the greatest scope for the tolerance of differences and a justification for that approach. At the same time it does not suggest that a system of government should be viewed merely as a system of accommodation.

The Centrality of Tolerance

Tolerance is an unheroic value. It stands for 'live and let live' or 'agreeing to disagree'. Sometimes differences about values seem to concern only 'second-order' differences – that is to say, the difference arises not over the value itself but, for example, over whether a value fits a particular situation or not. But tolerance is also, and more importantly, about clashes between values themselves, the different interpretations to be given to important values and the different weightings that may be given in situations where more than one value is relevant. Thus, toleration is about agreeing not to interfere with policies, measures and beliefs – even if they represent important values we do not agree with and believe we have reason not to agree with.[17] By contrast each of the previous accounts of coherence offers a 'heroic' vision of what a political system is about. Each suggests that there are at least some substantive values that Europe's system of politics should be designed to implement.

The practice of toleration is vulnerable to the criticism that all values are being treated as relative and that no one value is being treated as worthy of greater respect than another. This criticism is mistaken. Tolerance may appeal to those who consider all beliefs and values to be relative but it does not depend on such a view. On the contrary, people may hold clear views on what is good or bad, and how to interpret their most important values in particular circumstances, but still accept the idea that tolerance is a virtue in a political system so that different views about what is good are allowed.[18]

Despite its unheroic stature, toleration addresses fundamental questions about the design of political systems. It asks about the norms of accommodation within a political system. It asks how far the procedures and institutions of a political union should be designed deliberately to accommodate differences and in what way differences should be handled, and whether just accommodation itself should be seen as sufficient.[19]

One of the difficulties in answering these questions is that attitudes towards toleration can themselves vary enormously.[20] The scale of possible responses to diversity in society ranges from indifference and resigned acceptance, at one end, to a positive welcoming of diversity, at the other. Folk-sayings such as 'You mind your business and I'll mind mine' represent some kind of mid-ground where the implication is that society will be better off if people are allowed to get on with doing their own thing without interference from others. Another way of expressing the mid-ground is to see toleration as a way of expressing mutual respect in the face of disagreement.[21]

Nevertheless, despite the unheroic stature of toleration and ambiguous attitudes towards it, the questions are not ones that can be ducked. A continent-wide system of government for Europe will have to deal with a plurality of belief systems and values as well as huge differences in judgements about circumstance and aptness when applying values. Although differences in Europe are often presented as ones that are mainly about differences of interest, it is differences about how to interpret and weigh together important values in society that are every bit as important.[22]

Sometimes it is asserted that tolerance only concerns a limited range of issues in social choice: for example, those that involve religion or sex. According to this view, tolerance only becomes an issue when society is having to decide how to deal with the extremes of expression, such as homophobia or incitements to racial hatred. It is indeed the case historically that debate about tolerance had its origins in debates about religious belief and freedom of expression.[23] However, in today's societies it does not seem possible to regard questions of tolerance as arising only in limited circumstances. On the contrary, the issue arises wherever public policy brings about clashes in what people consider to be important values. Most ordinary choices involve plural values – often important ones. It therefore seems more reasonable to view tolerance not as referring to exceptions among the subject matter of choice, but as referring to a much more prevalent range of choices.[24]

Irreconcilable differences about values arise from four main sources in contemporary society. First the extent to which people hold fervent, systematic and incompatible religious beliefs has probably declined with the decline of organized religion generally. But religiously derived moral attitudes towards issues of public policy remain widespread and provide one continuing source of value differences. Attitudes towards family and partnership questions, towards genetic engineering and towards education are examples of many areas of public concern where religion plays a role in forming attitudes.

Leaving religion behind as a source of differences, a second source of value differences arises from the many non-religious value or belief systems that can lead to clashes that cannot be resolved by logic and reason alone. For example, many environmental organizations have an attitude towards environmental questions that has little to do with the science involved, or a willingness to acknowledge the gaps and uncertainties in scientific knowledge, and much to do with a belief system.

A third source of value difference is that, even in cases where fundamental beliefs are shared at some abstract and general level, there will still frequently be differences about how to interpret a basic value. For example, most people would subscribe in some general way to the view of the sanctity of human life. But society and the law have revealed changing boundaries over such aspects as the extent to which people are permitted to take a life when acting in self-defence, or in defence of another person or in the defence of property.

Finally, there is an even greater divergence of attitudes when new social issues are involved – such as arise with medical advances and the prolongation of lives. In such cases there may well be uncertainty about which values are relevant, as well as different views about their application.

The issue of pluralism has therefore become less a question of incompatible religious belief systems and much more a question of the different interpretations that people can put on values that may often be shared at a high level of generality. The differences frequently arise not from differences in basic values when a particular value is considered on its own at an abstract level, but because in typical circumstances the question is about how to weigh one value with another, or is about differing judgements about how to apply relevant values, or about their aptness in particular circumstances or in specific contexts. The clash is not about religious or moral absolutes but about interpretation.[25] The fact that different communities in Europe will bring different values and different interpretations to bear on public policy will thus need to be reflected as a central element in the design of Europe's system of political choice.

The Institutional Arrangements for Tolerance

A system of political choice can institutionalize arrangements for toleration, or for setting limits on the toleration of differences, in many different ways. But three distinctions seem particularly useful.[26]

One distinction is that of 'prescriptive' authority: the extent to which the system should prescribe values to be implemented in the union. A declaration of rights in a constitution is often seen as a way of providing the system with prescriptive authority. If a European charter of fundamental rights were to be treated in this way, then the rights and values selected for inclusion in the charter would be the ones to be prescribed and implemented across a continent-wide union.

A second distinction is that of 'decisiveness' authority. This refers to the circumstances in which the system specifies that the values are to be decisively applied. For example, within the existing European union there is a provision that says that measures about certain types of discrimination may be taken by the Council of Ministers. This is a way of saying that the circumstances and timing of applying some highly important values will be determined through a political process. Under these arrangements the Council has decisiveness authority because it can decide when and where to implement key values.

A third distinction concerns 'commitment' authority: the extent to which the institutions are charged with a commitment to implement fundamental values. It is possible to have a declaration of what a political union stands for without necessarily charging the institutions with the commitment authority to implement it. For example, the founding fathers of the American system of government saw the fundamental values being understood and guarded by the people themselves. Equally it would be possible for a charter of rights for Europe's political union to state what the union stands for without charging its institutions with a commitment to deliver those values.

For example, implementation could be left in the hands of the institutions of the member states and their regions and the Court of Human Rights in Strasbourg or it could vest them in the people themselves and not in government at all.

These distinctions make it possible to differentiate between three main approaches to providing different degrees of toleration in political association in Europe.

Comprehensive Authority for the Union   The first and least tolerant approach is that a political system should have comprehensive authority in asserting fundamental values. The system thus will prescribe key values, give commitment authority to its institutions and possess the authority to decide on the circumstances in which to apply the values. This far-reaching authority requires that the union must have sorted out its fundamental values in advance.

The advantage of this comprehensive approach is that it gives people a way of judging the overall nature of the bargain in agreeing to a political union. The disadvantage is that if the political system is viewed as one where fundamental values must be pre-set, then the scope for the tolerance for differences is limited. No exceptions are allowed in the areas of core values and differences are allowed only in other, less important areas. There is, moreover, no way of telling how large or small this area for allowable differences will be. Even minor issues of public policy may be seen to raise some fundamental point. Decision-taking techniques will correspondingly allow for differences in rather limited circumstances outside areas of core policy. Secession may not be permitted. Instead, in a case where a unit of government, such as a member state or region, attempts to interpret values in a way that is seen to be incompatible with the values authorized by the union, there will be an attempt to impose values.

Limiting Decisiveness   The second approach is to set time-limits to tolerance by reserving or conditioning the circumstances in which the system can act decisively. The main way this can be done is to allow the system to incorporate fundamental values over time – either as cases arise through the judicial system, or as legislative initiatives are taken.

The advantage of this approach is that differences are allowed in the initial position of starting out on political union, but the system achieves a common interpretation of fundamental values over time through the incorporation route. This enables movement from a starting position where there may be only a limited consensus on values towards a situation of much broader convergence.

This approach allows for a greater degree of tolerance in the sense that it sees convergence as taking place over time rather than being a condition to be insisted on at the outset. It sees convergence on fundamental values as something to be pursued as an objective by the institutions, but permits differences until the institutions have legislated or adjudicated. It is tolerant of differences and sub-systems up to that point.

The disadvantage is that the incorporation process is a highly discretionary one. The pace of incorporation lies entirely in the hands of the institutions with the authority to act decisively. In the case of the United States, it is the judicial branch – the Supreme Court – that has been the crucial actor. In the case of Europe, the pace of incorporation would likely be shared between the judiciary and other union institutions, such as the European Parliament and the Council.

It is possible that the institutions will act only when a consensus has emerged – in other words they will act to ratify generally accepted values. But such institutions are not necessarily well placed to judge whether a consensus has emerged, and the more likely stance of the institutions is to be activist in some way or another – in other words, to take the lead in proposing a common interpretation for important values. The more they move ahead of public opinion, the less tolerant the system. The less that the institutions are truly representative, the less tolerant the system. The more the institutions indulge in politically correct 'gesture politics', the less tolerant the system.

Limiting Commitment Authority   The third approach limits the commitment authority of the system of government. In the case of Europe, this would mean that the conditions of entry into the union could prescribe core values, but the institutions of the political association would have no further obligation to prescribe selected values, or the institutions given the commitment authority to implement them, or to decide in which circumstances they might be implemented. This would result either in 'trusting the people' to stand up for their own rights and values, as the founding fathers of the United States were inclined to trust, or it would mean trusting the different units that make up a union – in Europe's case, the member states and their regions – to look after fundamental values in their own ways.

This approach is the most tolerant of the three since it allows for tolerance for all values that are about policy principles and priorities within the system of political choice outside those that are conditions of membership.

The Arrangements for Tolerance and the Measures of Coherence

Different approaches to what would make Europe's system of government coherent result in a different evaluation of these possible treatments for tolerance:

- The benchmark of uniformity suggests that tolerance should be limited. The principles of justice and fairness are not principles to be applied in different ways in different places. The more expansive the definitions of justice and fairness, the less room there is for the tolerance of differences. In order to ensure a uniform application of norms of justice and fairness, a political union will need comprehensive authority over all key values related to justice and fairness in society.
- The criterion of consistency also suggests that tolerance should be limited. Europe's system of government needs comprehensive authority in order to implement a complete, integrated and consistent set of values.
- The model of core values limits the prescriptive and commitment authority of the union's system of government to the core area of overlapping values. At the same time, it allows union institutions to have limited decisiveness in other areas so that other values can be joined to the core as consensus is reached.

What each of these measures of a coherent and reasonable system of political choice therefore does is to set limits on tolerance. The idea that coherence can be defined around core values allows for a greater degree of tolerance than do the approaches that stress uniformity and consistency. Nevertheless, the limits could still, in practice, be severe. What constitutes 'core values' could be interpreted in expansive ways to cover almost all that is important in a society (as is the case in the proposed charter of fundamental rights of the existing union). Thus, a charter of fundamental rights becomes a means to impose values.[27]

What distinguishes 'simplicity' as a guide to the coherence of a system of government is that it is consistent with arrangements for the widest degree of tolerance in Europe – where the institutions of the union would not have the commitment authority to implement key values. The model for a simple system of governance for Europe looks to the conditions of membership to establish the coherence of the union. The conditions ensure respect for society's two systems of choice: the market and democratic political choice. Beyond this point, however, the framework allows for different interpretations and applications of key values in society.[28]

Justifying a Simple Framework for Tolerance

The justification for institutional arrangements that allow for the widest scope for tolerance is that the model of 'simplicity' looks on a political system as a way to learn and to sift good ideas from the bad.[29] It is this that leads it towards accepting the greatest degree of tolerance in a political association where the institutions of the union need no commitment authority over how key values are interpreted within the system of political choice.

Because there are many different ideas in Europe about what is good and worth pursuing and differences of opinion on how to interpret important values, the model of 'simplicity' does not try to put in place arrangements for organization and authority that promote or impose a single view about how to interpret important values. Instead, it views a coherent system of government as one that is about setting procedural standards that may lead communities to greater knowledge about their most important values, rather than trying to impose a conception of the truth about those values. Thus it allows for different rules to coexist alongside each other in the union so that rules with different interpretations of 'richness' can coexist with rules with reach. In some cases, jurisdictions will find that the variations they wanted are not as good as they thought. In other cases, the variations may prove their worth and the union will want to modify the general rule. Similarly, the model allows for maximizing the value of the language of rights as a way to explore values in society and to bring together those who feel very differently about the interpretation of important values. It accepts that this will lead to great variety in the interpretation and application of such values, but this is tolerated up to the point that the basic conditions for membership are violated. 'Simplicity' is not just accommodation.

The practical expectation is that in a political union where everything is subject to media examination, public debate and public comparison and peer review, a learning process will take place. The best setting for a learning process, and for ideas to be sorted between the good and the bad, is to allow for both good and bad to be fully expressed and for convergence to follow, if at all, from discussion and practice.

When the method of democratic politics is viewed in terms of learning, the criteria of both completeness and uniformity are seen to be lacking an extremely important aspect of procedural coherence. In order for the framework of politics to be reasonable, the system of political choice must be able to adapt and respond to changing circumstances. Ways are needed in which new information can be absorbed, local learning processes are utilized and outside influences can register. There is a need to allow for 'system effects' where changes in one part of the system will ripple across to another, and the system must be able to respond to feedback. All of this can be achieved under a simple form of government for Europe. Little or none of this can be done if the aim is to look for how best to implement a uniform and consistent system.[30]

The model of a simple system of government also adopts a different approach to coherence than that suggested by an emphasis on core values. This difference arises because the model of simplicity sees consensus around core values as a highly imperfect basis for achieving the kind of tolerance that will be needed in a highly diverse society. If core values are defined too broadly, then little room will be left for the tolerance of differences at all. Even if they are defined narrowly, the fact that a consensus exists may still not justify their imposition on those who are not part of the consensus.

The model of 'simplicity' suggests that a single interpretation of core beliefs and values is unnecessary for making choices within politics. What is needed instead is a method for choosing that makes it possible to separate superior concepts of what is substantively good from inferior concepts. This cannot be done unless different concepts are allowed to coexist alongside each other. The widest allowance for tolerance needs to be institutionalized.

Placing such a large stress on tolerance is not value-free from a procedural perspective since it assumes that society should encourage systems of governance that give people the widest possibilities of pursuing whatever their goals and values are. It allows for consensus to emerge over time, since it is through exposing beliefs and exposing conflicting interpretations of values and different policies to examination that people will gradually discard what does not stand up to inspection and examination. Even if consensus on the interpretation of important values does emerge, consensus cannot itself be the test. A consensus may change and it may be mistaken.

The approach offered to coherence by a simple model for Europe's political framework therefore identifies 'tolerance' as the key quality that would make Europe's democratic system of government reasonable. The criticism that a simple system of government for Europe will fail to provide a coherent system of government is thus a mistaken one.

The criticism that can be made of a simple system of government for Europe is of a different type. It is a criticism of tolerance itself. First, there are those who say that tolerance must be limited since Europe's system of government must project a European identity expressed in terms of key substantive values. Secondly, there are those who say that tolerance must be limited because Europe's system of government must work in ways that promote Europe's highest values in order for it to have legitimacy.[31] These views are explored in the next chapter.

9 The Spirit of Europe

When each nation has its distinct opinions, belief, laws, and customs, it looks upon itself as the whole of mankind, and is moved by no sorrows but its own.

Alexis de Tocqueville, *Democracy in America*

Introduction

The 'Spirit of Europe' symbolizes the view that Europe's system of government must clearly express the key values that Europe stands for – the soul of Europe. It is a view that, if accepted, would limit tolerance in Europe because tolerance allows for dissenting views about how to express and weigh key values. It is also a view that, if accepted, would object to a simple system of government for Europe on the grounds that a political union that is so open, so adaptable and so tolerant of differences will not be able to express the most important things that political union in Europe stands for.

The idea that Europe's system of government must in some way reflect a special spirit of Europe evokes an uncomfortable echo of nineteenth-century nationalism when poets and musicians searched for a vocabulary to reflect the unique spirit of their nation. What started as a genuine source of inspiration ended by tarnishing both art and politics. If this is all there is to the idea of the 'Spirit of Europe', then it should be quickly dismissed. In practice, for the reasons discussed below, and despite uncomfortable echoes of nationalism, the ideas behind the 'Spirit of Europe' cannot be so easily dismissed.

Definitions of what the 'Spirit of Europe' actually is aim to invoke two things. They aim to select what are the most important values for European society and they aim to identify what is uniquely European about them. Sometimes the invocation is to 'Christian Europe'. But this is offensive to the many millions in Europe who are not believers in Christian doctrine. Also, with the actual practice of religious belief in Europe much less pronounced than, say, in the Middle East or in the United States, it can hardly stand for what is unique about Europe. So much harm has been done in the world, not least in Europe itself, under the banner of religious belief that Christian belief would be an extraordinarily retrograde way of trying to express what Europe now stands for. Nowadays, even the British monarchy has the good sense to talk in terms of being a defender of all the faiths.

Leaving religious belief aside, the most frequent invocation of values refers to the ideas behind a European eco-social state. The suggestion is that in addition to the fundamental political freedoms, such as free expression, and in addition to providing a free and open marketplace, Europe places the highest value on social and environmental concerns. Social solidarity is singled out, not only in the sense of an obligation of society to provide material security for the poorest social groups, but also in the sense of the need to provide a safe environment by placing the highest value on sustainable development and the precautionary principle – in other words, on solidarity between generations.

It is this blend of values that is said to stand for something unique in the 'Spirit of Europe'. It seems to be believed by some that this combination places a higher value on social and environmental goals than, say, the American system of government and also a higher value on political freedoms than some other systems of government (in, say, the Middle East or in Asia). The suggestion that this is a unique combination of values also gives a moral dimension to the idea that Europe needs to develop as a global power. It suggests that Europe will bring its own special ethical flavour to international rule-making and rule-keeping and something that is visibly more than pure power politics, or a naked attempt to assert Europe's self-interest. In this it echoes a historical strand in the American approach to foreign policy: the sense that America has a moral calling in the world.

The idea that the 'Spirit of Europe' should somehow be crystallized in Europe's system of government is intended to serve three main purposes:

- Setting out the special character of the union would provide a target for success of the union and a measure of progress.
- It will help construct a sense of European identity and in particular help people identify with their new system of European government.
- It will help legitimate Europe's system of government because it will help ensure that the system is indeed consonant with Europe's highest social and moral values.

These views are important. What is deeply mistaken in them is to suppose that the idea of the 'Spirit of Europe' provides either a path to success for the system of government or a recipe for stimulating a sense of identity with it. Nor does the idea of the 'Spirit of Europe' provide a way of legitimizing Europe's system of government. This chapter discusses why.

Success

Alexis de Tocqueville made a famous long-range prediction in the 1830s, in his *Democracy in America*, that the future would belong to two great powers: the United States and Russia. At the time when he made it, when the world was still dominated by European powers such as France and Austria, it seemed far-fetched. Yet for much of the period after the Second World War his prediction seemed to have come true. Ironically, it is the collapse of Russia as a great power that is a truer test of Tocqueville's analysis. Communist Russia suppressed both systems of choice: the market and political choice. If Russia had continued strong, this would have constituted a decisive falsification of Tocqueville's approach to government, which stressed the importance of both systems' full functioning.

Winners and Losers in the Twenty-First Century

Tocqueville's insistence that societies can only flourish if they make best use of two mutually supportive systems of choice enables us to speculate on the winners and losers in the twenty-first century. If Russia succeeds in re-establishing both the market and democratic choice, it will be a winner. At the moment, with neither the market nor the system of democratic political choice fully established, it does not look like a future success story. But extraordinary success of the type predicted by Tocqueville could yet be in the making. At the same time, although there have been many predictions about the pending eclipse of the United States, there seems no reason to believe that America will not continue to be an extraordinarily successful society as long as its system of governance remains healthy.

Suggestions about the inevitable decline of the United States range from pessimism about the moral climate to fears about 'imperial overstretch'.[1] The arguments in this book support neither view. On the contrary, as far as America's international role is concerned, the analysis suggests that America is more likely to find its success eroded by trying to close itself off from the external world than by over-involving itself. Its embrace of market choice can only succeed in the context of a global economy where market rules are respected inter-nationally, and this means that the United States will have to remain fully involved in setting the international rules. In addition, its system of political choice will need to remain open to learn from what is going on in other systems of government elsewhere in the world. Its broad self-interest in rule-based international behaviour means also that America will need to keep generally involved in international rule-making. It will need to remain an active convenor of rule-making and rule-enforcing alliances in the world.

As far as the moral climate in America is concerned, the problem is that there are too many strongly held moral beliefs rather than too few. It is this that helps make tolerance such a critical quality for America, as for other modern societies. In many ways the United States is an extraordinarily tolerant society, and in welcoming immi-grants it has provided a refuge for generations of victims of intoler-ance elsewhere. At the same time it harbours many groups, including immigrant groups, whose views are themselves very intolerant. The incorporation doctrine of the Supreme Court has been developed in part to combat intolerance. Nevertheless, it remains questionable whether the process of providing a single interpretation to important values, where differences could be allowed, has not gone too far and is now more likely to provoke rather than allay intolerance. In the interplay between rights-based political expression and vote-based expression, possibly too much weight is now given to rights claims and there is too great a propensity to try to settle such claims cen-trally.

Tocqueville contrasted the vigour of the early United States with the poor performance of countries elsewhere in the Americas. Yet at this point there seems reason to speculate that countries in Latin America will have much greater success in this century than in the last two. For most of the twentieth century, Latin American countries distorted the system of market choice and suppressed or semi-suppressed political choice as well. More recently there has been an attempt to reinstate both systems of choice. Whether and how far this will succeed is still not clear. If it does succeed, Tocqueville's analysis would lead us to believe that Latin America will finally deliver on its promise.

Conversely, there is reason to be gloomy about the prospects for Africa and parts of East Asia. Few countries in Africa have a democratically functioning system of political choice; few allow the market to function properly. As long as this situation persists, Africa will remain a basket-case. In Asia the prospects depend critically on China. On the one hand, the regime increasingly allows for market choice – but it is a conditional and qualified support. At the same time, China suppresses political choice. Tocqueville's analysis would suggest that this is a combination that cannot deliver success. A repressive political regime can survive for a long time – since, as noted earlier, a situation of permanent or long-term disequilibrium in systems of choice is possible. But the current combination will not make China a successful society. At some point its people will wish to change their political system.

For Europe, the success of a continent-wide union hangs in the balance. The great majority of political forces favour a democratic system of political choice and also accept the need for market choice. The risk to Europe's future is not that either system of choice will be repudiated. Instead it comes from a danger that both systems will become clogged and unable to deliver.

The risk arises because there will be a huge reluctance to refocus systems of government away from the old task of provisioning and to see the long-term future of a continent-wide union in the making of rules with reach. There is little trust in market choice and there will be many voices singing the old refrains of redistribution and reallocation. The happy illusion that government is a benign counterpart that can correct any imperfection in the market is one that many will strongly cling to – despite any evidence to the contrary. This will tempt Europe to over-prescribe rules and regulations and to try to monopolize rule-making in detail. Thus, the system of market choice will be under constant pressure from political forces.

At the same time, there will be great resistance to the idea of putting in place a framework for a simple system of political choice. It will seem too great a leap away from the kinds of government that people have become used to in the context of their own countries. It seems more 'European' to say that Europe's system of government should do everything that a contemporary state does. The willingness to think afresh about the principles of good government that inspired America's founders is thus largely absent. Hence, unless Europe reconsiders the approach it is taking to the creation of a continent-wide union, the prospects are for a poorly functioning system of political choice accompanied by a poorly functioning system of market choice. The continent will become immobile and unable to offer the best of either individual or social choices.

The Benefits of the Indirect Approach

The difficulties in the way of creating a system of government for Europe lead politicians to look for short-cuts. One of the most tempting of these is to think that success can be achieved by writing the goals of success into the institutional framework. This is the bait dangled in the water by those who argue that incorporating the aims and objectives symbolized by the 'Spirit of Europe' into the system of government will help ensure its success.

When Tocqueville predicted the success of America, he did not attribute this to any ambitions that the young republic had set for itself. On the contrary, he noted the limited public ambitions of the United States – particularly in the area of foreign policy. According to Tocqueville, America's foreign policy stance was one based on abstaining from intervention. He noted that, far from actively seeking the status of a great power, 'the foreign policy of the United States is reduced by its very nature to await the chances of the future history of the nation' (p. 160).

Instead what impressed Tocqueville was what he called the 'indirect advantages' of the American system. It was, according to his assessment, innovation-minded and characterized by a 'ceaseless agitation' for improvements including social improvements. He noted 'an all-pervading and restless activity, a superabundant force, and an energy... which may... beget the most amazing benefits' (p. 180). Nor did he see these benefits just in terms of individual prosperity. On the contrary, he saw them as promoting the growth of public spirit, respect for law, the well-being of the greatest number rather than particular interests, and as offering checks against the abuse of power.

The lesson of Tocqueville's analysis is that the success of a system of governance is achieved through indirect means rather than by trying to promote a special character or setting direct goals for success. In everyday life we are all familiar with the indirect approach when we fail to find something that we are looking for but that mysteriously turns up when we are not looking for it. Sometimes our goals cannot be expressed in direct form at all. We all wish to lead happy and contented lives, but these are not goals we can set in those terms. They emerge from the pursuit of other things that make us happy or give us contentment. Similarly businesses often see success as the indirect outcome of other corporate qualities. A firm may declare its intention to be the market leader in its field, but if it succeeds, it will owe its success to other qualities, such as the speed with which it can adapt to changing business circumstances, or the trust it can inspire in client relationships. Tocqueville was fully prepared to predict the rise of the power of the United States but this, as he saw it, was because of the indirect advantages and incentives provided by its system of governance and not because the young republic had set ambitious goals.[2]

The idea that Europe's leaders can identify a 'Spirit of Europe' to stand as a target of success and a measure of progress is fundamentally mistaken because it ignores the importance of the indirect. Europe's influence in the world, whether as a power in international trade and finance or in global environmental issues or in international security matters, will be an indirect outcome of how well its system of governance actually works. Immobile and clogged systems of choice in Europe will mean that Europe will not only be unable to project itself effectively internationally but, in addition, will not provide an example any other country or region will wish to emulate or be influenced by. Social cohesion too will be the indirect outcome of a society that puts in place a system of governance that makes the best of individual and social choice. The importance of the indirect is a lesson that Europe's politicians need to take to heart.

Mistaken Identity

The second purpose noted earlier for looking to Europe's system of government to reflect the 'Spirit of Europe' is about fostering the sense of European identity, and in particular the need to encourage people to identify with a European system of government.

This concern with identity is well intended. It reflects the view that the union must stand for more than the self-interest of the states that make up its membership and must serve more importantly as a source of inspiration able to bind its citizens with a larger sense of loyalty.[3] To some, the vision of a continent-wide union represents no more than a marriage of convenience and self-interest among the nation states of Europe. The individual states have lost their ability and self-confidence to act alone in the world and turn naturally to act together instead. But to others this vision is sadly deficient. If the union is no more than a reflection of national self-interest, then support for the union in each member state will always be conditional on whether the national interest is being seen to be served. Such a union will always be fragile and liable to erosion. Some other binding force is necessary.

Identity as Participation

When Tocqueville described the spirit of America, he did so in terms of what he called the 'manners' and customs of its people. He pointed to their self-reliance and love of independence; he noted their mistrust of social authority and preference for forming private associations to get things done; he described their respect for the law and propensity towards litigation; he observed an unbounded desire for riches and saw the American people as much more motivated by commercial passion than by political passion.

Thus Tocqueville did not doubt, even at an early stage in the life of the nation, that the American people had a strong sense of individual and collective identity. On the contrary, he referred to the pride of American people in their achievements, their readiness to defend America against any criticism and their over-sensitivity in taking any criticism of America as personal criticism.

What is important about Tocqueville's observations on American identity was the way he attributed it not to the result of a system of government that tried to promote an identity, but to something bound up in the processes of the American system. According to Tocqueville, it was the benefits of democratic participation that made American citizens, as he put it, look on public prosperity as resulting from their own exertions and equate the public interest with their private interest. The secret of American identity was that for each citizen the great work of society went on 'beneath his eyes, and... under his hands' (p. 245). He noted that because American citizens were mainly new immigrants, 'the instinctive love of their country can scarcely exist in their minds; but everyone takes as zealous an interest in the affairs of his township, his county, and of the whole state, as if they were his own, because everyone, in his sphere, takes an active part in the government of society' (p. 169).

Tocqueville was making two important points in this diagnosis of the 'Spirit of America'. The first is that identity is not something that is primarily bestowed by government – on the contrary, it flows from the people to the system of government. He stated, 'if I have hitherto failed in making the reader feel the important influence which I attribute... to the manners of the Americans, upon the maintenance of their institutions, I have failed in the principal object of my work' (p. 251). Secondly, what enables people to identify with their system of government is the way it pulls them into its processes, not the material benefits it promises. Tocqueville saw the sense of individual participation as the secret ingredient that enabled the American people to identify with their form of government and to see it as their system.

The lesson for Europe is that a sense of identity with Europe and its institutions will not be achieved by politicians or by treaties proclaiming the symbols of identity. Instead people will identify with Europe's system of government if the system is arranged so as to avoid distant government and to achieve responsive government. For the many reasons discussed in this book, this is an extraordinarily difficult thing to achieve in a continent-wide union. It cannot be achieved by promising to replicate on a European scale the forms and functions of government that people are familiar with in their own state. It can only be achieved by a clear focus on what a union government possesses a comparative advantage in doing, and by leaving other choices much closer to the citizen. The existing European union has taken symbolism to its lowest point. It flies a flag and it plays an anthem. This does nothing to help people feel that they participate in the choices made in the union. All it has achieved is to ruin a fine piece of music.

Negative Identity

The idea of some of Europe's political leaders that identifying the special 'Spirit of Europe' can help construct a sense of identity in

Europe also appeals to a sense of identity in the negative. It defines what Europe is not: for example, it is not uncaring of the poor and unmindful of the environment. Because these qualities are in some way held to be uniquely combined in Europe, the implication is that other countries do not share these qualities and have not got the combination right. Above all, Europe is not America.

While commenting positively on the sense of identity that he found in America, Tocqueville specifically warned against making a sense of identity an objective of political association. He seemed particularly concerned with a sense of identity expressed in the negative. He noted that observations by Americans on Europe at that time were usually based on ignorance and that identity in the negative could distort perceptions of the outside world in ways that were actually damaging to the interests of the society that made them.

It is a warning that unfortunately applies to contemporary Europe just as much as it did to early nineteenth-century America. Much of the comment made by Europe's politicians about contemporary America is based on a profound ignorance, as are many popular views. The idea that Europe values social cohesion more than do Americans is one of them. At the end of the twentieth century the unemployment rate in the United States was less than half that of the European Union and the unemployment rate for young people and women was about half that in the EU. More than seven out of every ten persons aged 55 to 64 were not working in Italy, Austria and Belgium, and six out of ten in the EU as a whole, compared with four out of ten in the United States. Against the background of such facts it is difficult to claim that the United States reflects a socially uncaring attitude while Europe offers social solidarity. Projecting a negative identity – that Europe is not the United States – is a powerful political tool. But it panders to ignorance and will only make it more difficult for the union to have productive relations with the outside world – not least with the United States itself.

Morality and Knowledge-Based Government

The 'Spirit of Europe' is also about how to give legitimacy to a system of government for Europe. It stands for the idea that unless the system of government embodies Europe's highest moral and social values, that system will not be legitimate.[4] Even if invoking the 'Spirit of Europe' represents a misplaced way to project success in Europe and also a misguided way to think about how to build a sense of identity in Europe, nevertheless, the view it embodies about what makes a system of government legitimate has a clear historical rationale and a clear moral purpose. In the real world it is this search for a moral underpinning to Europe's system of government that has in large part motivated the desire for the existing union to have its own charter of fundamental rights and has led at the same time to the existing treaties being increasingly filled with high-sounding objectives such as respect for sustainable development, social cohesion and other important values.[5]

It is impossible and it would be wrong to ignore the historical and moral background to the search for a unified form of government for the continent. The fact that so many people passively acquiesced in the overthrow of democratic governments and actively participated in atrocities is something that cannot and should not be forgotten. The experience of moral complicity in Europe between people and their governments leads straight to the emphatic conclusion that people do not owe allegiance to *any* kind of government, even if it is their own, but only to a government that commands their moral respect. It also seems to lead straight to the further conclusion that the best way to ensure that governments command moral respect is to insist that the rules of the system of government themselves incorporate the highest values of society. It is this further conclusion that is a matter of debate.

On whatever view one takes about legitimation, there is a shared starting point. This is the view that the legitimacy of any system of government in Europe should rest on its consonance with people's highest moral values. In other words, any sense of obligation people have to respect and obey a system of government terminates when individuals or communities feel that the system, or what it is doing, runs counter to their highest moral values. At that point the least that is required is for people to speak out against the system of government and its acts.

Despite this shared starting point to the debate, there is a difference of view as to how to reflect this moral yardstick. One set of arguments favours incorporating society's highest moral and social values into the framework itself. This is the view that lies behind the idea that the system of government must incorporate what the 'Spirit of Europe' stands for. The other set of arguments stresses the unique features of systems of political choice, the way in which they differ from systems of moral choice, and suggests that people must keep their highest moral values as an independent measuring rod outside the system of political choice.

If the latter approach is followed, then a different theory is needed to justify the procedures and institutions of Europe's system of governance. The main alternative is 'epistemic'. What this means is that the system of government is justified to the extent to which it helps to improve the quality of individual and collective decisions in society, including their moral quality. It suggests that what is really important in a system of government is not whether the system says it will respect society's highest values – because that does not provide any assurance that either the political or legal system will actually do so – but that the system should work to improve the understanding of the content and application of the most important values. This means looking at the system of government as a system of knowledge.

The idea that Europe's system of government will be better as a simple system can be justified in these terms of knowledge-based government. The openness, adaptability and tolerance that a simple system encourages will make it much easier for Europe to learn about how to interpret and apply its most important values. This approach to the justification of a system of government and its alternative is therefore discussed further below.

Legitimacy and Embedded Morality

As noted above, the idea that the political system that people support should in some way be consonant with their deepest convictions about what is right or wrong is a common point of departure for two different views about how this consistency is best expressed. One view is that this consistency can be achieved by ensuring that the system itself incorporates a society's most important moral and social values. The other view is that this consistency can be achieved by holding moral and social values apart from the political system and applying them to criticize or support the system depending on the procedures it adopts and the outcomes from them. Allegiance, or the withholding of allegiance, comes therefore from applying a viewpoint that is held outside the system.

At first sight, the view that the system of government should itself embody a society's fundamental moral and social values appears the most straightforward way to ensure consistency. The arguments in favour of this approach are as follows.

First, it provides a way of linking the political system with the society it serves. Incorporation conveys the sense that the state and its rules and procedures are not some abstraction but are rooted in a concrete society that has its own core values and beliefs. It conveys the sense that the system of government is about more than representing interests and is, in addition, about a community that is bound also by ethical concerns. Moreover, it is not possible to understand the function and authority of rules unless the context in which they have been framed is accepted. And that context must involve some prior account of the social and moral life of the community.

Secondly, incorporation of a moral and social code is not just of symbolic value; it will also help the political system to work better in practice. This is because the moral and social norms of a community provide a basis for the consensual resolution of conflicts. A sense of agreement on basic beliefs should make it easier for people to reach agreement in other areas where there is not a consensus. At a minimum, people can still agree on the ideal of trying to reach agreements that all can go along with. This is not the same as saying that everyone agrees with compromise politics; it is saying that people will try to reach agreement on the substance of differences.[6]

Thirdly, if people have reason to believe that their political system does in some sense serve the common good, they will themselves have reasons and incentives to act in ways that serve this good. They will be more inclined to participate in the political system, more inclined to obey the law and be more disposed to accept different interpretations of the common good.[7]

Finally, it is important for a system of government to offer continuity. Policies change over time; so too may institutional roles and procedures and the balance of power within a political system. The incorporation of values offers a different kind of assurance about continuity.[8]

Systems of Government and the Independence of Moral Standards

The arguments set out above seem both plausible and attractive. The counter-arguments in favour of the separation of moral and political systems essentially revolve around the ways in which political systems differ from moral systems and have their own features, which have to be addressed on their own terms.

First, it is important to recognize that systems of government are not just about trying to resolve differences through negotiation, rational discussion and other mediation techniques, but also provide governments with the power to impose and to enforce – even against what a sizeable part of society may want. This power to coerce is what makes political systems special and needs to be addressed as a central concern. This special feature of systems of political choice is not addressed by being able to say that, in general, the system works to fulfil important moral and social values. This would be far too permissive for institutions that hold political power. It would also encourage the abuse of procedures because it would open the door to those who claimed that the end justified the means.

Secondly, the idea that a system of government must incorporate procedures to achieve the highest expression of the values of a society is too demanding a criterion for systems of political choice. Systems of political choice serve less elevated functions than systems of moral choice. Often they help society to reach agreements on what they can go along with rather than achieve what is 'best'. Societies also may favour moderate solutions to social issues.[9] In either case political choice involves much less prescriptive standards than does moral choice. Similarly, mediation techniques may look for agreement in very limited areas. For example, a technique such as mutual recognition provides a way of resolving disagreements without any appeal to any wider concept.

Thirdly, as noted earlier, political choice is often about the aptness of choice rather than the justification of a particular value. In making a personal moral choice a person is also making a judgement about whether the value is appropriate or aptly applied in the context. But in politics, judgements about aptness or context play a more important role and may provide good reasons why a high moral or social value is not applied.

Finally, the appeal to fundamental moral and social values does not solve the problem of how to achieve a sense of continuity in a system of political choice. This is because the interpretation placed on values, and the way in which people think they can best be applied, will change. Political systems are inevitably about matters under continual negotiation.

These arguments and counter-arguments about the merits of whether or not a system of political choice should incorporate a society's highest values may seem rather finely balanced and so abstract as to offer little clear practical guidance. But in practice the difference in approach matters in two absolutely basic ways. First, the incorporation of a society's highest values in a political system affects the span of authority in the system that can be used to impose interpretations of values on matters that people regard as of the highest importance to them. Secondly, in the final analysis, legitimacy asks the question of whether an individual or a group owes a duty or an allegiance to a system of government. This question cannot be answered by looking at the social or moral values that the political system claims to be incorporating. Communism claimed to be fulfilling the widest range of moral and social goods. Fascism also claimed to be acting in favour of a social state. The claims of a system of government cannot be taken as a measure of the moral or social worth of that system. In the end, in order to answer the question of allegiance, people have to be prepared to form their own moral judgements and be prepared to stand by these. A system of government cannot do it for us.[10]

If it is accepted that systems of political choice have special features, such as the power to coerce, that set them apart from a system of moral choice and that their incorporation of values does not absolve people from their own moral responsibilities, then a different approach to legitimation is required. The main alternative is that a system of government can be justified when it helps us to improve a society's knowledge of how to make the individual and social choices that reflect its highest values.

Knowledge-Based Government

Historically, the 'epistemic' approach to justification was associated with an emphasis on the educative effect of the democratic right to vote and to participate in politics. It was argued that having the right to vote would encourage everyone to participate in political debate and to learn by so doing. This way of linking democratic systems of government to the accumulation of knowledge in society now appears patronizing about the ability of individual voters to make informed choices and one that focuses far too much on the vote.[11] Lower voter turn-out, the many ways in which votes and procedures can be manipulated, the remoteness of the individual from a meaningful impact on choice – all have weakened any learning rationale that centres exclusively on the vote. The need is to look much more broadly at how systems of government can be said to hold out the prospects for acting as learning systems. The parallel is with the system of market choice. Economic activity is increasingly seen to be 'knowledge-based'. Similarly, there is a need to see how frameworks for systems of government can encourage knowledge-based political choices.

The idea of knowledge-based governance is not amoral. On the contrary, it treats social values as of the highest importance. But at the same time it views moral and social standards as subjects of learning just as much as any other aspect of choice.[12] A knowledge-based system of government thus finds its moral justification insofar as it helps improve the quality of a society's most important moral and social choices.

The question for any knowledge-based approach to systems of government then becomes how to set up the rules of a system of political choice in the best way to help a society improve the quality of its most important choices. In this context, 'simplicity' is justified as a deliberate design criterion for systems of government because it incorporates the very features that will help a society to learn, including learning about its moral values.

To justify a European system of government on the basis of how well it encourages informed choices may seem to demand a standard of rational behaviour in politics that is quite unrealistic. The question can, however, be posed the other way round. A system of government that takes decisions without gathering relevant facts, that applies values without taking account of different interpretations that may be placed on them, that tries to insulate itself from the outside world, or that cannot gather signals that changes in its rules and regulations may be needed and that cannot adapt constitutes a system of government that will satisfy individual and social choices only by accident rather than by design. As a result, a system of government that scorns the knowledge base of politics will frustrate all of a society's choices, even those that represent its highest moral and social values.

In the end, therefore, the idea that Europe's system of governance must reflect and be infused by some kind of 'Spirit of Europe' that reflects the high moral and social values to be found in Europe sets a false ideal:

- It provides an erroneous approach to achieving success in the system. Success will come as an indirect outcome, not from setting targets.
- It also provides a false approach to establishing a sense of European identity. People will identify with Europe's system of government not because it promises them the earth but because its

procedures encourage people to see the system of choice as theirs and not one that belongs to distant elites.

- It provides a false route to legitimizing a system of government because, however much a system of government claims to incorporate a society's highest moral and social values, it has to be judged independently – not on the basis of what it claims, but on the basis of how its procedures actually work and what its outcomes actually are. The judgement of whether a system of government deserves support or not is a moral judgement that people have to make for themselves. It is dangerous to suggest that the choice can be made for them because the system itself pronounces in favour of high moral and social values.

Moving away from the idea that Europe's system of government can be justified by the high moral and social values that it incorporates and claims to be acting in concordance with means finding a different way of justifying the system. The main alternative is that systems of government should be viewed not as ways of trying to impose the highest principles, but as ways to learn more about those principles and the context and circumstances in which they can be aptly applied. Only in this manner will a society increase its knowledge about how to make sensible individual and social choices. This is what a simple system of government for Europe will achieve.

10 Conclusions

No man upon the earth, can as yet affirm absolutely and gener-
ally that the new state of the world is better than its former one;
but it is already easy to perceive that this state is different.
Alexis de Tocqueville, *Democracy in America*

Continent-Wide Governance

At the start of the twenty-first century the peoples of Europe have
every reason to feel optimistic and confident about their future.
Twice, in the century just past, Europe almost destroyed itself through
war and dragged much of the rest of the world into conflict as well.
Now Europe has no enemies on its borders and within the continent
there is a general and widespread support for a democratic way of life
and for economies organized along market lines. What has not yet
been found is agreement on how to put everything together so as to
organize a new system of government for the continent of Europe as a
whole that takes full advantage of this historically unprecedented
opportunity. Thinking remains rooted in the past, relying far too
much on projecting forward the traditional national models of state
and market that politicians are accustomed to from recent history,
and imagining Europe as though it is just a question of scaling up in
size the kinds of systems of government people are most familiar with.
There has been a reluctance to face up to the fact that, in order to be
successful, a continent-wide system of political choice will have to
be both new and different.

The theme of this book has been that in order to achieve the success that is within its grasp, Europe has to get the connection right between the two systems of individual and social choice that societies have available to them. This means bringing together a system of market choice and a system of political choice in ways that enable people to make the most of the opportunities in their lives. This is not as straightforward as it sounds. There can be no convenient assumption that systems of political choice can be relied on to correct the market automatically when people find that it does not deliver the choices they want. Instead, in order to get Europe's system right, there is a need to stand back and to take a detached look at what is happening to systems of choice in the world.

When we place ourselves in the position of an outside observer, what we see is that systems of market choice are operating not perfectly, but with far more responsiveness to what people want than are systems of political choice. The market is more direct, faster, offers tailor-made and customized products and is generally easier to use. It has adapted to what are loosely referred to as globalization and the information revolution in much more effective ways than have systems of political choice. Moreover, the market is also likely to deliver people more of what they want as they live longer lives, make different life-style choices and approach life-cycle risks in different ways. By contrast, politicians are long on promises but short on delivery. Systems of political choice are slow, indirect, offer only generalized products and are difficult to access and influence. Thus, if Europe is to get the best out of the two systems of choice, it has to upgrade the system of political choice.

Upgrading the system of political choice for Europe means jettisoning much conventional thinking about Europe's future. None of the conventional models for Europe's future provides a convincing response to the challenges identified at the start of this book.

- The first question concerned the shifting functions of government. This means thinking afresh about where a system of government for the continent can most add value. Businesses have had to refocus their core activities; political systems cling to what they have delivered in the past. The answer does not lie in trying to create an 'Eco-social Europe' that models Europe in the image of the traditional welfare state.
- The second question focused on the huge extension in the use of the language of rights – from their original, restricted use as a means of underpinning the fundamental conditions for a demo-

cratic form of government, to their current, much more expansive use as a means of signalling directly what people want out of politics. Markets respond increasingly directly to what people want; political systems do not. The answer does not lie with the model of 'Jurists' Europe' that Europe's system of government should seek to impose a uniform interpretation of values across Europe in order to be coherent about what is important in public policy.

- The third question focused on the discontinuity between political boundaries based on territory and the boundaries of public policy. Markets connect seamlessly from the global to the local; political systems do not. The answer lies neither with the model of a 'Super-power Europe', nor with the model of an 'Order of States'.

The answers offered to these questions by this book have suggested instead the need to think about the future shape of European government in much more radical ways.

Reorienting the Activities of Government

The need to refocus the activities of government means that it cannot be assumed that a continent-wide system of government will, over the course of time, carry out the functions associated with the traditional state, and in particular with Europe's post-war welfare state. It is ingrained in Europe's thinking that the modern state is there to tax people so as to be able to reallocate resources, to redistribute income and to provide social safety nets. This large-scale provisioning function has hit its limits in most countries. It is not where Europe's system of government offers increasing returns. Instead, the rule-making and regulatory role of government needs to be placed at the centre of thinking about what European government actually should do.

In this rethinking of the functions of governments, Europe starts from a position of advantage because the existing union has developed mainly as a rule-making rather than as a resource-reallocating form of government. What has not been sufficiently appreciated is that this is its long-term future too. Rules become more valuable the more people follow them. By contrast, in a continent-wide system of government the provisioning role of government faces diminishing returns because limits on the revenue-raising possibilities have been reached, or exceeded, by national governments, so that the same volume of resources would have to be recycled or spread more thinly.

Where Europe is at a disadvantage in thinking about the rule-making functions of a continent-wide system of government is that many of the member states abuse their regulatory powers. Moreover, the existing union has compounded the problem by attempting to regulate in detail and to exclude alternate standards. The idea that people and communities might benefit from a choice of regulatory regimes in the same way as they benefit from a choice of goods and services has seemed foreign to thinking in the existing union. The aim has been to print the hand of Brussels on as much as possible.

Big business has colluded in this centralized vision of rule-making. Confident of its own access to the levers of power in Brussels, it prefers 'one-stop' shopping in the union. Regulatory capture is easier when there is only one regulator to capture. This is the wrong approach for European society and a short-sighted approach even for big business.

There are two underlying reasons for the abuse of the rule-making functions of government in Europe. The first has stemmed from not thinking carefully enough about the way in which systems of political choice and market choice interact, so that there has been an erroneous assumption that politics can correct any faults in the market in easy ways. Europe has to shed its twentieth-century illusion that politics is benign and the market is not. The second has been the failure of most governments and the existing union to realize the importance of constitutional rules that can set the framework for the use of regulatory powers in a system of government and that guard against their abuse.

In the case of a continent-wide system of government, the concentration of government on the rule-making role should involve a much more selective approach to rules and regulations than has been adopted by the existing union. It means that Europe's system of government should concentrate on putting in place rules with reach. The rules should not be over-detailed. Neither should the standards aim too high. Instead a general standard should be offered that will provide the convenience of applicability throughout the union. At the same time, the general rules provided by the union should allow room alongside for different rules that could offer alternative standards, either higher or lower, and that will provide a warning if the union's own rules are becoming out of date or lagging behind what people want. The rule-making role of a continent-wide system of government is therefore not about making detailed rules for everybody, everywhere. It is about making a certain limited class of general rules that will have a general applicability. The union will provide the McDonald's standard. It is the development of this rule-making function, in ways that offer rules which reach across the continent, and in ways that support the development of rule-based behaviour at the international level, that is crucial for the long-term future of Europe's system of government.

Signals and Rights

Systems of political choice cannot offer direct and speedy responses to what people want through the indirect methods of representative democracy. The vote is crucial for people's ability to get rid of those in positions of political power. But it is crude as a method of conveying signals about what people really want. The main way in which people now convey what they want, particularly in new areas of social choice, is through claims based on assertions about 'rights'. As a result of the much more widespread use of the language of rights, together with the organization of groups focused on rights, politics within the different states of Europe is becoming much more 'rights-based'. Therefore, the key challenge for the democratic design of a continent-wide system of government is how to arrange vote-based politics in relation to rights-based politics.

The conventional response is to see Europe's system of government increasingly becoming the locus of rights claims decisions. The reason for this response is that if Europe's system of government does not become the focus for rights claims, then it appears to be cutting itself off from the way people talk about what is most important for them in the content of public policies, and European citizenship would mean different things to different people in different places. A greater role in rights-based politics would appear to compensate for the fact that Europe does not provide a strong platform for vote-based politics.

The analysis given in this book offers a strong warning against this response. The reason for this warning lies in the potential for conflict between the two methods of expression. Rights claims are particularly useful for society as a way in which people can express what they feel most strongly about. Votes, on the other hand, do not give special weight to intensity of feeling. The challenge is thus to make full use of this virtue of rights without running the risk of conflict between committed minorities claiming rights and a possibly indifferent, or even defensive, public exerting a different, majority view at the ballot box. If rights claims dominate, the danger is a populist backlash of the 'silent majority' in the voting booth. In Europe, such backlashes are likely to take a nationalist and anti-European form.

The analysis in this book thus suggests a different response. It suggests that the different purposes of rights in a system of government must be kept distinct. In particular, systems of government must distinguish between the traditional role of rights as 'preconditions' for systems of political choice, and the more extensive purposes for which they are now used for debating priorities within systems of political choice. For most of the purposes for which they are now used, rights are not about the preconditions for political choice; they are about principles and priorities within systems of choice, and in particular about new areas of public policy and about moral and social standards on which people, often a minority, feel very strongly.

In a continent-wide system of government for Europe, the preconditions for systems of choice can be established by the conditions of membership and the conditions for the suspension of membership. In this context a common approach and standard is important. The next question then becomes where in Europe to recognize claims about rights that are being used to talk about priorities within politics.

The answer to this further challenge is to distinguish between the way rights are used to debate the 'right allocation' of resources in society and their use to ground public policy in 'right reason'. It is the setting for 'right reason' that must prevail since claims about allocation must themselves be justified.

Turning to think about the setting that can best make use of rights as guides to right reason, what is crucial is that rights claims are particularly useful for exploring new areas of social concern. In this role, rights claims are inherently contestable and context is key to their interpretation and aptness of application. A decentralized setting for the recognition of rights claims is thus most fitting. It allows for the fullest range of exploration and for the greatest variety of interpretation. Conflicting interpretations would become a positive rather than a negative feature of such a setting because they would invite further exploration of the reasons for such differences. Such a setting is less likely to provoke a clash between vote-based expression and rights-based expression because it allows for the fullest weighting of local context and for the fullest expression of local judgement about what is apt. If a conflict were to occur, the clash would be localized.

Connecting the Local with the Global

The third ingredient for the success of a continent-wide system of government involves looking at the extraordinary way in which systems of market choice connect the local with the global. Europe's system of political choice also has to look at the way it can provide similar connections to link people with local choices and global choices.

Unification of the European continent in itself does not answer the key questions about how exactly the continent is to organize its internal relationships or in what way it is to orchestrate external relationships. Neither is it an answer to state that Europe represents some kind of new 'network' government. The transfer of theories of network organization from business to political organization overlooks the most important aspects of form that political systems have to address. To refer to the existing union as a 'network' has become an indolent way of rationalizing the present muddle over form.

Business organizations achieve their success in part because they distinguish between the span of control they need to manage their internal connections and the different organizational techniques they need to manage external relationships. Europe's system of government also needs to distinguish between the span of control it needs for connecting up units of government within the union and the way it relates to the wider world outside.

The appropriate span of control within the union is defined and delineated by the rule-making function itself. This means that the span of control of the union does not need to go beyond that needed for the making of rules with reach. In areas within the continent other than the union's general rule-making function, the system of government should allow complete flexibility as to which units of government link up, what they do together and how they do it.

For external relations, the authority of the union should be seen as one that needs to be shaped by the different types of relationships involved. It is a mistake to think of external relationships just in terms of power politics between nations and of 'threat' relationships. The world's present system of global governance is highly imperfect, but it cannot be characterized in these terms alone.

The international system, such as it is, revolves around the different international regimes that exist in different areas of policy and that are developing different norms, codes of conduct, means of enforcement and ways of settling disputes. In many of these evolving international regimes, the member states of the union may wish it to act on their behalf. But this will not always be the case. Ultimately what is important for people in the union is that the reach of the different regimes of global governance should be extended and that the normative content of their rules is properly understood, developed, observed and upheld. This can best be achieved if each member state of the union maintains its own relationship with the different international regimes in addition to working as a union. The fact that members of the union have the possibility of acting independently, or with other allies, will encourage them to take a continuing responsibility for the development of the content of international rules and rule-keeping and will itself act as a restraint on the union's own approach to international rule-keeping. Paradoxically, this makes it more likely, not less likely, that the union will often act on behalf of all of Europe, because the union will have an incentive to be fully responsive to all its members.

Simplicity

The various components of a system of government for the continent described above have been brought together under the theme that Europe needs a simple system of democratic government and should deliberately try to build 'simplicity' into its organization. What 'simplicity' therefore stands for in the context of a democratic, continent-wide union is as follows:

- The functions of the union should be simplified so that it concentrates on the core role of making rules with reach;
- The role of the institutions should be simplified so that they cut back on their ambitions to replicate the institutions they see as their counterparts in the member states and focus instead on their specialized place in a continent-wide system of rule-making and rule enforcement;
- The internal span of authority of the union within the continent should be defined as that needed for the making of rules with a general applicability. This would allow for flexible forms of association between political units (states and regions) in other areas of public policy;

- The external span of authority of the union should be limited in respect of the various international regimes that make up the system of global governance to an authority that is contingent on its respect for international rules and the rule-keeping fostered by the different regimes. Member states of the union need to keep their own relations with the various international regimes in case other alliances offer greater support to the formation and enforcement of international rules.

- A decentralized system for the recognition of rights should be put in place that allows for the widest exploration of values in different communities in new areas of social concern under basic conditions of membership that insist on democratic methods of political choice and economies organized around market choice.

Simplicity and the Qualities of Europe's System of Government

The virtues of a simple system of democratic government for the continent are not just or even mainly about the responsiveness of Europe's system of political choice in relation to the system of market choice. A simple system of government will also fulfil two extraordinarily important underlying qualitative criteria. First, it makes tolerance the key test for the coherence of Europe's system of government in a pluralist continent. Secondly, it makes the way in which Europe's system of political choice can mobilize the greatest use of knowledge the key to justifying its procedures and responsibilities.

Tolerance needs to be specifically built into Europe's system of government. The continent will include a wide variety of belief systems that deserve respect. It would be nice to think that tolerance would happen by itself without need of encouragement. In Europe's multicultural setting, however, toleration has to be deliberately provided for in the constitutional framework.

It might seem superficially attractive for Europe to put in place a limited overlay of moral and social norms to be applied uniformly and consistently throughout the union. In this way it might seem as though it would be possible to reconcile the desire for a common set of values to be applied consistently throughout the union with a recognition of the existence of plural values in the continent. The means of doing this is often seen to be through a declaration of fundamental rights that specify the values on which all can agree – even if there is no agreement on other areas.

This approach does not work. Going down this route means that rights become, as they have been throughout their history, a means to impose authority as much as a defence against authority. The basic question that has to be confronted is the extent to which the design of the continent's system of government should provide for a central authority to impose values.

Creating the conditions for tolerance means insisting that the basic conditions for membership of the union demand adherence to democratic methods of choice as far as political choice is concerned and to market choice as far as economic organization is concerned – but going no further than this. Within this framework, toleration is about agreeing to disagree. The requirements for toleration reject any further imposition of values, however much they seem to command respect at some high level of generality. A simple framework is a tolerant framework.

The requirement for Europe's system of government to give proper attention to the way in which its policies can be based on knowledge tends to get overlooked as other qualities are stressed – in particular, the perceived need for the system to help create a sense of European identity in its domestic and external policies. Knowledge-based government requires a continent-wide system of government to limit what it tries to do, to have in place an early warning system for when changes are necessary and to ensure openness to the outside world. The system must guard against the misrepresentation of the external world. It must also allow for important individual and social values to change. Even values that are durable over generations need to be capable of being refreshed and updated in the way in which they are interpreted and applied. A simple framework provides the structure within which a rich and complex social order can best develop.

Tear Up the Treaties

Simplicity also provides a guide as to what Europe should not try to do. It should not try to extend the arrangements for the existing union over the rest of Europe. The current system is a muddle and will not work for the continent as a whole. The present union and its institutions aspire to do too much and already the union regulates in excessive detail rather than trying to identify where general rules with reach are most necessary. Already, the existing treaties have started down the road of centralizing the recognition of rights. Already the treaties provide pegs for the union to develop as a taxing, spending, reallocating and redistributing union. The present treaties should be torn up and replaced by a new continent-wide system. Europe should also not try to replicate on a large scale any model either from a state within the continent or from the United States. It has the chance to think afresh about the functions of modern government and to be guided by the maxim that simpler will be better.

It is very tempting for Europe – in the name of uniformity, the need for a 'level playing field', equality and social cohesion – to try to put in place an over-ambitious system of political choice that tries to regulate in detail, that tries to perform every traditional function of government, and where each unit of government is interlocked with another. Such a system will not work for a continent-wide system of government. It will neither be responsive to what people want, nor be adaptable to changing conditions, nor be open to outside influences. The existing union has only gone a small way down the road to traditional government, and in particular the redistributive and re-allocative functions of such government. However, a continent-wide union should not go down this path at all. It will take it in the direction of functions that are likely to be phased out by governments as markets offer products that are more suited to individual life-cycle risks and preferences. Most of the spending of the existing union is unproductive. A continent-wide system of governance does not need a budget at all.

Updating Classical Liberalism

This book has also offered a secondary theme: about the nature of liberalism in Europe. There always has been a liberal tradition in Europe, but it too needs to be updated. The battle against communism has been won. Therefore a liberal message that focuses on the evils of a system of governance that suppressed both political choice and market choice has lost its resonance. Moreover, when liberalism preaches the wilder forms of libertarianism – that society does not need a system of political choice – it flies in the face of human experience.

The message about liberalism in this book is that both systems of choice are needed: the market and politics. It suggests that the system of political choice should be refocused around a core function – the making of rules and regulations of general applicability – and that the authority needed by systems of government can be delineated by this role. Rules of good behaviour at the international level are needed in order to underpin the regimes that govern global markets and other codes of international conduct. Rules of general applicability are needed for Europe as a whole, while rules suited to their particular circumstances are also needed by smaller political units.

Liberals have been reluctant to endorse the rule-making and regulatory roles of government because rules and regulations have been seen as providing instruments for interference in market choice and involving attaching strings and conditions to freedom of contract. Rules and regulations have thus been seen as a step down the road that leads ultimately to total government control of both politics and the market. The discussion, however, has suggested that the problem is not rule-making as such but the abuse of the regulatory role. The right kind of rules can reduce risk and uncertainty in people's lives, economize on the costs of gathering and disseminating information, reduce the cost of transactions and make contracts more secure. They make it possible for people to operate comfortably in geographical and social settings that are otherwise unfamiliar.

With rules goes enforcement. It is not possible to get away from the fact that systems of government possess, and need to possess, coercive power – from the global level to the local. The liberal perspective, however, is that coercive power has to be framed around the central reality of the plurality of belief systems in the modern world and that systems of government should be consciously designed to protect a pluralist interpretation of values.

In much of the recent liberal tradition, thinking about the rules of democratic politics has been framed in terms of the way in which democratic or majoritarian systems of government might turn against minorities. This is not an idle fear, but it misrepresents what has actually happened in democracies. In the twentieth century the main problem was that ideologically committed minorities manipulated the political system through taking advantage of the passivity and inertia of the silent majority. The majority woke up to what had been happening far too late. The key problem, therefore, is to ensure that the rules of the system are designed to mediate effectively between minorities that feel very strongly about an issue and the majority that does not. In democratic politics this issue comes to a head in the relationship between vote-based politics and rights-based politics. In trying to get this relationship defined, the liberal tradition stresses the continuing priority of grounding rights claims on reason.

Tolerance, pluralism and reason are themselves values. It can therefore be said that in favouring a system of governance that gives priority to such values, the liberal is imposing a value system. The justification for the liberal concept lies in seeing systems of market and political choice as about how society can put in place a framework that helps provide better knowledge for making individual and social choices. The need for knowledge is even greater when it comes to the interpretation and application of a society's highest values. Liberalism is about knowledge-based governance, especially in respect of a society's most important values.

Constitutional Form

Sooner rather than later, Europe's system of government will need to be put into the form of a constitution. The present treaties are unintelligible and will become even less comprehensible when all the adjustments are made to accommodate new members and a total membership of thirty-plus states. An effort is underway to sift the provisions in the treaties that are of constitutional importance from a lot of detail that is not. This exercise will not, however, address the substantive defects of the present treaty base. The discussion in this book suggests, moreover, that the constitution needed for Europe will differ in six fundamental respects from traditional constitutions.

First, the constitution should start with clear provisions about the conditions of membership. Rights such as the right to free expression, which are about the preconditions of political and market choice, have their place among these provisions. However, the constitution should not give the union institutions authority to legislate and adjudicate on rights that are about priorities within the system of political choice. Instead it should guide the citizens of Europe to where they can best take up particular rights-based claims in their member state and elsewhere. In its approach to legitimacy it should make clear that the ultimate moral responsibility for judging whether a system of government deserves allegiance rests with each person and each community; it is not vested in the government itself.

Secondly, in defining the tasks of the union the constitution should not try to divide the functions of government between the union and the member states along territorial lines. Instead it should set out the procedures for ensuring that the union focuses on the making of rules with reach. It is this activity that is the key for defining the necessary span of authority of the union. The constitution would protect the rule-making role of other jurisdictions and would allow for flexibility of association in other policy areas.

Thirdly, because the rule-making and regulatory function will lie at the heart of Europe's long-term system of government, the constitution must contain explicit provisions to guide this role and to guard against its abuse. The procedures needed to justify a proposed rule on the basis of the benefits of reach, whether the justification is that a proposed regulation will reduce costs or that it will reduce net risks for societies in Europe, must be treated as of major constitutional importance. For modern systems of government, constitutional provisions about the regulatory role are no less important than the provisions that set out the roles of the institutions. What this will mean more precisely is as follows:

- The framework should remove all references to harmonization as an objective and specifically allow for coexisting rules. Concurrent rule-making widens the choice for users of rules, helps ensure that rules are based on the best knowledge available and helps keep rules up to date.
- The test for whether the continent needs to adopt legislation should be framed not, as with the present union, in terms of a subjective judgement as to whether it may be more effective than individual countries acting by themselves, but in terms that the continent will not act unless it can demonstrate the public benefit of rules with reach across the union.
- The procedural tests for measuring the public interest, such as cost–benefit analysis and risk–risk analysis, have to be entrenched as necessary prerequisites for action by the union – and not, as in the case of the existing union, as optional add-ons.

Fourthly, qualitative aspects of association in Europe have to be specifically provided for. This means that there need to be specific provisions in the design for pluralism, tolerance and openness to the outside world.

Fifthly, in delineating the role of the institutions, the constitution should not attempt to model them after the roles played by their analogues within the individual countries of Europe. Instead their tasks should be defined in relation to their role in the rule-making, management and enforcement process and in terms of the qualities of association that the union aspires to foster.

Finally, the union needs no revenue-raising and taxing powers of its own. It will need only an administrative budget provided by the member states as well as provision that allows member states to make payments for common purposes, such as peace-keeping and cross-border cooperation.

Influence and Strength

A simple system of governance for Europe that offers people the best of market choice and the best of political choice will enable the continent to make the most of its chances in the future. With success will come influence in the world and a sense of allegiance from its people. Success will not come from targeting superpower status for Europe and trying to organize government around it. People's willingness to identify with Europe will not come from artificial construction either. The two will emerge as the indirect outcomes of a system of government that limits its focus to doing only what it alone can do and that is tolerant and does not try to impose a uniform interpretation on what people most value.

When Alexis de Tocqueville looked at the United States in the 1830s he saw a system of governance that did not set ambitious goals but instead unleashed the energy and creativity of its people. That led him to predict a most marvellous future for the country. When we look on Europe's system of governance, we also should see success as flowing from its citizens, rather than from setting ambitious goals and making sweeping promises about what government can deliver. With this as our guide, we too can look forward to a future where Europe makes the most of its chances and the most of the talents of its people.

Notes

Introduction

1 This classical liberal tradition is represented today in the conservative movement in the US and mainly within European conservative politics.

Chapter 1   How to Look at European Governance

1 For two accounts of the American debate and its dynamics, see Rakove (1996) and Riker et al. (1996).
2 Lewis (1986) stresses the continuing importance of counterfactuals in political thought: 'Counterfactuals are by no means peripheral or dispensable to our serious thought. They are as central as causation itself' (p. 23).
3 One of a variety of 'endisms' stimulated by Fukuyama (1992).
4 As an example of this kind of argument, see Wallerstein (1995).
5 Associated most notably with the work of Buchanan and Tullock (1962) and Rawls (1971).
6 See Rawls (1971) for one account of the development of a political morality.
7 For a discussion of different types of proceduralism, see Estlund (1997).
8 See Sandel (1982) for this kind of argument.
9 See Rawls (1971).
10 Binmore (1998) provides a game theory account but earlier emphasized the need to distinguish between the game of life and the game of morals (1994).
11 See Wallerstein (1999).
12 See, for example, the perspective given by Höffe (1995).
13 One elaborate attempt at reconciliation is made by Beitz (1989). Gutmann and Thompson (1996) also attempt to combine procedural

criteria with substantive accounts of the content of politics relying on the notions of basic opportunity and fair opportunity.

14 Stephen Holmes (1993b) notes: 'What sets Tocqueville apart from other theorists, then, is that he refuses to rely on political or economic mechanisms alone, but insists on seeing them in tandem' (p. 43).

15 From a rational choice perspective Herbert Simon (1982) has written: 'There is no a priori reason why the community should select the competitive market as the institutional means of organizing its activities, any more than it should select a governmental organization. It is only after the institutional framework has been constructed that the 'rationality' of consumers' behaviour in the market has any meaning in economic theory' (p. 75).

16 See, for example, Bell (1996 [1976]), Fukuyama (1995) and Harrison (1992) for well-known accounts.

17 See Dahl (1997, pp. 671–90).

18 It has been suggested by Jon Elster (1992, 1995) that we should look at this point of intersection as a third system of choice – a system largely influenced by administrative decision-taking following principles that belong neither to the market nor to politics. However, this seems unnecessary. We are facing an area where both systems are operating – and often operating badly – together.

19 This not only undermines naïve critics of the market but also weakens Gauthier's much more sophisticated analysis of the relationship as involving a system of individual utility maximization in the case of the market and 'constrained' maximization in the case of politics (see Gauthier, 1990).

Chapter 2   Adapting to Shock: The New Setting for Governance

1 For discussion of how much of today's international system has nineteenth-century roots, see Holsti (1992).

2 Posner (1995) defines opportunity costs only in terms of information costs: 'People array their opportunities and choose the one that is best; but the costs of identifying opportunities will limit the size of the array, so sometimes a person will make a different choice from the one he would have made had the costs of information been zero' (p. 442).

3 For a discussion, see Arrow (1974) and Schotter (1981).

4 For these and other reasons, economists have tended to downplay the role of entry costs as a competitive factor. See, for example, Geroski and Schwalbach (1991).

5 The classic account is provided by Tullock (1965). See also Demsetz (1989).

6   For a critique of Orwell, see Huber (1994).

7   See the discussion in Ferejohn and Kuklinski (1990).

8   See ibid.

9   The best account is that of Esping-Andersen (1990), who distinguished between three types of welfare state: the conservative, the liberal and the social democratic.

10   See Rosenberg and Birdzell (1986) for the view that the political sphere maximizes the wealth it can extract from the economic sphere.

11   Riker (1982) notes that the revelation of institutional disequilibrium is probably a longer process than disequilibrium of tastes and preferences more generally. See the discussion in the same volume (Shepsle and Ordeshook, 1982).

12   See the discussion in Neuman, McKnight and Solomon (1997).

13   Broadly speaking, the risk of permanent disequilibrium because those with political power will try to block change is consistent with Olson's view of path dependency (Olson, 1982), while North (1990) notes that the causality between institutions and the market works in both directions. See also the discussion in Bernholz, Streit and Vaubel (1998) of different types of path dependency.

Chapter 3   Projecting the Past: Conventional Scenarios for Europe's Future

1   For a discussion of what he calls 'the holism inherent in ecology', see Nash (1989). 'The implication of all biocentric and . . . universal ethical philosophy . . . is that the whole is more important than the parts' (p. 158). Gaia theory is one type of green holism (see Lovelock, 1988).

2   For a discussion of the way in which the environmental movement crosses traditional left–right divides, see Bramwell (1989). Goodin (1992) notes that the green philosophy involves a theory of value, based on the value of natural resources, that underlies an opposition to market economics in part of the movement.

3   This view of the continuing role of the nation state can be linked loosely with the 'realist' tradition among the scholars of international relations (see Bull, 1977).

4   For the classic account, see Cappelletti, Seccombe and Weiller (1986b): 'If we conceive of "integration" as free of any ideological connotations, the ultimate "test" of success applying the standard would be uniformization and unification' (1986a, p. 12).

5   The pre-emption doctrine has been defined as follows: 'Community law, when it substantially regulates a subject matter, is generally taken to pre-empt Member State legislation except in cases in which Community law provides for the contrary' (Gaja, Hay and Rotunda, 1986, p. 122).

6   See Mancini (2000). Wincott (1996) refers to as 'a piece of judicial activism' (p. 172) the doctrine of direct effect under which individuals can rely on community laws applying certain provisions of the Treaty of Rome directly without a requirement for national implementing legislation.

7   For this type of view, see Reiman (1990).

8   It provides a large space for what has been called 'symbolic' politics – seen by some as a new path for democratic debate. (For this view see Castells, 1997.)

9   Gellner (1997) writes about constructed identity: 'My own view is that some nations possess genuine ancient navels, some have navels invented for them by their own nationalist propaganda, and some are altogether navel-less' (p. 96). In his view the largest category is the second.

10 Taylor (1982) suggests three attributes of a community: beliefs and values in common, direct and many-sided relations between members, and a practice of reciprocity.

11 There is also a technical factor predisposing that the bargains struck by Europe's politicians could go in the wrong direction. As each politician is framing his or her objectives in the light of the negotiating objectives of the other, any agreement arrived at through this type of bargaining situation will reflect what is known as Nash equilibrium, where, strictly speaking, given my claim you could not do better by changing yours, and given your claim I could not do better by changing mine. The key feature of this type of situation is that more than one outcome is possible where everybody is satisfied and there is no guarantee of the nature of that equilibrium. (See Skyrms, 1996.)

Chapter 4   The Reach of Rules

1   For a debate on this orthodoxy, see Buchanan and Musgrave (2000).

2   See Sunstein (1990) for the view that the problem is not regulation as such but the need for constitutional safeguards in a new situation. He notes that regulations, 'can fit quite comfortably with a system that provides a prescriptive right to freedom of contract and private ordering – while at the same time providing reasons to reject private ordering in identifiable areas' (p. 3).

3   See Smith (1976 [1776], p. 15).

4   See Buchanan and Yoon (1994) for an updated discussion of the classical doctrine, and in particular see Arrow, Ng and Yang (1998).

5   Evans and Wurster (1999, p. 112) refer to 'Metcalfe's law', which defines the value of a network as proportional to the square of the number of people using it.

6   Kolm (1996) also distinguishes between compensation theories of justice and risk accounts of justice.

7   The best-known exponent of the importance of risk as what is distinctive in modern society is Ulrich Beck (see Beck, 1992).

8   Beck (1995) takes the view that many of these risks are large and of a type that cannot be compensated for.

9   Rose-Ackerman (1992) sees targeted regulation both as a way of reducing the costs of political action to bring about broad change and as a way of saving on the costs of case-by-case adjudication in law.

10 See Majone (1996) for a description of the incentives, such as the absence of a large budget, that have contributed to this evolution.

11 This is consistent with the observation of Steven K. Vogel (1996) that attempts at deregulation are followed by re-regulation, and what is called deregulation is usually the reorganization of the regulatory effort.

12 This distinction is taken from Evans and Wurster (1999), who argue that business is now able to provide both reach and richness.

13 See Ellickson (1991) for an analysis of when an informal approach is preferred to formality. He notes the limits of informality when social distance increases, when the magnitude of what is at stake rises, and when legal systems give disputants an opportunity to externalize costs to a third party.

14 Knight (1992) notes that, 'As the size of a community increases, the stability of informal rules is threatened by the incentives for non-compliance' (p. 181). Becker (1986) sets out a number of conditions that will make people more likely to observe rules, including the likelihood of compliance, each of which tends to favour formality over large social spaces.

15 See Graham and Wiener (1995).

16 See Scharpf (1999) for an elaboration of this view. Sagoff (1988) makes a similar distinction.

17 See the discussion in Yang and Ng (1998).

18 See Buchanan and Yoon (1994).

19 Chirot (1994) distinguishes between internal and external sources of information for ways in which large societies change. He argues, 'As far as societies are concerned, then, the vitality and diversity of a culture and its resistance to uniformity now as always offer the best chances for successfully meeting future challenges' (p. 125). For the benefits of the periphery, see Kennedy (1988).

20 For a discussion, see David Vogel (1995).

21 See Romano (1999).

22 From a different perspective Beck (1997) calls 'not just for rule-enforcing but rule-altering politics' (p. 7).

23 'Soft law' (a recommendation that falls short of a uniform legal obligation) provides an alternative to allowing the coexistence of hard laws. It

is a technique that performs many of the same purposes. Both techniques are about ways to ensure that rules and regulations can be based on the best knowledge and practice around the union and can be kept up to date. Cram (1997) notes that soft laws can pave the way for future hard laws. A continent-wide union is likely to use both techniques.

24 See Arrow (1995).

Chapter 5 Signals and Noise: The Role of Rights

1 Tuck (1979) provides a broad historical overview. The authoritative account of the medieval origin of rights is provided by Tierney (1997).

2 See Lacey and Haakonssen (1991a) for an account of the rise in the importance of the American Bill of Rights: 'Today it seems to many observers that federalism, once the potent principle, has become rather like a vestigial organ among the living tissues of the Constitution, while the Bill of Rights, once something of a useless appendix, has become a symbol of the Constitution itself' (1991b, p. 5).

3 The best-known critique of unrestrained rights talk is that of Glendon (1991). See also Schlesinger (1991).

4 For an account of the essentially indirect nature of representative democracy, see Manin (1997).

5 See Hinich and Munger (1994) for an analysis of party platforms (party ideology) as an entry barrier in politics: 'An ideology is an extraordinarily complex mechanism for transmitting information and persuading others about what is "good" in politics and social intercourse' (p. 72).

6 Zaller (1992) discusses the relationship between spatial differences and value differences in getting political messages across to electorates: 'The amount of added resistance due to awareness increases as value distance from the message increases' (p. 166).

7 A brief transactions cost perspective is given in Mueller (1996). A much more extended discussion of rights as a means to reduce the costs of communication is given in Hardin (1988).

8 David Beetham (1998) notes: 'Human rights are more consistently universalist, and more readily identifiable with a global politics, than the idea of democracy has been' (p. 59).

9 The launch of much subsequent discussion of different classes of rights is usually attributed to Hohfeld 1966 [1919].

10 See, for example, Martin (1992) for a theory of rights that relates rights to the justification of democratic forms of government.

11 The proclamation of the General Assembly of the United Nations referred to the 1948 Universal Declaration of Human Rights as a 'common standard of achievement for all peoples and all nations' (see Brownlie, 1992, p. 107).

12   Alan Gewirth (1992) puts forward this view.

13   Donnelly (1989) argues that human rights are rights simply because one is a human being and that they take priority over other moral, legal and political claims: 'No other rights appeal is available' (p. 13).

14   Shue (1980) argues the case for social rights as follows: 'A person who has a right has especially compelling reasons . . . on his or her side' (p. 13).

15   See Thomson (1986): 'It seems to me that very very few of the rights a human being can plausibly be thought to have are truly absolute' (p. 255).

16   Hardin (1988) states: 'The point of the institutionalization of various protections is not to spare us as individuals of the need to make judgements of right and wrong but to secure certain outcomes that would otherwise not be secured' (p. 104).

17   See Waldron (1993) for a discussion of the opposing view that one type of right entails another.

18   Wellman (1999) discusses the use of rights claims in these terms.

19   This aspect of rights claims is elaborated in Holmes and Sunstein (1999).

20   The view of rights as trumps stems from Dworkin (1977, 1985).

21   For an example of arguments that link rights with the common good, see Kagan (1989). For an explicit link between rights and Madison's views on 'faction', see, for example, Pitkin (1972).

22   Dahlgren (1995) makes a useful distinction between the notion of the common domain (a space for impartiality) and the 'advocacy domain' (where there is space for advocacy groups).

23   See Krehbiel (1991) for an analysis of the extent to which the organization of the US Congress reflects distributional concerns or the information needs that can help lead to the preferred solutions of the majority. He sees uncertainty about the consequences of legislative action as a key force driving the need to give priority to information.

24   See the discussion in Brett (1997) and Tierney (1997).

25   The ways in which rights are guides to right reason has been expressed in a number of different ways. Hardin (1988) refers to them as 'institutional choices for reducing the burden of gathering information and calculating consequences' (p. 78). Primus (1999) views them as 'waystations' of an argument, 'a kind of shorthand for an accepted normative idea' where the underlying norm provides the reason (p. 236). Thomson (1990) sees them as reducing certain types of moral inconsistency that can arise when we fail to connect a proposition we believe in with another that shares something in common with that belief.

26   The assumptions underlying accounts of deliberative democracy are given by Cohen (1989). The vote-based focus is exemplified by Fishkin (1991, 1995). Dryzek (1990, 1996) emphasizes the need for communicative rationality to be seen in a wider setting.

27   The notable exception is provided by Nino (1996), who sees the relationship between rights-based communication and vote-based expression as essentially adversarial: 'If . . . rights cover the whole of the moral space, there is very little space left for the operation of the democratic system. In short, this shrinking space for democracy is the problem the recognition of rights poses for the democratic process' (p. 13). See also the discussion of Nino in Koh and Slye (1999).

28   Sosa (1991) distinguishes between the justification of a claim (derived from deep principles) and the aptness of a claim (where the claim achieves virtue relative to the environment): 'Aptness is relative to environment' (p. 289).

29   Becker (1973) notes that the standards used in determining the fittingness of valuations 'are as much given by the situation (i.e. the needs and wishes of the valuers involved) as by any context-free features of the objects' values or of notions of "compatibility", "consistency", etc.' (p. 47).

30   Rawls (1971) takes this view: 'Basic human rights express a minimum standard of well-ordered political institutions for all people who belong, as members in good standing, to a just political society of peoples' (p. 552). This formulation by Rawls fails to distinguish between rights that are about conditions of membership and rights that are about priorities within a political society. It further assumes that the notion of a 'well-ordered' society helps define a coherent political framework.

Chapter 6   Networks and Nexus

1   In the 1970s Dahl and Tufte (1973) noted: 'The locus of democracy is shifting from the nation state to a multiplicity of interrelated units, some below, some above, and some at the level of the nation state. It seems fair to say that democratic theory has not yet received the restatement it needs to provide adequate guidance in this new and complex institutional setting' (p. 79). This diagnosis remains valid.

2   See Alesina and Spolaore (1997). Their main finding is that the stable number of countries is larger than the efficient one and that the efficient number is not stable.

3   See, for example, Wallerstein (1991).

4   See Dahl (1989).

5   See Castells (1998).

6   See Castells (1997, 1998).

7   A distinction made by Herbert Simon (1969).

8   There is a discussion in Aoki (1988) and in Thompson et al. (1991).

9   For illustrative discussions of different types of informal networks, see Risse, Ropp and Sikkink (1999) on international human rights networks and Thatcher (1998) for a survey of policy networks.

10 For the contrary view that some kind of unitary nation was always intended, see Beer (1993).

11 See Demsetz (1988) for a discussion of the firm as a nexus of contracts. Aoki, Gustaffson and Williamson (1990) prefer to discuss the firm as a nexus of treaties on the grounds that it is less legalistic in approach.

12 See Williamson (1975) for the launch of the discussion.

13 See Reve (1990).

14 Pitelis (1993) identifies a number of different classes of relevant costs.

15 International regimes have been formally defined as 'sets of governing arrangements that affect relationships of interdependence' (see Keohane and Nye, 1977, p. 19).

16 For example, Helleiner (1994), Kapstein (1994) and Mittelman (1996).

17 Waltz (1979, 1986).

18 See, for example, Beitz (1979), Crane and Amawi (1991), Kratochwill and Mansfield (1994) and Ruggie (1993).

19 The distinction between world government in the sense of a global democracy and global governance in terms of international regimes that affect behaviour is discussed in Bohman and Lutz-Bachman (1997). Held (1995) argues in favour of the development of a global democracy.

20 For a discussion, see Risse-Kappen (1995).

21 These distinctions have been taken from Boulding (1985).

22 Alesina and Spolaore (1997) note that the benefits of country size should decrease with an increase in international economic integration and the removal of trade barriers. It is also important to remember that it is firms and not nations that compete in international markets (see Porter, 1990).

23 See Kreps (1990). For an earlier statement, see Kreps and Wilson (1982).

24 For example, Ridley (1996) describes reputation as a 'vital ingredient of reciprocity' (p. 70).

25 See Krugman (1996) for a discussion of this type of misrepresentation in the case of international trade.

26 From this perspective, European union can be seen as a putative ideological union rather than as a reaction to threat (see Walt, 1987).

27 This goes well beyond the kind of precautionary motives suggested by Walzer (1985).

28 See Thies (1980) for some lessons from Vietnam.

29 The concept of policy space in international policy is discussed from a different perspective in Haftendorn, Keohane and Wallander (1999).

30 Geographical proximity could lead to what Walt (1987) describes as the 'bandwagon' effect, where neighbours align with a potential source of danger rather than with what is 'right'.

31 Linklater (1998) suggests that the pooling of sovereign powers is only one of three possible models of institutionalizing rules of international behaviour.

32   See Buchanan and Faith (1987) for a discussion of the incentive effects of exit.

33   Alesina and Spolaore (1997) also mention the potentially unifying effect of opt-out clauses.

Chapter 7   Simplicity

1   Elster (1998b) states, 'I believe that for modern societies this is an exhaustive list' (p. 5).

2   See the account in Bessette (1994).

3   Lewis (1986) makes this point when he states, 'what fits behaviour is not a system of belief alone but rather a combined system of belief and desire' (p. 36).

4   See, for example, Gutmann and Thompson (1996) and Cohen (1998).

5   There is a discussion in my earlier book (Vibert, 1995). See also the discussion in Tsebelis (1995) on the role of veto players.

6   Epstein (1995) provides an example of this approach.

7   Quine (1996) links simplicity with confirmation procedures rather than truth.

8   See Quine (1990) and Nozick (1997, pp. 182–90) and, for a much fuller discussion, Lycan (1988).

Chapter 8   Coherence

1   The criterion advanced by Rawls (1971).

2   There is a major line of argument linking coherence with rationality in moral argument. See Blackburn (1998) and Broome (1991).

3   This is a far weaker test than tests of rationality that require preferences to be ranked and for the system to produce results in line with the rankings.

4   For this perspective, see Dworkin (1986).

5   For example, Bonjour (1985) argues, 'Coherence is a matter of how well a body of beliefs "hangs together", how well its component beliefs fit together, agree or dovetail with each other, so as to produce an organ- ized, tightly structured system of beliefs, rather than a helter-skelter collection or a set of conflicting sub-systems' (p. 93).

6   For a discussion of the importance and types of incompletely theorized agreements, see Sunstein (1996, pp. 35–7).

7   Gellner (1994) suggests that a coherent civil society can be thought of in 'modular' terms: 'Modular man is capable of combining into effective associations and institutions, *without* these being total, many-stranded,

underwritten by ritual and made stable through being linked to a whole set of relationships, all of these being tied in with each other and so immobilized' (p. 100).

8 Gibbard (1990) suggests, 'Ordinarily, a person will accept only a system of norms that is incomplete' (p. 88).

9 Binmore (1994, p. 305) suggests that consistency is not a virtue in a large world because probabilities about outcomes can be better taken into account in small worlds.

10 For a discussion of the need for inconsistency as a safeguard against abuse, see Buchanan (1954).

11 See Sunstein (1996).

12 The idea of the overlapping consensus is set out and discussed in Rawls (1993a, 1993b). Gibbard (1990) also argues that in a world of overlapping 'communities of judgement' there is a 'need to form widespread communities of judgement on a restricted range of norms' (p. 234).

13 See Moser (1989, pp. 183–6).

14 Swanton (1992, pp. 26–9) suggests beliefs accepted by the many are one factor to be taken into account in arriving at a coherent belief system, alongside other criteria such as the extent to which the beliefs have been subject to the pressure of rival viewpoints.

15 Copp (1995, p. 143) argues that a society needs a coherence constraint so as to dampen the influence of moral differences in situations of overlapping moral demands.

16 Newey (1999) points out correctly that the fact of pluralism does not by itself justify toleration: 'There has to be some basis in value for valuing the existence of the diverse conceptions themselves. This basis need have nothing to do with pluralism' (p. 126).

17 Morally grounded or reasoned disapproval is integral to the concept of toleration. See Heyd (1996) and Mendus (1989).

18 See Mendus (1989).

19 Bohman (1996, p. 100) suggests that the key to accommodating pluralism is not convergence but conditions that allow for ongoing cooperation with others that is not unreasonable. Tully (1995) argues that cultural diversity requires that contemporary constitutions should be seen as a 'form of accommodation' (p. 30). Another view of toleration as representing norms of accommodation is given in Kymlicka (1995).

20 Walzer (1997) identifies a spectrum of attitudes.

21 See Gibbard (1990).

22 Discussing the legitimacy of systems of government, Nagel (1991) states that 'the most intellectually difficult problem . . . arises not from conflicts of interest but from conflicts over what is truly valuable' (p. 154).

23 For a discussion, see Simmons (1992).

24   Stocker (1989) argues that 'plural values are the rule rather than the exception ... many, if not most, ordinary choices involve plural values' (pp. 168–9).

25   Larmore (1987) notes, 'Usually our disagreements fix not upon the validity of general moral rules, but rather upon whether the rules are being properly applied, how they are to be satisfied, and what to do when they come into conflict' (p. 14).

26   These distinctions have been taken from Hampton (1998).

27   See Rawls (1999, pp. 554–5).

28   Holmes (1993a, p. 242) argues that this kind of proceduralism does not exclude substantive moral values.

29   'Coherence requires you to believe in the value of knowledge' (Skyrms, 1990, p. 87).

30   See Cohendet and Llerena (1992) for a discussion of responsiveness as a test of procedural coherence. Holmes (1990) asserts that rationality requires listening to a multiplicity of voices.

31   Nagel (1991) argues that legitimacy requires toleration, and qualifies this view: 'Legitimate government would be impossible if it were never legitimate to impose a policy on those who reasonably rejected the values on which it was based' (p. 163). This, however, is a much more limited formulation than the case that a system of government must promote its highest values in order to be legitimate.

Chapter 9   The Spirit of Europe

1   An idea popularized by Paul Kennedy (1988).

2   A contemporary account of the importance of the indirect is given in Jervis (1997).

3   Kristeva (1993) makes a relevant distinction between organic nationhood and a nation of contracts.

4   MacIntyre (1981) reflects this type of rationale in arguing that 'we need to attend to virtues in the first place in order to understand the function and authority of rules' (p. 119).

5   Mulhall and Swift (1992) reflect this family of views when they suggest that 'no vision of politics can be articulated or justified except by making reference to some conception of human well-being' (p. 349).

6   See Habermas (1999).

7   See Schmidtz (1995) for this kind of argument.

8   See the discussion in Copp (1995), in particular pp. 192–5.

9   This is sometimes expressed in terms that debate within a political framework is about 'satisficing' rather than 'optimizing' (see Slote, 1989).

10   Dworkin (1977, p. 186) notes that a general duty to obey the state and its laws cannot be an absolute duty.

11 For an updated version of the epistemic value of vote-based democracy, see Hurley (1989).
12 Simon (1969) notes, 'Problem-solving systems and design procedures in the real world do not merely assemble problem solutions from components but must search for appropriate assemblies' (p. 69).

Bibliography

Alesina, Alberto and Spolaore, Enrico (1997) 'On the Number and Size of Nations', *Quarterly Journal of Economics*, 112, 1027–56.

Alt, James E. and Shepsle, Kenneth A., eds (1990) *Perspectives on Positive Political Economy*. Cambridge: Cambridge University Press.

Aoki, Masahiko (1988) *Information, Incentives and Bargaining in the Japanese Economy*. Cambridge: Cambridge University Press.

Aoki, Masahiko, Gustafsson, Bo and Williamson, Oliver E., eds (1990) *The Firm as a Nexus of Treaties*. London: Sage.

Archibugi, Danielle, Held, David and Köhler, Martin, eds (1998) *Re-imagining Political Community*. Cambridge: Polity.

Arrow, Kenneth J. (1974) *The Limits of Organization*. New York: W.W. Norton.

Arrow, Kenneth J. (1984) *Individual Choice under Certainty and Uncertainty*. Cambridge, MA: Belknap Press.

Arrow, Kenneth J. (1995) 'Information Acquisition and the Resolution of Conflict', in Kenneth J. Arrow, ed., *Barriers to Conflict Resolution*. New York: W.W. Norton, pp. 259–72.

Arrow, Kenneth J., Ng, Yew-Kuang and Yang, Xiao-kai, eds (1998) *Increasing Returns and Economic Analysis*. Basingstoke: Macmillan.

Beck, Ulrich (1992) *Risk Society: Towards a New Modernity* (trans. Mark Ritter). London: Sage.

Beck, Ulrich (1995) *Ecological Politics in an Age of Risk* (trans. Amos Weisz). Cambridge: Polity.

Beck, Ulrich (1997) *The Reinvention of Politics: Rethinking Modernity in the Global Social Order* (trans. Mark Ritter). Cambridge: Polity.

Becker, Lawrence C. (1973) *On Justifying Moral Judgements*. London: Routledge and Kegan Paul.

Becker, Lawrence C. (1986) *Reciprocity*. London: Routledge and Kegan Paul.

Beer, Samuel H. (1993) *To Make a Nation: The Rediscovery of American Federalism*. Cambridge, MA: Belknap Press.

Beetham, David (1998) 'Human Rights as a Model for Cosmopolitan Democracy', in Danielle Archibugi, David Held and Martin Köhler, eds, *Re-imagining Political Community*. Cambridge: Polity, pp. 58–71.

Beitz, Charles R. (1979) *Political Theory and International Relations*. Princeton, NJ: Princeton University Press.

Beitz, Charles R., ed. (1985) *International Ethics*. Princeton, NJ: Princeton University Press.

Beitz, Charles R. (1989) *Political Equality*. Princeton, NJ: Princeton University Press.

Bell, Daniel (1995) *Communitarianism and Its Critics*. Oxford: Clarendon Press.

Bell, Daniel (1996) [1976] *The Cultural Contradictions of Capitalism*. New York: Basic Books.

Bernholz, Peter, Streit, Manfred E. and Vaubel, Roland, eds (1998) *Political Competition, Innovation and Growth*. Berlin: Springer Verlag.

Bessette, Joseph M. (1994) *The Mild Voice of Reason*. Chicago: University of Chicago Press.

Binmore, Ken (1994) *Playing Fair: Game Theory and the Social Contract, Vol. I*. Cambridge, MA: MIT Press.

Binmore, Ken (1998) *Just Playing: Game Theory and the Social Contract, Vol. II*. Cambridge, MA: MIT Press.

Blackburn, Simon (1998) *Ruling Passions: A Theory of Practical Reason*. Oxford: Clarendon Press.

Bohman, James (1996) *Public Deliberation: Pluralism, Complexity and Democracy*. Cambridge, MA: MIT Press.

Bohman, James and Lutz-Bachmann, Matthias, eds (1997) *Perpetual Peace: Essays on Kant's Cosmopolitan Ideal*. Cambridge, MA: MIT Press.

Bohman, James and Rehg, William, eds (1997) *Deliberative Democracy: Essays on Reason and Politics*. Cambridge, MA: MIT Press.

Bonjour, Laurence (1985) *The Structure of Empirical Knowledge*. Cambridge, MA: Harvard University Press.

Bormann, F. Herbert and Kellert, Stephen R., eds (1991) *Ecology, Economics, Ethics: The Broken Circle*. New Haven, CT: Yale University Press.

Boulding, Kenneth E. (1985) *The World as a Total System*. Beverley Hills, CA: Sage.

Bramwell, Anna (1989) *Ecology in the Twentieth Century: A History*. New Haven, CT, and London: Yale University Press.

Brett, Annabel S. (1997) *Liberty, Right and Nature: Individual Rights in Later Scholastic Thought*. Cambridge: Cambridge University Press.

Broome, John (1991) *Weighing Goods*. Oxford: Blackwell.

Brownlie, Ian, ed. (1992) *Basic Documents on Human Rights* (3rd edn). Oxford: Clarendon Press.

Buchanan, James M. (1954) 'Social Choice, Democracy and Free Markets', *Journal of Political Economy*, 62, 114–23.

Buchanan, James M. and Faith, Roger L. (1987) 'Secession and the Limits of Taxation: Towards a Theory of Internal Exit', *American Economic Review*, LXXVII, 1023–31.

Buchanan, James M. and Musgrave, Richard A. (2000) *Public Finance and Public Choice*. Cambridge, MA: MIT Press.

Buchanan, James and Tullock, Gordon (1962) *The Calculus of Consent*. Ann Arbor: University of Michigan Press.

Buchanan, James M. and Yoon, Yong J., eds (1994) *The Return to Increasing Returns*. Ann Arbor: University of Michigan Press.

Bull, Hedley (1977) *The Anarchical Society*. London: Macmillan.

Buzan, Barry, Jones, Charles and Little, Richard (1993) *The Logic of Anarchy: Neorealism to Structural Realism*. New York: Columbia University Press.

Cappelletti, Mauro, Seccombe, Monica and Weiler, Joseph (1986a) 'A General Introduction', in Mauro Cappelletti, Monica Seccombe and Joseph Weiler, eds, *Integration Through Law: Europe and the American Federal Experience, Vol. 1: Methods, Tools and Institutions*. Berlin: Walter de Gruyter, Book 1, Part I, pp. 3–18.

Cappelletti, Mauro, Seccombe, Monica and Weiler, Joseph, eds (1986b) *Integration Through Law: Europe and the American Federal Experience, Vol. 1: Methods, Tools and Institutions*. Berlin: Walter de Gruyter.

Carroll, Glenn R. and Teece, David J., eds (1998) *Firms, Markets and Hierarchies*. Oxford: Oxford University Press.

Castells, Manuel (1996) *The Rise of the Network Society: The Information Age, Vol. 1*. Oxford: Blackwell.

Castells, Manuel (1997) *The Power of Identity: The Information Age, Vol. 2*. Oxford: Blackwell.

Castells, Manuel (1998) *End of Millennium: The Information Age, Vol. 3*. Oxford: Blackwell.

Chirot, Daniel (1994) *How Societies Change*. Thousand Oaks, CA: Pine Forge Press.

Cohen, Joshua (1989) 'Deliberation and Democratic Legitimacy', in Alan Hamlin and Philip Pettit, eds, *The Good Polity: Normative Analysis of the State*. Oxford: Basil Blackwell, pp. 17–34.

Cohen, Joshua (1998) 'Democracy and Liberty', in Jon Elster, ed., *Deliberative Democracy*. Cambridge: Cambridge University Press, pp. 185–231.

Cohendet, Patrick and Llererna, Patrick (1992) 'Integration and Learning Process', in Paul Bourgine and Bernard Walliser, eds, *Economics and Cognitive Science*. Oxford: Pergamon Press, pp. 181–9.

Copp, David (1995) *Morality, Normativity and Society*. Oxford: Oxford University Press.

Copp, David, Hampton, Jean and Roemer, John E., eds (1993) *The Idea of Democracy*. Cambridge: Cambridge University Press.

Cram, Laura (1997) *Policy-Making in the European Union: Conceptual Lenses and the Integration Process*. London: Routledge.

Crane, George T. and Amawi, Abla M., eds (1991) *The Theoretical Evolution of International Political Economy: A Reader*. Oxford: Oxford University Press.

Dahl, Robert A. (1989) *Democracy and Its Critics*. New Haven, CT: Yale University Press.

Dahl, Robert A. (1997) *Toward Democracy: A Journey. Vol. II*. Berkeley: Institute of Governmental Studies Press. University of California.

Dahl, Robert A. and Tufte, Edward, R. (1973) *Size and Democracy*. Stanford, CA: Stanford University Press.

Dahlgren, Peter (1995) *Television and the Public Sphere*. London: Sage.

Demsetz, Harold (1988) *Ownership, Control and the Firm: The Organization of Economic Activity, Vol. 1*. Oxford: Blackwell.

Demsetz, Harold (1989) *Efficiency, Competition and Policy: The Organization of Economic Activity, Vol. 2*. Oxford: Blackwell.

Donnelly, Jack (1989) *Universal Human Rights in Theory and Practice*. Ithaca, NY: Cornell University Press.

Dryzek, John S. (1990) *Discursive Democracy: Politics, Policy and Political Science*. Cambridge: Cambridge University Press.

Dryzek, John S. (1996) *Democracy in Capitalist Times*. Oxford: Oxford University Press.

Dworkin, Ronald (1977) *Taking Rights Seriously*. London: Duckworth.

Dworkin, Ronald (1985) *A Matter of Principle*. Cambridge, MA: Harvard University Press.

Dworkin, Ronald (1986) *Law's Empire*. Cambridge, MA: Harvard University Press.

Ellickson, Robert C. (1991) *Order without Law*. Cambridge, MA: Harvard University Press.

Elster, Jon (1992) *Local Justice*. Cambridge: Cambridge University Press.

Elster, Jon, ed. (1995) *Local Justice in America*. New York: Russell Sage Foundation.

Elster, Jon, ed. (1998a) *Deliberative Democracy*. Cambridge: Cambridge University Press.

Elster, Jon (1998b) 'Introduction', in Jon Elster, ed., *Deliberative Democracy*. Cambridge: Cambridge University Press, pp. 1–18.

Epstein, Richard A. (1995) *Simple Rules for a Complex World*. Cambridge, MA: Harvard University Press.

Esping-Andersen, Gøsta (1990) *The Three Worlds of Welfare Capitalism*. Cambridge: Polity.

Estlund, David (1997) 'Beyond Fairness and Deliberation', in James Bohman and William Rehg, eds, *Deliberative Democracy: Essays on Reason and Politics*. Cambridge, MA: MIT Press, pp. 173–204.

Evans, Philip and Wurster, Thomas S. (1999) *Blown to Bits*. Cambridge, MA: Harvard Business School Press.

Ferejohn, John A. and Kuklinski, James H., eds (1990) *Information and Democratic Processes*. Urbana: University of Illinois Press.

Fishkin, James S. (1991) *Democracy and Deliberation*. New Haven, CT: Yale University Press.

Fishkin, James S. (1995) *The Voice of the People*. New Haven, CT: Yale University Press.

Fukuyama, Francis (1992) *The End of History and the Last Man*. London: Hamish Hamilton.

Fukuyama, Francis (1995) *Trust: The Social Virtues and the Creation of Prosperity*. London: Hamish Hamilton.

Gaja, Giorgio, Hay, Peter and Rotunda, Ronald (1986) 'Legal Techniques for Integration', in Mauro Cappelletti, Monica Seccombe and Joseph Weiler, eds, *Integration Through Law: Europe and the American Federal Experience, Vol. 1: Methods, Tools and Institutions*. Berlin: Walter de Gruyter, Book 2, Part II, pp. 113–60.

Gauthier, David (1990) *Moral Dealing*. Ithaca, NY: Cornell University Press.

Gellner, Ernest (1994) *Conditions of Liberty: Civil Society and Its Rivals*. London: Hamish Hamilton.

Gellner, Ernest (1997) *Nationalism*. London: Weidenfeld and Nicolson.

Geroski, Paul A. and Schwalbach, Joachim, eds (1991) *Entry and Market Contestability*. Oxford: Blackwell.

Gewirth, Alan (1992) 'Human Dignity as the Basis of Rights', in M.J. Meyer and W.A. Parent, eds, *The Constitution of Rights*. Ithaca, NY: Cornell University Press, pp. 10–28.

Gewirth, Alan (1996) *The Community of Rights*. Chicago: University of Chicago Press.

Gibbard, Alan (1990). *Wise Choices, Apt Feelings*. Oxford: Clarendon Press.

Glendon, Mary Ann (1991). *Rights Talk: The Impoverishment of Political Discourse*. New York: Free Press.

Goodin, Robert E. (1992) *Green Political Theory*. Cambridge: Polity.

Graham, John D. and Weiner, Jonathan Baert, eds (1995) *Risk vs Risk*. Cambridge, MA: Harvard University Press.

Gutmann, Amy and Thompson, Dennis (1996) *Democracy and Disagreement*. Cambridge, MA: Harvard University Press.

Habermas, Jürgen (1984) *The Theory of Communicative Action, Vol. 1* (trans. Thomas McCarthy). Cambridge: Polity/Boston: Beacon.

Habermas, Jürgen (1987) *The Theory of Communicative Action, Vol. 2* (trans. Thomas McCarthy). Cambridge: Polity/Boston: Beacon.

Habermas, Jürgen (1999) *The Inclusion of the Other: Studies in Political Theory* (ed. Ciaran Cronin and Pablo De Greiff). Cambridge: Polity.

Haftendorn, Helga, Keohane, Robert O. and Wallander, Celeste A. (1999) *Imperfect Unions*. Oxford: Oxford University Press.

Hamlin, Alan and Pettit, Philip, eds (1989) *The Good Polity: Normative Analysis of the State*. Oxford: Blackwell.

Hampton, Jean. E. (1998) *The Authority of Reason*. Cambridge: Cambridge University Press.

Hardin, Russell (1988) *Morality within the Limits of Reason*. Chicago: University of Chicago Press.

Harrison, Lawrence E. (1992) *Who Prospers? How Cultural Values Shape Economic and Political Success*. New York: Basic Books.

Held, David (1995) *Democracy and the Global Order*. Cambridge: Polity.

Helleiner, Eric (1994) *States and the Reemergence of Global Finance*. Ithaca, NY: Cornell University Press.

Heyd, David, ed. (1996) *Toleration: An Elusive Virtue*. Princeton, NJ: Princeton University Press.

Hinich, Melvin J. and Munger, Michael C. (1994) *Ideology and the Theory of Political Choice*. Ann Arbor: University of Michigan Press.

Höffe, Otfried (1995) *Political Justice* (trans. Jeffrey C. Cohen). Cambridge: Polity.

Hohfeld, W.N. (1966) [1919] *Fundamental Legal Conceptions* (ed. W.W. Cook). New Haven, CT: Yale University Press.

Holmes, Stephen (1990) 'Liberal Constraints on Private Power', in Judith Lichtenberg, ed., *Democracy and the Mass Media*. Cambridge: Cambridge University Press, pp. 21–65.

Holmes, Stephen (1993a) *The Anatomy of Anti-Liberalism*. Cambridge, MA: Harvard University Press.

Holmes, Stephen (1993b) 'Tocqueville and Democracy', in David Copp, Jean Hampton and John E. Roemer, eds, *The Idea of Democracy*. Cambridge: Cambridge University Press, pp. 23–63.

Holmes, Stephen (1995) *Passions and Constraint: On the Theory of Liberal Democracy*. Chicago: University of Chicago Press.

Holmes, Stephen and Sunstein, Cass R. (1999) *The Cost of Rights*. New York: W.W. Norton.

Holsti, K.J. (1992) 'Governance without Government: Order and Change in Nineteenth-Century European International Politics', in James N. Rosenau and Ernest Otto, eds, *Governance without Government: Order and Change in World Politics*. Cambridge: Cambridge University Press, pp. 30–57.

Huber, Peter (1994) *Orwell's Revenge: The 1984 Palimpsest*. New York: Free Press.

Huntington, Samuel P. (1996) *The Clash of Civilizations and the Remaking of World Order*. New York: Simon and Schuster.

Hurley, Susan L. (1989) *Natural Reasons: Personality and Polity*. Oxford: Oxford University Press.

Jervis, R. (1997) *System Effects: Complexity in Political and Social Life*. Princeton, NJ: Princeton University Press.

Kagan, Shelly (1989) *The Limits of Morality*. Oxford: Clarendon Press.

Kapstein, Ethan B. (1994) *Governing the Global Economy: International Finance and the State*. Cambridge, MA: Harvard University Press.

Kellert, Stephen (1993) *In the Wake of Chaos*. Chicago: University of Chicago Press.

Kelly, Kevin (1998) *New Rules for the New Economy*. London: Fourth Estate.

Kennedy, Paul (1988) *The Rise and Fall of Great Powers*. London: Fontana Press.

Keohane, Robert O., ed. (1986) *Neo-Realism and its Critics*. New York: Columbia University Press.

Keohane, Robert O. and Nye, Joseph S. (1977) *Power and Interdependence*. Boston: Little Brown & Co.

Khalil, Elias L. and Boulding, Kenneth E., eds (1996) *Evolution, Order and Complexity*. London: Routledge.

Knight, Jack (1992) *Institutions and Social Conflict*. Cambridge: Cambridge University Press.

Koh, Harold Hongju and Slye, Ronald C., eds (1999) *Deliberative Democracy and Human Rights*. New Haven, CT: Yale University Press.

Kolm, Serge-Christophe (1996) *Modern Theories of Justice*. Cambridge, MA: MIT Press.

Kratochwil, Friedrich and Mansfield, Edward D., eds (1994) *International Organization: A Reader*. New York: HarperCollins.

Krehbiel, Keith (1991) *Information and Legislative Organization*. Ann Arbor: University of Michigan Press.

Kreps, David M. (1990) 'Corporate Culture and Economic Theory', in James E. Alt and Kenneth A. Shepse, eds, *Perspectives on Positive Political Economy*. Cambridge: Cambridge University Press, pp. 90–143.

Kreps, David M. and Wilson, Robert (1982) 'Reputation and Imperfect Information', *Journal of Economic Theory*, 27, 253–79.

Kristeva, Julia (1993) *Nations without Nationalism* (trans. Leon S. Roudiez). New York: Columbia University Press.

Krugman, Paul (1996) *Pop Internationalism*. Cambridge, MA: MIT Press.

Kymlicka, Will (1995) *Multicultural Citizenship*. Oxford: Clarendon Press.

Lacey, Michael J. and Haakonssen, Knud (1991a) *A Culture of Rights: The Bill of Rights in Philosophy, Politics and Law 1791–1991*. Cambridge: Woodrow Wilson International Centre for Scholars and Cambridge University Press.

Lacey, Michael J. and Haakonssen, Knud (1991b) 'Introduction', in Michael J. Lacey and Knud Haakonssen, eds, *A Culture of Rights: The Bill of Rights in Philosophy, Politics and the Law 1791–1991*. Cambridge: Woodrow Wilson International Centre for Scholars and Cambridge University Press, pp. 1–18.

Larmore, Charles E. (1987) *Patterns of Moral Complexity*. Cambridge: Cambridge University Press.

Lewis, David (1986) *On the Plurality of Worlds*. Oxford: Blackwell.

Lichtenberg, Judith, ed. (1990) *Democracy and the Mass Media*. Cambridge: Cambridge University Press.

Lijphart, Arend (1977) *Democracy in Plural Societies*. New Haven, CT: Yale University Press.

Linklater, Andrew (1998) *The Transformation of Political Community*. Cambridge: Polity.

Lovelock, James (1988) *The Ages of Gaia: A Biography of Our Living Earth*. Oxford: Oxford University Press.

Lycan, William G. (1988) *Judgement and Justification*. Cambridge: Cambridge University Press.

MacIntyre, Alasdair (1981) *After Virtue: A Study in Moral Theory*. London: Duckworth.

Majone, Giandomenico (1996) *Regulating Europe*. London: Routledge.

Mancini, G.F. (2000) *Democracy and Constitutionalism in the European Union*. Oxford: Hart Publishing.

Manin, Bernard (1997) *The Principles of Representative Government*. Cambridge: Cambridge University Press.

Martin, Rex (1992) *A System of Rights*. Oxford: Clarendon Press.

Mendus, Susan (1989) *Toleration and the Limits of Liberalism*. Basingstoke: Macmillan.

Meyer, M.J. and Parent, W.A., eds (1992) *The Constitution of Rights*. Ithaca, NY: Cornell University Press.

Mittelman, James H., ed. (1996) *Globalization: Critical Reflections*. Boulder, CO: Lynne Rienner.

Moser, Paul, K. (1989) *Knowledge and Evidence*. Cambridge: Cambridge University Press.

Mueller, Dennis C. (1996) *Constitutional Democracy*. Oxford: Oxford University Press.

Mulhall, Stephen and Swift, Adam (1992) *Liberals and Communitarians*. Oxford: Blackwell.

Murphy, Craig N. (1994) *International Organization and Industrial Change*. Cambridge: Polity.

Nagel, Thomas (1991) *Equality and Partiality*. Oxford: Oxford University Press.

Nash, R.F. (1989) *The Rights of Nature: A History of Environmental Ethics*. Madison: University of Wisconsin Press.

Neuman, Russell W., McKnight, Lee and Solomon R.J. (1997) *The Gordian Knot*. Cambridge, MA: MIT Press.

Newey, Glen (1999) *Virtue, Reason and Toleration*. Edinburgh: Edinburgh University Press.

Nino, C.S. (1996) *The Constitution of Deliberative Democracy*. New Haven, CT: Yale University Press.

North, Douglass C. (1990) *Institutions, Institutional Change and Economic Performance*. Cambridge: Cambridge University Press.

Nozick, Robert (1997) *Socratic Puzzles*. Cambridge, MA: Harvard University Press.

Olson, Mancur (1982) *The Rise and Decline of Nations: Economic Growth, Stagflation, and Social Rigidities*. New Haven, CT: Yale University Press.

Pitelis, Christos, ed. (1993) *Transaction Costs, Markets and Hierarchies*. Oxford: Blackwell.

Pitkin, Hannah F. (1972) *The Concept of Representation*. Berkeley: University of California Press.

Porter, Michael E. (1990) *The Competitive Advantage of Nations*. London: Collier Macmillan.

Posner, Richard A. (1995) *Overcoming Law*. Cambridge, MA: Harvard University Press.

Primus, Richard A. (1999) *The American Language of Rights*. Cambridge: Cambridge University Press.

Quine, Willard V. (1976) [1966] *The Ways of Paradox*. Cambridge, MA: Harvard University Press.

Quine, Willard V. (1990) *Pursuit of Truth*. Cambridge, MA: Harvard University Press.

Rakove, Jack N. (1996) *Original Meanings: Politics and Ideas in the Making of the Constitution*. New York: Alfred Knopf.

Rawls, John (1999) [1971] *A Theory of Justice*. Oxford: Oxford University Press.

Rawls, John (1993a) 'The Domain of the Political and Overlapping Consensus', in David Copp, Jean Hampton and John E. Roemer, eds, *The Idea of Democracy*. Cambridge: Cambridge University Press, pp. 245–69.

Rawls, John (1993b) *Political Liberalism*. New York: Columbia University Press.

Rawls, John (1999) *Collected Papers* (ed. Samuel Freeman). Cambridge, MA: Harvard University Press.

Reiman, Jeffrey H. (1990) *Justice and Modern Moral Philosophy*. New Haven, CT: Yale University Press.

Reve, Torger (1990) 'The Firm as a Nexus of Internal and External Contracts', in Masahiko Aoki, Bo Gustaffson and Oliver E. Williamson, eds, *The Firm as a Nexus of Treaties*. London: Sage, pp. 133–61.

Richardson, Jeremy, ed. (1996) *European Union: Power and Policy-Making*. London: Routledge.

Ridley, Matt (1996) *The Origins of Virtue*. New York: Viking.

Riker, William (1982) 'Implications from the Disequilibrium of Majority Rule for the Study of Institutions', in Kenneth A. Shepsle and Peter C. Ordeshook, eds, *Political Equilibrium*. Boston: Kluwer-Nijhoff, pp. 3–24.

Riker, William, Calvert, Randall L., Mueller, John and Wilson, Rick K., eds (1996) *The Strategy of Rhetoric: Campaigning for the American Constitution*. New Haven, CT: Yale University Press.

Risse-Kappen, Thomas, ed. (1995) *Bringing Transnational Relations Back In*. Cambridge: Cambridge University Press.

Risse, Thomas, Ropp, Stephen C. and Sikkink, Kathryn, eds (1999) *The Power of Human Rights: International Norms and Domestic Change*. Cambridge: Cambridge University Press.

Romano, Roberta (1999) 'Corporate Law and Corporate Governance', in Glenn R. Carroll and David J. Teece, eds, *Firms, Markets and Hierarchies*. Oxford: Oxford University Press, pp. 365–427.

Rose-Ackerman, Susan (1992) *Rethinking the Progressive Agenda: The Reform of the American Regulatory State*. New York: Free Press.

Rosenau, James N. and Czempiel, Ernest Otto, eds (1992) *Governance without Government: Order and Change in World Politics*. Cambridge: Cambridge University Press.

Rosenberg, Nathan and Birdzell, L.E. (1986) *How the West Grew Rich*. New York: Basic Books.

Ruggie, J.G., ed. (1993) *Multilateralism Matters: The Theory and Praxis of an Institutional Form*. New York: Columbia University Press.

Sagoff, Mark (1988) *The Economy of the Earth: Philosophy, Law and the Environment*. Cambridge: Cambridge University Press.

Sandel, Michael J. (1982) *Liberalism and the Limits of Justice*. Cambridge: Cambridge University Press.

Scharpf, Fritz (1999) *Governing in Europe: Effective and Democratic?* Oxford: Oxford University Press.

Schlesinger, Arthur M., Jr (1991) *The Disuniting of America*. New York: W.W. Norton.

Schmidtz, David (1995) *Rational Choice and Moral Agency*. Princeton, NJ: Princeton University Press.

Schotter, Andrew (1981) *The Economic Theory of Social Institutions*. Cambridge: Cambridge University Press.

Shapiro, Carl and Varian, Hal R. (1998) *Information Rules: A Strategic Guide to the Network Economy*. Boston: Harvard Business School Press.

Shepsle, Kenneth A. and Ordeshook, Peter C., eds (1982) *Political Equilibrium*. Boston: Kluwer-Nijhoff.

Shue, Henry (1980) *Basic Rights*. Princeton, NJ: Princeton University Press.

Simmons, A. John (1992) *The Lockean Theory of Rights*. Princeton, NJ: Princeton University Press.

Simon, Herbert A. (1969) *The Sciences of the Artificial*. Cambridge, MA: MIT Press.

Simon, Herbert A. (1982) *Models of Bounded Rationality, Vol. I: Economic Analysis and Public Policy*. Cambridge, MA: MIT Press.

Skyrms, Brian (1990) *The Dynamics of Rational Deliberation*. Cambridge, MA: Harvard University Press.

Skyrms, Brian (1996) *Evolution of the Social Contract*. Cambridge: Cambridge University Press.

Slote, Michael (1989) *Beyond Optimizing: A Study of Rational Choice*. Cambridge, MA: Harvard University Press.

Smith, Adam (1976) [1776] *An Inquiry into the Nature and Causes of the Wealth of Nations*. Oxford: Clarendon Press.

Sosa, Ernest (1991) *Knowledge in Perspective*. Cambridge: Cambridge University Press.

Stocker, Michael (1989) *Plural and Conflicting Values*. Oxford: Clarendon Press.

Sunstein, Cass R. (1990) *After the Rights Revolution: Reconceiving the Regulatory State*. Cambridge, MA: Harvard University Press.

Sunstein, Cass R. (1996) *Legal Reasoning and Political Conflict*. Oxford: Oxford University Press.

Swanton, Christine (1992) *Freedom: A Coherence Theory*. Indianapolis, IN: Hackett Publishing Co.

Taylor, Michael (1982) *Community, Anarchy and Liberty*. Cambridge: Cambridge University Press.

Thatcher, Mark (1998) 'The Development of Policy Network Analyses', *Journal of Theoretical Politics*, 10(4), 389–416.

Thies, Wallace (1980) *When Governments Collide*. Berkeley: University of California Press.

Thompson, Grahame, Frances, Jennifer, Levacíc, Rosalind and Mitchell, Jeremy, eds (1991) *Markets, Hierarchies and Networks*. London: Sage.

Thomson, Judith J. (1986) 'Afterword', in William Parent, ed., *Rights, Restitution and Risk*. Cambridge, MA: Harvard University Press, pp. 251–60.

Thomson, Judith J. (1990) *The Realm of Rights*. Cambridge, MA: Harvard University Press.

Tierney, Brian (1997) *The Idea of Natural Rights*. Atlanta, GA: Scholars Press.

Tilly, Charles, ed. (1975) *The Formation of National States in Western Europe*. Princeton, NJ: Princeton University Press.

Tsebelis, George (1995) 'Decision Making in Political Systems: Comparison of Presidentialism, Parliamentarianism, Multicameralism and Multipartyism', *British Journal of Political Science*, 25, 289–325.

Tuck, Richard (1979) *Natural Rights Theories*. Cambridge: Cambridge University Press.

Tullock, Gordon (1965) 'Entry Barriers in Politics', *American Economic Review*, 55 (1), 458–66.

Tully, James (1995) *Strange Multiplicity: Constitutionalism in an Age of Diversity*. Cambridge: Cambridge University Press.

Vibert, Frank (1995) *Europe: A Constitution for the Millennium*. Aldershot: Dartmouth.

Vogel, David (1995) *Trading Up: Consumer and Environmental Regulation in a Global Economy*. Cambridge, MA: Harvard University Press.

Vogel, Steven K. (1996) *Freer Markets, More Rules: Regulatory Reform in Advanced Industrial Countries*. Ithaca, NY: Cornell University Press.

Waldron, Jeremy (1993) *Liberal Rights*. Cambridge: Cambridge University Press.

Wallerstein, Immanuel (1991) *Geopolitics and Geoculture: Essays on the Changing World System*. Cambridge: Cambridge University Press.

Wallerstein, Immanuel (1995) *After Liberalism*. New York: New Press.

Walt, Stephen M. (1987) *The Origins of Alliances*. Ithaca, NY: Cornell University Press.

Waltz, Kenneth (1979) *Theory of International Politics*. Reading, MA: Addison-Wesley.

Waltz, Kenneth (1986) 'Reductionist and Systemic Theories', in Robert O. Keohane, ed., *Neo-Realism and Its Critics*. New York: Columbia University Press, pp. 47–69.

Walzer, Michael (1985) 'The Moral Standing of States: A Response to Four Critics', in Charles R. Beitz, ed., *International Ethics*. Princeton, NJ: Princeton University Press, pp. 217–37.

Walzer, Michael (1997) *On Toleration*. New Haven, CT: Yale University Press.

Wellman, Carl (1999) *The Proliferation of Rights*. Oxford: Westview Press.

Williamson, Oliver E. (1975) *Markets and Hierarchies: Analysis and Antitrust Implications*. New York: Free Press.

Wincott, Daniel (1996) 'The Court of Justice and the European Policy Process', in Jeremy Richardson, ed., *European Union: Power and Policy-Making*. London: Routledge, pp. 170–84.

Wright, Eric Olin, ed. (1995) *Associations and Democracy*. London: Verso.

Yang, Xiao-Kai and Ng, Yew-Kuang (1998) 'Specialization and Division of Labour', in Kenneth J. Arrow, Yew-Kuang Ng and Xiao-Kai Yang, eds, *Increasing Returns and Economic Analysis*. Basingstoke: Macmillan, pp. 3–63.

Zaller, John R. (1992) *The Nature and Origins of Mass Opinion*. Cambridge: Cambridge University Press.

Index